Grade 5

Vocabulary
for Making Meaning®
SECOND EDITION

Thinking and Talking About Words

DEVELOPMENTAL STUDIES CENTER™

Copyright © 2009 by Developmental Studies Center

All rights reserved. Except where otherwise noted, no part of this publication may be reproduced in whole or in part, or stored in a retrieval system, or transmitted in any form or by any means, electronic, mechanical, photocopying, recording, or otherwise, without the written permission of the publisher. For information regarding permissions, write to the Editorial Department at Developmental Studies Center.

First edition published 2009.

Making Meaning is a registered trademark of Developmental Studies Center.

Developmental Studies Center wishes to thank the following authors, agents, and publishers for their permission to reprint materials included in this program. Many people went out of their way to help us secure these rights and we are very grateful for their support. Every effort has been made to trace the ownership of copyrighted material and to make full acknowledgment of its use. If errors or omissions have occurred, they will be corrected in subsequent editions, provided that notification is submitted in writing to the publisher.

"Zoo" by Edward D. Hoch, originally published in Fantastic Universe. Copyright ©1958 by Edward D. Hoch. Reprinted by permission of the Sternig & Byrne Literary Agency. "Is Dodge Ball Too Dangerous?" from TimeForKids.com Sports News, May 15, 2001. Copyright © TIME For Kids. Used with permission from TIME For Kids Magazine. Excerpt from "Turn It Off!" from TIME For Kids World Report Edition, April 12, 2002. Copyright © TIME For Kids. Used with permission from TIME For Kids Magazine.

All articles and texts reproduced in this manual and not referenced with a credit line above were created by Developmental Studies Center.

All book covers reproduced in this manual by the permission of the publishers.

Developmental Studies Center
2000 Embarcadero, Suite 305
Oakland, CA 94606-5300
(800) 666-7270, fax: (510) 464-3670
www.devstu.org

ISBN-13: 978-1-59892-362-9
ISBN-10: 1-59892-362-5

Printed in China

1 2 3 4 5 6 7 8 9 10 RSL 18 17 16 15 14 13 12 11 10 09

Table of Contents

VOLUME 2

Lessons

Week 13 287
Week 14 307
Week 15 327
Week 16 347
Week 17 375
Week 18 401
Week 19 425
Week 20 445
Week 21 465
Week 22 483
Week 23 505
Week 24 523
Week 25 541
Week 26 563
Week 27 585

Appendices 607
  Making Meaning Vocabulary Lessons and *Making Meaning* 609
  Grade 5 Words and Definitions 610
  Independent Word-learning Strategies 615
  Extension Activities 619
  Word Checks 620
  Student Self-assessment Instructions 634
  Vocabulary Words K–6 636
  Bibliography 640

Week 13 Overview

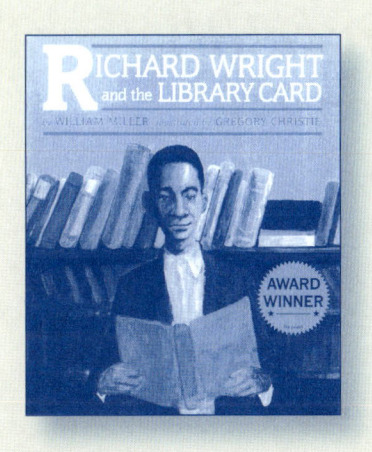

Richard Wright and the Library Card
by William Miller,
illustrated by Gregory Christie
(Lee & Low, 1997)

Words Taught

frugal

hunger

apprehensive

discourteous

prejudice

episode

Word-learning Strategies

- Using the prefix *dis-* to determine word meanings (review)

- Recognizing antonyms (review)

- Using the prefix *pre-* to determine word meanings (review)

Words Reviewed: advantage, conspicuous, ordeal, thoughtful, widespread

DO AHEAD

- Prior to Day 3, preview the "Author's Note" on page 32 of *Richard Wright and the Library Card*. (You did not read this part of the book during the *Making Meaning* lesson.) You will read the "Author's Note" aloud to the students to introduce the word *episode*.

- Prior to Day 5, collect these word cards for Ongoing Review: 35, 42, 58, 63, and 69.

Week 13 ▶ Day 1

Day 1

Introduce *Frugal, Hunger,* and *Apprehensive*

Materials
- *Richard Wright and the Library Card*
- Chart paper
- A marker

Words Taught

frugal
Frugal means "careful in spending money or not wasteful."

hunger (p. 12)
Hunger is "a strong desire or want."

apprehensive
Apprehensive means "uneasy or worried and slightly afraid."

INTRODUCE AND PRACTICE USING *FRUGAL*

▶ **1** **Introduce and Define *Frugal***

Briefly review *Richard Wright and the Library Card*.

Show pages 12–13 and review that Richard has a job in an optician's office. He is trying to earn enough money to move to Chicago and make a new life for himself. Read the first paragraph on page 12 aloud.

Explain that the first word the students will learn today is *frugal* and that *frugal* means "careful in spending money or not wasteful."

Remind the students that Richard wants to save enough money from what he earns to pay for a trip to Chicago. Explain that when he buys beans, an inexpensive food, he is being frugal, or careful about how he spends his money. Being frugal will help Richard save money.

288 | Making Meaning® Vocabulary

Week 13 ▶ Day 1

Have the students say the word *frugal*, and then write it on a sheet of chart paper.

2 Discuss Being Frugal

Remind the students that frugal people are careful about how they spend money and that they look for ways to save money. For example, a frugal person might check a book out of the library instead of buying it at a bookstore. A frugal person might use coupons at the grocery store to save money on food purchases. A frugal person might buy new clothes only when the clothes are on sale.

Use "Think, Pair, Share" to discuss:

Q *What other things might a person do to be frugal?* [pause] *Turn to your partner.*

PROMPT: "To be frugal, a person might…."

Explain that a frugal person also is not wasteful. For example, a frugal person saves plastic bags from the grocery store, rather than throwing them away, so that she can use the bags later for other purposes.

Explain that frugal people are also careful about saving valuable resources such as electricity and water. Discuss as a class:

Q *What might a frugal person do to save electricity?*

PROMPT: "To save electricity, a frugal person might…."

In the same way, discuss:

Q *What might a frugal person do to save water?*

Review the pronunciation and meaning of the word.

◀ **Teacher Note**

Support struggling students by suggesting other frugal actions, such as buying things at yard sales, eating at home instead of in restaurants, and renting movies instead of going to the theater, or by asking questions such as, "What do you do to be frugal?" and "What do your friends or family do to be frugal?"

◀ **Teacher Note**

Have a few students share their thinking with the class. Hearing from only a few students keeps the lesson moving.

Grade Five | 289

Week 13 ▶ Day 1

INTRODUCE AND PRACTICE USING *HUNGER*

3▶ Introduce and Define *Hunger*

Show pages 12–13 again. Remind the students that Richard loves to read and that as a child he read anything he could find. Read the last two paragraphs on page 12 aloud, emphasizing the word *hunger*.

Tell the students that the next word they will learn today is *hunger* and that *hunger* is "a strong desire or want." Point out that Richard has a hunger, or strong desire, for words and books. He wants with all his heart to read and learn.

Have the students say the word *hunger*, and write it on the chart.

> **Teacher Note**
>
> Point out that *hunger* has two other familiar meanings, "pain or weakness caused by not eating enough food" and "the feeling of wanting and needing food."

4▶ Discuss Hungering to Learn About Something

Explain that, like Richard, many people hunger for knowledge, or have a strong desire to learn things. Give a couple of examples of things you have hungered to learn. (You might say, "When I was your age, I hungered to learn about the ancient Egyptians. I was especially fascinated by mummies and read everything I could find about them. These days I hunger to learn all I can about gardening. I want to grow my own vegetables, so I'm learning about vegetables that will grow in our climate.")

Explain that you will ask partners to discuss things they hunger to learn about, and then a few of them will share their partners' thinking with the class.

Ask:

Q *What is something you hunger to learn about? Why? Turn to your partner.*

PROMPT: "I hunger to learn about [kites] because…."

Have a few volunteers share their partners' thinking.

Review the pronunciation and meaning of the word.

INTRODUCE AND PRACTICE USING *APPREHENSIVE*

▶ 5 Introduce and Define *Apprehensive*

Show pages 16–17 and review that Richard asks Jim Falk to help him get books from the library. Read the following sentences from page 16 aloud: "'All right,' Jim said nervously. 'But don't tell anyone else. I don't want to get into trouble.'"

Tell the students that the last word they will learn today is *apprehensive* and that *apprehensive* means "uneasy or worried and slightly afraid."

Point out that Jim is apprehensive, or worried and slightly afraid, about giving Richard his library card, because only white people are allowed to have library cards. Jim might get into trouble if Richard is caught using his card.

Have the students say the word *apprehensive*, and write it on the chart.

◀ **Teacher Note**

You might remind the students that *uneasy* means "nervous, worried, or anxious." You might explain that *uneasy* and *apprehensive* are synonyms and add the words to the synonym chart.

▶ 6 Discuss Being Apprehensive

Explain that, like Jim, people often feel apprehensive, or uneasy, when they are doing things they think might get them into trouble. Explain that people also feel apprehensive when they are doing things that are a little risky or dangerous or when they are doing things they have never done before. Give a couple of examples of times you have been apprehensive. (You might say, "I was a little apprehensive the first time I flew on an airplane. Even though I know flying is a safe way to travel, it was a new experience for me, and I was a little scared. Recently, I was apprehensive about letting my son play football. I was worried that he might get hurt.")

Week 13 ▶ Day 1

Use "Think, Pair, Share" to discuss:

Q *When have you been apprehensive? Why were you apprehensive? [pause] Turn to your partner.*

PROMPT: "I was apprehensive when [I tried out for the choir at my church] because [I wasn't sure my singing was good enough]."

Review the pronunciation and meaning of the word.

Day 2

Review *Frugal, Hunger,* and *Apprehensive*

Words Reviewed

frugal
Frugal means "careful in spending money or not wasteful."

hunger
Hunger is "a strong desire or want."

apprehensive
Apprehensive means "uneasy or worried and slightly afraid."

Materials
- Word chart from Day 1

REVIEW THE WORDS

1 Briefly Review the Words

Review the pronunciation and meaning of each word.

Ask:

Q *Which of the words we learned yesterday do you think was interesting or fun to talk about? Why? Turn to your partner.*

PROMPT: "I think the word [*frugal*] was [interesting/fun] to talk about because…."

Week 13 ▶ Day 2

PRACTICE USING THE WORDS

2 Do the Activity "Create a Sentence"

Explain that partners will do the activity "Create a Sentence." Review that partners will work together to create sentences that use the vocabulary words.

Point to the word *frugal* on the chart, and review that a frugal person is careful in spending money or not wasteful.

Use "Think, Pair, Share" to discuss:

Q *How might you use the word* frugal *in a sentence?* [pause] *Turn to your partner.*

Have a few pairs share their sentences.

Follow up by asking:

Q *Does it make sense to say, ["My brother is saving money for college so he has to be frugal"]? Why?*

In the same way, have partners work together to use *hunger* and *apprehensive* in sentences.

Teacher Note

Support struggling students by asking questions such as, "Who is a frugal person you know? What does he or she do to be frugal?" and "When might someone need to be frugal?" If they continue to struggle, provide a sentence starter such as, "I was frugal when…" or "To be frugal, my mom…."

Teacher Note

[*hunger*] Support struggling students by asking questions such as, "What is something you hunger to do?" and "Where is a place you hunger to visit?" If they continue to struggle, provide a sentence starter such as, "After the cold winter, I hungered for…" or "When I finished the first book in the series, I hungered…."

[*apprehensive*] Support struggling students by asking questions such as, "What is something you are apprehensive about doing at school?" and "When have you been apprehensive about something?" If they continue to struggle, provide a sentence starter such as, "My parents were apprehensive when…" or "I was apprehensive when…."

294 | Making Meaning® Vocabulary

Week 13 ▶ Day 3

Day 3

Introduce *Discourteous, Prejudice,* and *Episode*

Words Taught

discourteous
Discourteous means "not courteous, or disrespectful or rude."

prejudice
Prejudice is "an unfair opinion of someone based on the person's race, religion, or other characteristic."

episode (p. 32)
An *episode* is "an event or series of events in a person's life."

Materials

- *Richard Wright and the Library Card*
- Word chart from Day 1
- A marker

INTRODUCE AND PRACTICE USING *DISCOURTEOUS*

▶ 1 Introduce *Discourteous* and Review the Prefix *dis-* and Antonyms

Show pages 22–23 of *Richard Wright and the Library Card*, and review that Richard uses Jim Falk's library card to check out books. Read page 22 aloud. Use a loud voice and sharp tone when the librarian says, "Are you sure these books aren't for you?"

Tell the students that the first word they will learn today is *discourteous* and that *discourteous* means "not courteous, or disrespectful or rude."

Explain that the librarian is discourteous when she loudly asks Richard if the books are his. She's discourteous again when she laughs at him when he says he cannot read. She makes Richard feel embarrassed and uncomfortable.

Grade Five | 295

Week 13 ▶ Day 3

Have the students say *discourteous*, and then add the word to the chart.

Point to the prefix *dis-* in *discourteous* on the chart, and review that *dis-* is a prefix that means "not." Explain that when *dis-* is added to the word *courteous*, which means "polite and respectful," it makes the word *discourteous*, which means "not courteous, or disrespectful or rude." Point out that *discourteous* and *courteous* are antonyms.

▶ **Teacher Note**

If you started an antonym chart, add *courteous* and *discourteous* to it. If you started a chart of *dis-* words, add *discourteous* to it.

2 Play "Is Tulip Discourteous?"

Explain that partners will play "Is Tulip Discourteous?" You will describe something that Tulip is doing, and partners will discuss whether or not Tulip is discourteous and why they think so.

Begin by reading the following scenario aloud twice, slowly and clearly:

- *Tulip is studying in the library. The people next to her are whispering and giggling. Tulip turns to them and says, "Shhh! I'm trying to study!"*

Ask:

Q *Is Tulip discourteous? Why? Turn to your partner.*

PROMPT: "Tulip [is/is not] discourteous because…."

In the same way, discuss:

- *Tulip is waiting in line at the movie theater. The person in front of her steps out of line to talk to a friend, and then gets back in line in front of Tulip. Tulip says to her, "Excuse me, you stepped out of line, so you need to go to the end of the line."*

Q *Is Tulip discourteous? Why? Turn to your partner.*

- *Tulip is eating crackers during recess. Her friend asks if she can have one. Tulip says, "I'm really hungry, so I'm not going to share my snack today."*

296 | Making Meaning® Vocabulary

Q *Is Tulip discourteous? Why? Turn to your partner.*

Review the pronunciation and meaning of the word.

INTRODUCE AND PRACTICE USING *PREJUDICE*

3 Introduce and Define *Prejudice*

Show pages 22–23 again, and review that the librarian questions Richard about the library books. Reread the following sentences from page 22 aloud: "But Richard told the lady what she wanted to hear, what she believed was true about all black boys like him. 'No ma'am,' he said. 'These books aren't for me. Heck, I can't even read.'"

Explain that the next word the students will learn is *prejudice*. Explain that *prejudice* is "an unfair opinion of someone based on the person's race, religion, or other characteristic."

Explain that the librarian's prejudice is her unfair belief that African Americans cannot read. Explain that when Richard says, "Heck, I can't even read," he is using the librarian's prejudice, or unfair opinion about his race, to trick her into thinking that the library books cannot possibly be for him.

Have the students say *prejudice*, and then add the word to the chart.

4 Review the Prefix *pre-*

Point to the prefix *pre-* in *prejudice* on the chart and review that *pre-* is a prefix that means "before." Review that the students discussed the prefix earlier when they learned the word *prearrange*.

Week 13 ▶ Day 3

Teacher Note ▶

You might explain that *judice* is an example of a root and that a root is a part of a word to which prefixes and suffixes can be added to make new words. Many roots come to English from other languages, such as Latin and Greek. For more about roots, see the Extension on page 300–301.

If you started a list of *pre-* words, add *prejudice* to it.

Point to *judice* in *prejudice* and explain that *judice* comes from the Latin language, which was spoken by the people of ancient Rome. Explain that in Latin *judice* means "judgment." Explain that when you add *pre-* to *judice*, you make the word *prejudice*. Explain that prejudice is forming an opinion or making a judgment about someone before you know the person, and that prejudice can be based on the person's race, religion, or other characteristic.

5 Discuss Whether People Are Prejudiced

Tell the students that we use the word *prejudiced* to describe someone who has a prejudice. Explain that the librarian can be described as prejudiced, because she has an unfair opinion about Richard based on his race. Explain that, in addition to race, people are sometimes prejudiced because of another person's religious beliefs, age, or gender (whether the person is male or female).

Write the word *prejudiced* next to *prejudice* on the chart.

Tell the students that you will describe a situation and partners will decide if the person in the situation is prejudiced and why they think so.

Begin with:

- *Sheila goes to a tryout for a youth hockey team. The hockey coach says to Sheila, "You can't try out for the hockey team. Girls aren't tough enough to play hockey."*

Use "Think, Pair, Share" to discuss:

Q *Is the coach prejudiced? Why?* [pause] *Turn to your partner.*

PROMPT: "The coach [is/is not] prejudiced because…."

In the same way, discuss:

- *An elderly couple wants to buy a car. The salesperson says, "Elderly people are unsafe drivers. I don't feel comfortable selling you a car."*

Q *Is the salesperson prejudiced? Why?* [pause] *Turn to your partner*

PROMPT: "The salesperson [is/is not] prejudiced because…."

- *Gilroy's neighbor offers him a babysitting job. When Gilroy asks his father if he can babysit, his father says, "Boys don't know how to take care of children. Babysitting is a job only a girl can do."*

Q *Is Gilroy's father prejudiced? Why?* [pause] *Turn to your partner.*

PROMPT: "Gilroy's father [is/is not] prejudiced because…."

Review the pronunciation and meaning of the words *prejudice* and *prejudiced*.

INTRODUCE AND PRACTICE USING *EPISODE*

6 Introduce and Define *Episode*

Show the "Author's Note" on page 32, read the title aloud, and tell the students that on this page the author gives more information about Richard Wright's life and explains where the idea for the book *Richard Wright and the Library Card* came from. Read page 32 aloud, emphasizing the word *episode* in the first sentence.

Tell the students that the last word they will learn today is *episode* and that an *episode* is "an event or series of events in a person's life." Explain that gaining access to the public library in Memphis was an important episode, or event, in Richard's life.

Have the students say the word *episode*, and write it on the chart.

Week 13 ▶ Day 3

7 Discuss Important or Memorable Episodes in Our Lives

Explain that, like Richard Wright, all of us have episodes, or events, in our lives that are important or memorable. We might remember an episode because it led to a big change in our lives or because it was an event that was especially happy or exciting or especially sad or scary. Give an example of an important or memorable episode in your life. (You might say, "An important episode in my life was when I volunteered at an animal shelter when I was 15. It was important because I became aware of the number of animals that need homes and I learned how important it is to take care of a pet.")

Use "Think, Pair, Share" to discuss:

Q *What is an important or memorable episode from your life? Why is it important or memorable?* [pause] *Turn to your partner.*

PROMPT: "An [important/memorable] episode in my life was when [I learned how to read] because…."

Review the pronunciation and meaning of the word.

> **Teacher Note**
> Support struggling students by asking questions such as, "When have you learned something that has helped you to be successful in school?" "When have you done something that you didn't think you could do? How did that change you?" and "What was a moment in your life when you were very happy or excited or very sad or disappointed?"

EXTENSION

Exploring Roots

Write the word *prejudice* on the board and underline *judice*.

Explain that *judice* is an example of a root and that a root is a part of a word to which prefixes and suffixes can be added to make new words. Explain that many roots come to English from other languages, such as Latin and Greek. Remind the students that *judice* is a Latin word that means "judgment" and that when you add the prefix *pre-* to *judice*, you make the word *prejudice*, which is "a judgment about someone based on the person's race, religion, or other characteristic."

Week 13 ▶ Day 3

Write the word *spectacle* on the board and underline *spect*. Remind the students that they learned the word *spectacle* earlier and that a *spectacle* is "an unusual or remarkable sight." Explain that the word *spectacle* comes from the Latin root *spec* or *spect*, meaning "look or see." Explain that many other words also include the root *spect*, and discuss the meaning of each of the following words: *spectacles, spectator, spectacular, inspect, inspection,* and *inspector*.

Write the word *bicycle* on the board and underline *cycl*. Explain that the word *bicycle* comes from the Greek root *cycl*, meaning "circular." Explain that a *bicycle* is "a vehicle that has two circular wheels." Ask the students for other words that use the root *cycl*, and discuss the meaning of each one (for example, *motorcycle, cycle, tricycle, cyclone, cyclist,* and *recycle*).

◀ **Teacher Note**

For a list of common Latin and Greek roots, visit Developmental Studies Center's website at www.devstu.org.

Week 13 ▶ Day 4

Day 4

Review *Discourteous, Prejudice,* and *Episode*

Materials
- Word chart from Day 3
- A marker

Words Reviewed

discourteous
Discourteous means "not courteous, or disrespectful or rude."

prejudice
Prejudice is "an unfair opinion of someone based on the person's race, religion, or other characteristic."

episode
An *episode* is "an event or series of events in a person's life."

REVIEW THE WORDS

▶1 Briefly Review the Words

Review the pronunciation and meaning of each word.

Discuss as a class:

Q *If you were writing a report about Martin Luther King, Jr., which of these words might you use? Why?*

PROMPT: "If I were writing a report about Martin Luther King, Jr., I would use the word [*prejudice*] because…."

302 | Making Meaning® Vocabulary

PRACTICE USING THE WORDS

▶2 Do the Activity "What Do You Think About?"

Explain that partners will do the activity "What Do You Think About?" Point to the words on the chart, and explain that you want the students to notice what they think about, or what picture comes into their minds, when they hear each of the words.

Have the students close their eyes. Then use "Think, Pair, Share" to discuss:

Q *What do you think about when you hear the word* discourteous? *Why?* [pause] *Open your eyes and turn to your partner.*

PROMPT: "When I hear the word *discourteous*, I think of [graffiti] because…."

Discuss the remaining words the same way.

Teacher Note

If the students struggle to make associations, call for attention and think aloud about what comes into your mind when you hear the word *discourteous*. (You might close your eyes and say, "When I hear the word *discourteous*, I think of people who litter. I think it is discourteous to throw garbage on the ground instead of in the trashcan. I also think about manners. I think it is discourteous to use bad manners.") If the students continue to struggle, support them by asking questions such as, "When have you seen someone be discourteous?" "What might someone do to be discourteous?" and "How do you feel when someone is discourteous to you?"

Teacher Note

Support struggling students by thinking aloud about what you picture in your mind when you hear the word or by asking questions such as, [*prejudice*] "When have you seen an example of prejudice or heard about someone facing prejudice?" "Why might a person be prejudiced against another person or group of people?" and "Whom do you know about who has fought against prejudice?" [*episode*] "What is a memorable episode in your life?" and "What might happen to you to make an episode memorable?"

Week 13 ▸ Day 5

Day 5

Ongoing Review

Materials
- Pocket chart
- Word cards 35, 42, 58, 63, 69

Words Reviewed

advantage
An *advantage* is "something that is helpful or useful." An advantage can help you do something better or succeed at something.

conspicuous
Conspicuous means "obvious or noticeable." Something that is conspicuous stands out and can be seen easily.

ordeal
An *ordeal* is a "very difficult or bad experience."

thoughtful
Thoughtful means "full of thought for the feelings or needs of others."

widespread
Widespread means "spread, scattered, or happening over a large area."

REVIEW THE WORDS

▶ **1** **Display the Word Cards and Briefly Review the Words**

Review the pronunciation and meaning of the words.

PRACTICE USING THE WORDS

2 Play "Does That Make Sense?"

Explain that partners will play the game "Does That Make Sense?" Explain that you will read a scenario that includes one of the vocabulary words. Partners will decide whether or not the word makes sense in the scenario and why they think so.

Point to the word *advantage*, and explain that the first scenario includes the word *advantage*.

Then read the following scenario aloud twice:

- Greg's little brother Ivan wants to race. Greg gives Ivan a head start because Greg wants Ivan to have an advantage in the race.

Ask:

Q *Does the word* advantage *make sense in the scenario? Why do you think that? Turn to your partner.*

PROMPT: "The word *advantage* [does/does not] make sense in the scenario because…."

In the same way, discuss:

[conspicuous]

- Millie hid her money under her mattress because she wanted it to be conspicuous.

[ordeal]

- Hugo missed the bus and had to ride his bike to school. Along the way, a dog chased him, he ran into the curb, and his bike got a flat tire. When he finally got to school, he told his teacher, "I'm sorry I'm late, but getting to school this morning was an ordeal!"

◀ **Teacher Note**

If the students struggle to answer the questions, call for attention. Reread the scenario aloud, and explain that *advantage* does make sense because an *advantage* is "something that is helpful and useful." A head start is an advantage for Ivan, or something that will help him do well in the race with his big brother. Then read the story that uses the word *conspicuous*, and discuss it in pairs.

[thoughtful]

- *Abbie sent her grandmother a birthday card. When her grandmother received the card in the mail, she thought, "My goodness, Abbie is so thoughtful!"*

[widespread]

- *A tornado touched down near the town of Arcadia, but it did not destroy any property or hurt anyone. The damage from the tornado was widespread.*

Week 14

Overview

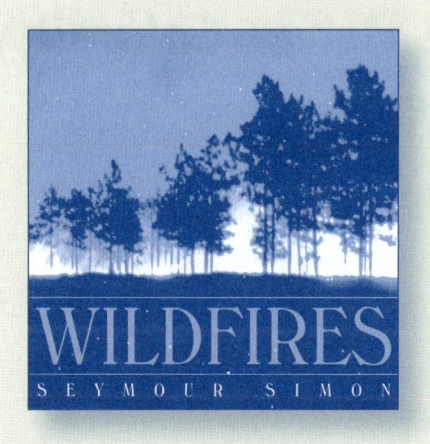

Widlfires
by Seymour Simon
(HarperTrophy, 1996)

Words Taught

merge

calamity

range

revive

flourish

deprive

Word-learning Strategies

- Recognizing synonyms (review)
- Recognizing words with multiple meanings (review)

Words Reviewed: comrade, dumbfounded, picturesque, reverie, scarce

DO AHEAD

- Prior to Day 1, review More Strategy Practice on page 312.
- Prior to Day 5, collect these word cards for Ongoing Review: 40, 56, 61, 70, and 72.

Grade Five | 307

Week 14 ▶ Day 1

Day 1

Introduce *Merge, Calamity,* and *Range*

Materials
- *Wildfires*
- Chart paper
- A marker

Words Taught

merge (p. 12)
Merge means "combine or join together to form one thing."

calamity
A *calamity* is "a terrible disaster."

range (p. 22)
Range means "vary or change within certain limits."

INTRODUCE AND PRACTICE USING *MERGE*

1 Introduce and Define *Merge*

Briefly review *Wildfires*.

Show pages 12–13 and review that, during the summer of 1988, eight major forest fires were burning in Yellowstone National Park. The fires threatened park buildings and caused tourists to leave the park. Read the first paragraph on page 12 aloud, stopping after the sentence, "The old fires continued to spread, while the small fires raced toward one another and merged into even bigger fires." Emphasize the word *merged*.

Tell the students that the first word they will learn today is *merge* and that *merge* means "combine or join together to form one thing." Point out that the small fires merged, or joined together, to form bigger and more dangerous fires.

308 | Making Meaning® Vocabulary

Have the students say the word *merge*, and then write it on a sheet of chart paper.

2. Discuss Things That Merge

Remind the students that in Yellowstone smaller fires merged to form a larger fire. Explain that other things merge, or join together to form one thing. For example, two companies sometimes merge to form one bigger company. Two lanes of traffic on a freeway sometimes merge to form a single lane of traffic.

Explain that sometimes two or more streams or rivers merge. Discuss as a class:

Q *What happens when streams or rivers merge?*

PROMPT: "When streams or rivers merge…."

Ask the students to imagine that it is lunchtime and three lines of students have formed outside the cafeteria. When the bell rings, the lines of students move forward together and merge at the cafeteria door.

Ask:

Q *What might happen when the lines of students merge at the door? Turn to your partner.*

PROMPT: "When the lines of students merge…."

Review the pronunciation and meaning of the word.

INTRODUCE AND PRACTICE USING *CALAMITY*

3. Introduce and Define *Calamity* and Review Synonyms

Show pages 12–13 again. Review that strong winds made the firefighters' job more difficult by blowing hot embers downwind, starting new fires and feeding the fires that were already burning.

Week 14 ▶ Day 1

Teacher Note ▶

You might explain that an acre is an area of land about the size of a soccer field.

Read the following sentences from the second paragraph on page 12 aloud: "On August 20, known as Black Saturday, 165,000 acres of forest, an area more than twice the size of the entire city of Chicago, were burning. But the worst was still ahead."

Tell the students that the next word they will learn today is *calamity*. Explain that a *calamity* is "a terrible disaster" and that *calamity* and *disaster* are synonyms. Point out that the Yellowstone fire was a calamity, or terrible disaster, because such a large area of forest was destroyed.

Teacher Note ▶

If you started a synonym chart, add *calamity* and *disaster* to it.

Have the students say the word *calamity*, and write it on the chart.

ELL Note

You might explain that a *disaster* is "an event that causes a lot of damage or suffering."

4 Play "Is It a Calamity?"

Remind the students that a *calamity* is "a terrible disaster," and explain that we use the word *calamity* to talk about situations in which there is a great deal of destruction or loss of life. Explain that you will describe a situation and partners will decide whether the situation is or is not a calamity and why they think so.

Begin with the following situation:

- *An earthquake strikes. It causes cans to fall off shelves in a few supermarkets.*

Ask:

Q *Is this situation a calamity? Why? Turn to your partner.*

PROMPT: "This situation [is/is not] a calamity because…."

In the same way, discuss:

- *A flood sweeps through a town. Several people drown, many homes are swept away, and hundreds of residents are left without shelter.*

Q *Is this situation a calamity? Why? Turn to your partner.*

Review the pronunciation and meaning of the word.

310 | Making Meaning® Vocabulary

INTRODUCE AND PRACTICE USING *RANGE*

5. Introduce and Define *Range*

Show pages 22–23.

Review that wildfires in lodgepole pine forests can be beneficial because they melt the resin that encases the seeds of the trees, which helps them reproduce. Read the following sentences from the second paragraph on page 22 aloud, emphasizing the word *ranging*: "Following the Yellowstone fires, seed counts in burned lodgepole stands were very high, ranging from fifty thousand to one million seeds per acre. All had come from sealed pinecones that were opened by the fire."

Tell the students that the last word they will learn today is *range* and that *range* means "vary or change within certain limits."

Point out that after the fire the number of seeds found on each acre of land ranged, or varied, from fifty thousand to one million. In other words, every acre had a different number of seeds, and the number on each acre was between fifty thousand and one million.

◀ **Teacher Note**

You might review that *vary* means "are different."

Have the students say the word *range*, and write it on the chart.

6. Discuss Ranges of Things

Explain that the word *range* can also be used to tell the lower and upper limits of things, and give examples of ranges. (You might say, "Our winter temperatures range from about 10 degrees Fahrenheit to 40 degrees Fahrenheit. That means that the temperature in winter might fall as low as 10 degrees or rise as high as 40 degrees. The distance my car can go on a gallon of gas ranges from 26 to 35 miles. In city driving, I get only about 26 miles per gallon, but in highway driving, I get as much as 35 miles per gallon. In our class, the number of students who are absent each day ranges from none to four or five. On some days, no student is absent. On other days, as many as four or five students are absent.")

Week 14 ▶ Day 1

Discuss as a class:

Q *What is the range, or upper and lower limit, of grade levels in our school?*

PROMPTS: "The range of grade levels in our school is from…" or "The grade levels range from…."

Then ask:

Q *What is the range of ages in our school? Turn to your partner.*

PROMPTS: "The range of ages in our school is from…" or "The ages range from…."

Review the pronunciation and meaning of the word.

MORE STRATEGY PRACTICE

Discuss Other Meanings of *Range*

Remind the students that words often have more than one meaning and that sometimes the meanings are very different. Point to the word *range* on the word chart, pronounce it, and review that *range* means "vary or change within certain limits."

Ask and discuss as a class:

Q *What else do you know about the word* range*? What is a mountain range? What is a kitchen range?*

PROMPTS: "*Range* also means…" or "A [mountain range/kitchen range] is…."

If necessary, explain that a *range* can also be "a row or line of connected mountains" and "a large stove with burners and an oven."

Teacher Note

You might explain that a *range* is also "a large area of flat land." In pioneer days, huge herds of buffalo roamed the ranges of the western United States. A *range* is also "the limits within which things can vary." Some stores carry a wide variety of fruit, ranging from ordinary fruits such as apples, oranges, and pears to more exotic fruits such as pomegranates and kiwis.

312 | Making Meaning® Vocabulary

Day 2

Review *Merge, Calamity,* and *Range*

Words Reviewed

merge
Merge means "combine or join together to form one thing."

calamity
A *calamity* is "a terrible disaster."

range
Range means "vary or change within certain limits."

Materials
- Word chart from Day 1

REVIEW THE WORDS

1 Briefly Review the Words

Review the pronunciation and meaning of each word.

Discuss as a class:

Q *Do you think our class should merge with [Mr. Henshaw's fifth-grade class]? Why?*

PROMPT: "I [think/do not think] our class should merge with [Mr. Henshaw's fifth-grade class] because…."

In the same way, discuss:

Q *Is spilling orange juice on a pair of new shoes a calamity? Why?*

PROMPT: "Spilling orange juice on a pair of new shoes [is/is not] a calamity because…."

Week 14 ▶ Day 2

Q *What is the range of ages of people in your family?*

PROMPT: *"The range of ages is from…."*

PRACTICE USING THE WORDS

▶ **2 Do the Activity "Tell Me a Story"**

Explain that partners will do the activity "Tell Me a Story." Review that you will tell the beginning of a story that includes one of the vocabulary words. The students will use what they know about the word and their imaginations to make up an ending for the story.

Begin by reading the following story aloud twice, slowly and clearly:

- *The weather forecaster said, "There are two hurricanes gaining strength off the east coast. If the two storms merge…."*

Use "Think, Pair, Share" to discuss:

Q *How might you finish the story? What might happen if the two storms merge? [pause] Turn to your partner.*

PROMPT: *"If the two storms merge…."*

In the same way, discuss:

- *A fire started in a shed behind Mr. Coble's house. The fire became a calamity when….*

Q *How might you finish the story? What might happen when a fire becomes a calamity? [pause] Turn to your partner.*

PROMPT: *"The fire became a calamity when…."*

314 | Making Meaning® Vocabulary

- *Holly is visiting her grandmother who lives in the desert. In the morning Holly is cold, but in the afternoon she is hot because the temperature ranges from….*

Q *How might you finish the story? What might be the range of temperatures if it is cold in the morning and hot in the afternoon? [pause] Turn to your partner.*

PROMPT: "The temperature ranges from…."

Week 14 ▶ Day 3

Day 3

Introduce *Revive, Flourish,* and *Deprive*

Materials

- *Wildfires*
- Word chart from Day 1
- A marker

Words Taught

revive
Revive means "bring back to a healthy, active condition or give new strength or freshness to."

flourish (p. 24)
Flourish means "grow well or be successful."

deprive (p. 24)
Deprive means "prevent from having something or take something away."

INTRODUCE AND PRACTICE USING *REVIVE*

▶ 1 Introduce and Define *Revive*

Show pages 24–25 of *Wildfires*, and review that in 1988 wildfires devastated the forests of Yellowstone. Then read the first paragraph on page 24 aloud.

Tell the students that the first word they will learn today is *revive* and that *revive* means "bring back to a healthy, active condition or give new strength or freshness to." Explain that, as you reread the paragraph aloud, you want the students to listen for examples of ways the forests revived, or returned to a healthy condition.

Reread the first paragraph on page 24 aloud.

Week 14 ▸ Day 3

Discuss as a class:

Q *What examples did you hear of ways the forests revived?*

PROMPT: "One way the forests revived is…."

If necessary, point out that ways the forest revived are that new plants sprouted and insects, birds, and other animals returned to the forests.

Have the students say the word *revive*, and write it on the chart.

2 Do the Activity "Imagine That!"

Have the students close their eyes and imagine:

- *You move into a new house. There is a garden in the backyard that is filled with weeds, dying plants, and plant-eating bugs.*

Use "Think, Pair, Share" to discuss:

Q *What might you do to revive the garden? Why?* [pause] *Open your eyes and turn to your partner.*

PROMPT: "I might revive the garden by…."

3 Discuss Things We Do to Revive

Explain that, when people are feeling tired, they do various things to revive themselves, or feel strong and fresh again. Give examples of ways you revive yourself when you are tired. (You might say, "When I am tired, I revive myself by taking a shower. Getting into the water helps to wake me up. A brisk walk or a bike ride also revives me.")

Ask:

Q *What do you to do revive yourself when you are tired? Turn to your partner.*

PROMPT: "When I am tired, I revive myself by…."

Review the pronunciation and meaning of the word.

Grade Five | 317

Week 14 ▶ Day 3

INTRODUCE AND PRACTICE USING *FLOURISH*

▶4 Introduce and Define *Flourish*

Show pages 24–25 again, and review that the forests revived after the fires. Then read the second paragraph on page 24 aloud, emphasizing the word *flourish*.

Tell the students that the next word they will learn today is *flourish* and that *flourish* means "grow well or be successful." Explain that the towering lodgepole pines blocked sunlight from the forest floor, so low-growing plants could not flourish, or grow well. When the fires destroyed the tall trees, low-growing plants got sunlight and flourished.

Teacher Note ▶
You might remind the students that *towering* means "very tall."

Discuss as a class:

Q *In addition to sunlight, what does a plant need to flourish?*

PROMPT: "A plant needs [water] to flourish."

Have the students say the word *flourish*, and write it on the chart.

▶5 Discuss Ways a Student Might Flourish in School

Review that *flourish* can also mean "be successful," and explain that we use the word *flourish* to talk about people who are doing well at things. For example, a student who is flourishing in school is doing well in her studies and learning lots of things.

Ask:

Q *What might a student do that would help him or her flourish, or be successful, in school? Turn to your partner.*

PROMPT: "To flourish in school, a student might…."

Review the pronunciation and meaning of the word.

318 | Making Meaning® Vocabulary

INTRODUCE AND PRACTICE USING *DEPRIVE*

6 Introduce and Define *Deprive*

Show pages 24–25 again, and review that many of the plant species found on the forest floor would die off without occasional fires. Then read the last paragraph on page 24 aloud, emphasizing the word *deprive*.

Tell the students that the last word they will learn today is *deprive* and that *deprive* means "prevent from having something or take something away." Review that, as the pines grow, they deprive low-growing plants of light, or prevent the light from reaching the plants. When the plants are deprived of light, they cannot grow.

Have the students say the word *deprive*, and write it on the chart.

7 Discuss *Deprive*

Point out that when people are deprived of, or prevented from having, food or sleep, they feel grumpy and tired and have trouble concentrating. Explain that people can also become grumpy when they are deprived of things they enjoy, like TV or video games.

Ask:

Q *What is something you would not like to be deprived of? Why? Turn to your partner.*

PROMPT: "I would not like to be deprived of…."

Review the pronunciation and meaning of the word.

EXTENSION

An Interesting Fact About *Revive*

Explain that *revive* is a word that was first used in 1432 and that it comes from the Latin word *revivere,* meaning "to live again." Write the word *revivere* on the board, and underline the prefix *re-*. Explain that the Latin word *revivere* contains the prefix *re-*, meaning "again," and the Latin root *vivere,* meaning "to live."

Day 4

Review *Revive, Flourish,* and *Deprive*

Words Reviewed

revive
Revive means "bring back to a healthy, active condition or give new strength or freshness to."

flourish
Flourish means "grow well or be successful."

deprive
Deprive means "prevent from having something or take something away."

Materials
- Word chart from Day 3
- A marker

REVIEW THE WORDS

1 Briefly Review the Words

Review the pronunciation and meaning of each word.

Discuss as a class:

Q *Which of the words we learned yesterday might you use when you are talking with your friends or family? How might you use the word?*

PROMPT: "I might use the word [*deprive*] when I'm talking with [my father]. I might say…."

Week 14 ▶ Day 4

PRACTICE USING THE WORDS

2 ▶ **Do the Activity "Imagine That!"**

Ask the students to imagine:

- *You and your family move into a new home. When you explore the backyard, you are stunned by what you see. In one half of the yard, there are patches of dried grass and tall weeds. In the other half of the yard, there is no grass at all. There are no flowers anywhere.*

> **Teacher Note** ▶
> You might review that *stun* can mean "shock or greatly surprise."

Use "Think, Pair, Share" to discuss:

Q *What might you do to revive the yard?* [pause] *Turn to your partner.*

PROMPT: "To revive the yard, I might…."

In the same way, imagine and discuss:

- *Because your new house has a big backyard, your parents decide you can have a dog. At the animal shelter you select a healthy, happy puppy and take it home.*

Q *What might you do to make sure your puppy flourishes in its new home? Why?* [pause] *Turn to your partner.*

PROMPT: "To make sure my puppy flourishes, I might…."

- *One of your chores in your new home is to take out the garbage each week, but you forget. Your parents tell you that as punishment you will be deprived of one of the following privileges for a week: watching TV, riding your bike, or talking on the phone.*

Q *Which would you miss the most if you were deprived of it: watching TV, riding your bike, or talking on the phone? Why?* [pause] *Turn to your partner.*

Teacher Note
For a crossword puzzle you can use to review words taught during weeks 13 and 14, visit Developmental Studies Center's website at www.devstu.org.

PROMPT: "I would miss [watching TV] the most if I were deprived of it, because…."

Day 5

Week 14 ▶ Day 5

Ongoing Review

Words Reviewed

comrade
A *comrade* is "a good friend or companion."

dumbfounded
Dumbfounded means "so surprised that you cannot speak."

picturesque
Picturesque means "beautiful or pleasant to look at."

reverie
A *reverie* is "a pleasant daydream."

scarce
Scarce means "difficult to get or find." If something is scarce, there is very little of it.

Materials
- Pocket chart
- Word cards 40, 56, 61, 70, 72

REVIEW THE WORDS

▶ **1** **Display the Word Cards and Briefly Review the Words**
Review the pronunciation and meaning of the words.

Week 14 ▶ Day 5

PRACTICE USING THE WORDS

2 **Play "Finish the Story"**

Tell the students that partners will play the game "Finish the Story." Explain that you will tell a story, leaving off the last word. Point to the word chart, and explain that partners will finish the story by choosing the word on the chart that makes the best ending for it.

Teacher Note ▶
For a fully written-out example of the activity, see page 66.

Begin by reading the following story aloud twice:

- *The severe weather delayed deliveries to grocery stores, so food and supplies were _____. (scarce)*

Ask:

Teacher Note ▶
You might explain that the students may need to change the form of the word to complete the sentence by adding an ending such as *-s, -ing,* or *-ed.*

Q *Which word makes the best ending for the story? Why? Turn to your partner.*

PROMPT: "I think [*scarce*] makes the best ending because…."

Retell the story, adding the word *scarce* at the end.

Continue the activity using the following stories:

- *Annie's family is driving through the desert. All she can see when she looks out the window are rocks and dirt. Annie turns to her mother and says, "Mom, this place is not _____." (picturesque)*

- *Orson and Boris often argue, but they never stay angry. They have remained _____. (comrades)*

- *For the magician's final act, she made a table float in mid-air. When the audience realized there were no strings attached to the table, they were _____. (dumbfounded)*

- *Maggie was staring into space, imagining she was a gymnast competing in the Olympic games. Her mother smiled at her and said, "Maggie, would you like to tell me about your_____." (reverie)*

324 | Making Meaning® Vocabulary

CLASS VOCABULARY PROGRESS ASSESSMENT

As you observe the students, ask yourself:

- Do the students' responses indicate that they understand the words' meanings?

- Are they using context clues, prefixes and suffixes, and other strategies to figure out words in their independent reading?

For more information about reviewing and practicing the words, see "Retaining the Words" on pages xviii–xix.

Week 15 Overview

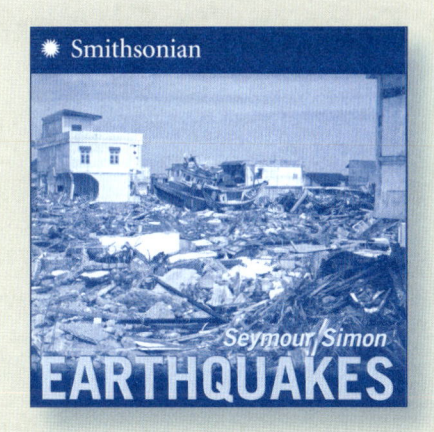

Earthquakes
by Seymour Simon
(Smithsonian/Collins, 2006)

Words Taught

topple

a shambles

thrust

churn

gush

batter

Word-learning Strategies

- Recognizing synonyms (review)
- Using context to determine word meanings (review)

Words Reviewed: a shambles, calamity, discourteous, jumble, thoughtless

DO AHEAD

- Prior to Day 1, review More Strategy Practice on pages 332–333.

- Prior to Day 2, write the "What's the Missing Word?" sentences on the board or a sheet of chart paper or make a transparency of the sentences (BLM11). (See Step 2 on page 335.)

- Prior to Day 3, review More Strategy Practice on pages 341–342. Write the "Use the Clues" sentences on the board or a sheet of chart paper or make a transparency of the sentences (BLM12).

- Prior to Day 5, collect these word cards for Ongoing Review: 62, 67, 76, 80, and 86.

Week 15 ▶ Day 1

Day 1

Introduce *Topple*, "a Shambles," and *Thrust*

Materials
- *Earthquakes*
- Chart paper
- A marker

Words Taught

topple (p. 5)
Topple means "fall over or make something fall over."

a shambles
When a place is a shambles, it is very messy or in complete disorder or ruin.

thrust (p. 9)
Thrust means "push or shove suddenly or with force."

INTRODUCE AND PRACTICE USING *TOPPLE*

▶ **1 Introduce and Define *Topple* and Review Synonyms**

Briefly review *Earthquakes*.

Show pages 4–5 and review that there are millions of earthquakes around the world every year. Then read the following sentence from page 5 aloud, emphasizing the word *toppled*, "A large earthquake in Kobe, Japan, in 1995, toppled this freeway onto its side and cracked the roadway in numerous places."

Tell the students that the first word they will learn today is *topple*. Explain that *topple* means "fall over or make something fall over" and that *topple* and *fall* are synonyms.

Teacher Note
If you started a synonym chart, add *topple* and *fall* to it. Remind the students that they can use a word like *topple* in their writing to replace an overused word like *fall*.

328 | Making Meaning® Vocabulary

Point to the photograph on page 4, and explain that when the earthquake toppled the freeway, or made it fall over, it caused the trucks that were on the road to topple, or fall.

Have the students say the word *topple*, and then write it on a sheet of chart paper.

2 Discuss *Topple*

Remind the students that a freeway toppled, or fell over, during the Kobe earthquake.

Discuss as a class.

Q *What other structures might topple in an earthquake?*

PROMPT: "A [building] might topple in an earthquake."

Discuss as a class:

Q *What might cause a tree to topple, or fall over?*

PROMPT: "A [wind storm] might cause a tree to topple."

Explain that we can also use the word *topple* to talk about people falling, especially from high places. For example, people sometimes topple from ladders or from chairs or footstools they are standing on. Children sometimes topple from trees or bikes. Construction workers sometimes topple from roofs or from scaffolding.

Use "Think, Pair, Share" to discuss:

Q *When have you toppled or seen someone topple?* [pause] *Turn to your partner.*

PROMPT: "I toppled [from my bike] when…."

Review the pronunciation and meaning of the word.

ELL Note

Using a photograph or other visual image as you discuss a word's meaning is especially helpful to English Language Learners, who may struggle with a verbal explanation.

Teacher Note

If the students struggle to answer the question, name other structures that might topple, such as a wall, house, office building, skyscraper, water tower, or bridge. Then repeat the question.

Teacher Note

Support struggling students by asking questions such as, "When have you toppled or seen someone topple from a high place?" "When have you toppled or seen someone topple [at home/at a park/on a playground]?" and "When have you seen someone in a movie or on TV topple?"

Week 15 ▸ Day 1

INTRODUCE AND PRACTICE USING "A SHAMBLES"

▶3 Introduce and Define "a Shambles"

Tell the students that next they will discuss the expression "a shambles," and explain that when a place is a shambles, it is very messy or in complete disorder or ruin.

Show pages 6–7 and review that the earthquake that struck Mexico City in 1985 killed or injured thousands of people and destroyed hundreds of buildings. Point to the photograph on page 7, and point out that the parking garage and surrounding buildings are a shambles, or in disorder or ruin, because of the earthquake. Then show the photograph on page 4 again, and point out that the Japanese freeway is a shambles because of the earthquake.

Have the students say the words "a shambles," and write them on the chart.

▶4 Do the Activity "Imagine That!"

Have the students imagine that they walk into the classroom one morning and discover that the room is a shambles, or very messy or in complete disorder.

Use "Think, Pair Share" to discuss:

Q *What might our classroom look like if it were a shambles?* [pause] *Turn to your partner.*

PROMPT: "If the classroom were a shambles…."

Have volunteers share their thinking.

Follow up by discussing as a class:

Q *How might the classroom have become a shambles?*

PROMPT: "The classroom might have become a shambles when…."

Review the pronunciation and meaning of the word.

Teacher Note ▶

Support struggling students by asking questions such as, "What might the [bulletin board/book shelves/desks/chairs] look like if the classroom were a shambles?"

330 | Making Meaning® Vocabulary

Week 15 ▶ Day 1

INTRODUCE AND PRACTICE USING *THRUST*

5 Introduce and Define *Thrust* and Review Synonyms

Show pages 8–9 and review that sections of the earth's crust sliding against each other cause earthquakes. Read page 9 aloud, emphasizing the word *thrust*.

Tell the students that the last word they will learn today is *thrust*. Explain that *thrust* means "push or shove suddenly or with force" and that *thrust*, *push*, and *shove* are synonyms.

Point to the right-hand photograph on page 9, and explain that it shows what happens when one section of the earth's crust thrusts upward, or pushes upward with force, during an earthquake.

Have the students say the word *thrust*, and write it on the chart.

◀ **Teacher Note**

If you started a synonym chart, add *thrust*, *push*, and *shove* to it.

6 Discuss *Thrust*

Tell the students that when you thrust something, you push or shove it *suddenly* or *with force*. For example, if you want to dig into hard ground with a shovel, you do not gently push the shovel into the ground. Instead, you thrust the shovel into the ground, or push it with force. Act out thrusting a shovel into the ground.

Explain that sometimes people thrust open doors, or open doors suddenly or with force.

Use "Think, Pair, Share" to discuss:

Q *Why might someone thrust open a door?* [pause] *Turn to your partner.*

PROMPT: "Someone might thrust open a door because…."

Explain that people sometimes thrust, or suddenly shove, things like notes or slips of paper into their pockets. Act out thrusting a note into your pocket.

ELL Note

You might act out thrusting open a door or invite a student volunteer to act it out.

◀ **Teacher Note**

Support struggling students by asking questions such as, "Why might a firefighter or police officer thrust open a door?" "Why might someone thrust open our classroom door?" and "Why might you thrust open a door at home?"

Grade Five | 331

Week 15 ▶ Day 1

Then discuss as a class:

Q *Why might a person thrust a note or slip of paper into his or her pocket?*

PROMPT: "A person might thrust a note or slip of paper into his or her pocket because…."

Review the pronunciation and meaning of the word.

MORE STRATEGY PRACTICE

Play "Synonym Match"

Write these words in two columns on a sheet of chart paper:

1	2
calamity	strange
forceful	fall
peculiar	shove
thrust	powerful
topple	disaster

Explain that partners will play the game "Synonym Match." Point to the words in column 1, and explain that these are vocabulary words the students have learned.

Point to the words in column 2, and explain that these are synonyms of the words in column 1, or words that mean the same thing or almost the same thing. Explain that partners will match each vocabulary word to its synonym.

Point to the word *calamity*, pronounce it, and have the students pronounce it.

continues

MORE STRATEGY PRACTICE *continued*

Then point to the words in column 2, and ask:

Q *Which word in column 2 is the synonym of* calamity? *Turn to your partner.*

PROMPT: "[*Disaster*] is the synonym of *calamity*."

Have volunteers share their thinking. Then have a volunteer draw a line from the word *calamity* to the word *disaster*.

Discuss the remaining words the same way. When you get to the final two words, have the students discuss them together by asking:

Q *Which word in column 2 is the synonym of* thrust, *and which word is the synonym of* topple? *Turn to your partner.*

Week 15 ▶ Day 2

Day 2

Review *Topple*, "a Shambles," and *Thrust*

Materials
- Word chart from Day 1
- Sentences or transparency (BLM10) for "What's the Missing Word?" (see Step 2 page 335)
- (Optional) Overhead projector and marker

Words Reviewed

topple
Topple means "fall over or make something fall over."

a shambles
When a place is a shambles, it is very messy or in complete disorder or ruin.

thrust
Thrust means "push or shove suddenly or with force."

REVIEW THE WORDS

1 **Briefly Review the Words**

Review the pronunciation and meaning of each word.

Ask:

Q *If you were writing a story about an angry gorilla, which of the words might you use? Why? Turn to your partner.*

PROMPT: "If I were writing a story about an angry gorilla, I might use the word [*topple*] because…"

PRACTICE USING THE WORDS

2 Review "What's the Missing Word?"

Display the transparency or write the following sentences (without the answers) on the board or on a sheet of chart paper, leaving blanks as shown:

> The landslide caused rocks and trees to _____ down the mountainside. (topple)
>
> The power of the rapids _____ the kayaks through the water. (thrust)
>
> The bear rummaged through the tents looking for food. When he left, the campsite was _____. (a shambles)

Explain that partners will play the game "What's the Missing Word?" Direct the students' attention to the sentences and point out that a word is missing from each sentence. Explain that you will read each sentence aloud and partners will discuss which vocabulary word they learned yesterday could replace the missing word and why they think so.

Begin by pointing to this sentence and reading it aloud twice:

- *The landslide caused rocks and trees to _____ down the mountainside.*

Ask:

Q *What is the missing word? Why do you think that? Turn to your partner.*

PROMPT: "I think [*topple*] is the missing word because…."

Have volunteers share their thinking with the class. Then reread the sentence, replacing the blank with the vocabulary word.

In the same way, discuss:

- *The power of the rapids _____ the kayaks through the water.*
- *The bear rummaged through the tents looking for food. When he left, the campsite was _____ .*

You might invite partners to write a "What's the Missing Word?" sentence of their own and share it with the class.

Day 3

Introduce *Churn*, *Gush*, and *Batter*

Words Taught

churn (p. 13)
Churn means "stir or move about with force."

gush (p. 24)
Gush means "flow or pour out quickly."

batter (p. 29)
Batter means "pound repeatedly with heavy blows."

Materials
- *Earthquakes*
- Word chart from Day 1
- A marker
- (Optional) "Use the Clues" sentences or transparency (BLM11; see More Strategy Practice on pages 341–342)
- (Optional) Overhead projector and marker

INTRODUCE AND PRACTICE USING *CHURN*

1 Introduce and Define *Churn*

Show pages 12–13 of *Earthquakes* and review that this part of the book tells what causes earthquakes in California. Read the first paragraph on page 13 aloud, emphasizing the word *churns*.

Tell the students that the first word they will learn today is *churn* and that *churn* means "stir or move about with force."

Explain that the mantle below the earth's crust is made up of hot rock that is slowly churning, or moving with force. The plates that make up the earth's crust float on the churning mantle. When the plates collide, earthquakes occur.

Have the students say the word *churn*, and write it on the chart.

◀ **Teacher Note**

You might explain that *churn* and *stir* are synonyms and add the words to the synonym chart.

Grade Five | 337

Week 15 ▶ Day 3

2 Do the Activity "Imagine That!"

Explain that, when something is churning, it is being stirred or moved quite forcefully. For example, the water in a washing machine churns, or moves about with great force, during the wash cycle. The churning, or forceful movement, of the water helps to clean the clothes.

Have the students close their eyes and imagine:

- *You are on a boat. You look behind the boat and see the propeller churning the water.*

Use "Think, Pair, Share" to discuss:

Q *What does the churning water look like?* [pause] *Open your eyes and turn to your partner.*

PROMPT: "The churning water looks like…."

In the same way, discuss:

- *You are walking near the park. You see a pile of leaves on the sidewalk. A gust of wind churns the leaves.*

Q *What do the churning leaves look like?* [pause] *Open your eyes and turn to your partner.*

PROMPT: "The churning leaves look like…."

Review the pronunciation and meaning of the word.

INTRODUCE AND PRACTICE USING *GUSH*

3 Introduce and Define *Gush*

Show pages 24–25 and review that earthquakes sometimes cause dangerous changes in the earth under buildings. Read page 24 aloud, emphasizing the word *gushing*.

Tell the students that the next word they will learn today is *gush* and that *gush* means "flow or pour out quickly."

Explain that an earthquake can cause water and soil to gush, or flow out quickly, from the ground like a miniature mud volcano. The gushing water and mud are called "sand boils."

Have the students say the word *gush*, and write it on the chart.

◀ **Teacher Note**

You might explain that *gush* and *flow* are synonyms and add the words to the synonym chart.

4 Do the Activity "Imagine That!"

Remind the students that, when something gushes, it flows quickly and powerfully. For example, when a volcano erupts, lava gushes from the volcano. When a firefighter opens a fire hydrant, water gushes from the hydrant.

Have the students close their eyes and imagine:

- *You are helping your mom fix a leaky pipe under your kitchen sink. Suddenly the pipe bursts and water gushes from the pipe.*

Use "Think, Pair, Share" to discuss:

Q *What does the gushing water look like?* [pause] *Open your eyes and turn to your partner.*

PROMPT: "The gushing water…."

Review the pronunciation and meaning of the word.

INTRODUCE AND PRACTICE USING *BATTER*

5 Introduce and Define *Batter*

Show pages 28–29.

Remind the students that a powerful earthquake shook Alaska in 1964. The center of the earthquake was beneath the sea, so the earthquake caused tsunamis, or huge sea waves. Read the following

Week 15 ▶ Day 3

sentences from page 29 aloud, emphasizing the word *battered*: "The earthquake acted like a giant paddle churning the waters. Tsunamis battered the land for hours."

Tell the students that the last word they will learn today is *batter* and that *batter* means "pound repeatedly with heavy blows." Point out that the giant waves of the tsunamis battered the coast of Alaska, or pounded the coast repeatedly, overturning boats and destroying buildings.

▶ **Teacher Note**

You might explain that *batter* and *pound* are synonyms and add the words to the synonym chart.

Show the photograph on page 28, and point out that the battering of the waves left this waterfront a shambles.

Have the students say the word *batter*, and write it on the chart.

6 Play "Battered or Not Battered?"

Remind the students that *batter* means "pound repeatedly with heavy blows." Explain that you will describe a situation and partners will decide whether or not the object in the situation is being battered and why they think so.

Begin with:

- A fireman hits a door repeatedly with his ax to break it down.

Ask:

Q *Is the door being battered? Why do you think that? Turn to your partner.*

PROMPT: "The door [is/is not] being battered because…."

Have volunteers share their thinking.

In the same way, discuss:

- A flag is gently waving in the breeze.

Q *Is the flag being battered? Why do you think that? Turn to your partner.*

340 | Making Meaning® Vocabulary

Week 15 ▶ Day 3

- *Cannonball after cannonball pounds the walls of the fort.*

Q Are the walls being battered? Why do you think that? Turn to your partner.

Review the pronunciation and meaning of the word.

MORE STRATEGY PRACTICE

Play "Use the Clues"

Write the following sentences on the board or a sheet of chart paper, leaving blanks as shown, or display the transparency of the sentences:

> When we started our nature walk, the park ranger said, "If you watch carefully, you will be able to see tiny tree frogs _____ from tree to tree."
>
> She also told us that the tree frogs have sticky toe pads, which help them _____ to leaves, bark, and glass.

Explain that partners will play the game "Use the Clues," in which they use clues to figure out a word that is missing from a sentence. Direct the students' attention to the first sentence, and review that, as you read the sentence aloud, you want them to think about what the missing word might be and what words in the sentence are clues to the missing word. Remind them that more than one word might make sense as the missing word and that the word does not have to be a vocabulary word.

Read the sentence aloud twice, slowly and clearly, saying "blank" for the missing word.

Use "Think, Pair, Share" to discuss:

Q *What's the missing word? What words are clues to the missing word?* [pause] *Turn to your partner.*

continues

Teacher Note

Listen as partners share. If the students cannot suggest a word or suggest words that are not supported by the context, call for attention. Provide a word and point out the context clues. Then have the students discuss the second example.

Grade Five | 341

Week 15 ▶ Day 3

Teacher Note

Although *jump* and *leap* are logical responses, the students may reasonably argue that *hop*, *bound*, or another word is also supported by the clues in the sentence. What is important is that the students explain their thinking.

Teacher Note

Possible responses include *cling*, *grasp*, *stick*, and *hold on*.

MORE STRATEGY PRACTICE *continued*

Have a few pairs share their ideas with the class.

If necessary, explain that the missing word might be *jump* or *leap* and that the words "tree frog" and "from tree to tree" are clues that the frog is jumping or leaping from one tree to another.

Discuss the second example the same way.

---

342 | Making Meaning® Vocabulary

Day 4

Review *Churn*, *Gush*, and *Batter*

Words Reviewed

churn (p. 13)
Churn means "stir or move about with force."

gush (p. 24)
Gush means "flow or pour out quickly."

batter (p. 29)
Batter means "pound repeatedly with heavy blows."

Materials
- Word chart from Day 3

REVIEW THE WORDS

1 Briefly Review the Words

Review the pronunciation and meaning of each word.

Discuss as a class:

Q *Which of the words we learned yesterday do you think was interesting or fun to talk about? Why?*

PROMPT: "I think the word [*gush*] was [interesting/fun] to talk about because…."

PRACTICE USING THE WORDS

2 Do the Activity "Which Word Goes With?"

Tell the students that partners will do the activity "Which Word Goes With?" Review that you will write a word on the board and partners

Teacher Note

For a fully written-out example of the activity, see page 77.

Week 15 ▸ Day 4

will discuss which of the vocabulary words they learned yesterday goes with the word. Then you will ask some pairs to share their thinking with the class.

Remind the students that the word you write might go with more than one of the vocabulary words and that partners may not always agree. Explaining *why* they think the words go together is the most important thing.

Write the word *thunderstorm* on the board, and read the word aloud. Use "Think, Pair, Share" to discuss:

> **Q** *Which of yesterday's words do you think goes with* thunderstorm? *Why do you think that?* [pause] *Turn to your partner.*

PROMPT: "I think [*churn*] goes with *thunderstorm* because…."

Teacher Note

If the students struggle to answer the questions, think aloud about associations you might make and why. (You might say, "I think *churn* goes with *thunderstorm*, because clouds churn during a storm. I think *gush* goes with *thunderstorm*, too, because when there is a lot of rain, rainwater gushes from gutters and down streets. I think *batter* can go with *thunderstorm* also, because the powerful winds of a thunderstorm can batter trees and houses.") Then discuss the word *water* as a class, rather than in pairs.

Write the word *water* on the board, and read the word aloud.

Use "Think, Pair, Share" to discuss:

> **Q** *Which of yesterday's words do you think goes with* water? *Why do you think that?* [pause] *Turn to your partner.*

PROMPT: "I think [*gush*] goes with *water* because…."

When most pairs have finished talking, ask one or two pairs to share their thinking with the class.

Teacher Note

If the students have trouble making associations, think aloud about associations you might make or ask questions such as, "How might the word *gush* go with *water*? When might water gush? Where might you see gushing water?" "How might the word *batter* go with *water*? When might water batter something or someone?" and "How might the word *churn* go with *water*? When have you seen water churn? What might cause water to churn?"

344 | Making Meaning® Vocabulary

Day 5

Ongoing Review

Words Reviewed

a shambles
When a place is a shambles, it is very messy or in complete disorder or ruin.

calamity
A *calamity* is "a terrible disaster."

discourteous
Discourteous means "not courteous, or disrespectful or rude."

jumble
A *jumble* is "a messy mixture of things."

thoughtless
Thoughtless means "without thought for the feelings or needs of others."

Materials

- Pocket chart
- Word cards 62, 67, 76, 80, 86

REVIEW THE WORDS

1 **Display the Word Cards and Briefly Review the Words**

Review the pronunciation and meaning of the words.

Week 15 ▶ Day 5

PRACTICE USING THE WORDS

▷ 2 Review the Game "Alike or Different"

Explain that partners will play the game "Alike or Different." Point to the review words, and explain that today you will ask the students to think about how some of the words are alike. Explain that, when you say "turn to your partner," partners will discuss their thinking. Then you will ask some pairs to share their thinking with the class.

Explain that the words may be alike in many ways and that partners may not always agree. Explaining why the words are alike is the most important thing.

Tell the students that, before they play the game in pairs, they will practice as a class.

Point to the words *discourteous* and *thoughtless* and ask:

▶ **Q** *How are the words* discourteous *and* thoughtless *alike?*

PROMPT: "The words *discourteous* and *thoughtless* are alike because…."

▷ 3 Play "Alike or Different" in Pairs

Point to the words *jumble*, "a shambles," and *calamity* and use "Think, Pair, Share" to discuss:

Q *How are the words* jumble, *"a shambles," and* calamity *alike?* [pause] *Turn to your partner.*

PROMPT: "The words *jumble*, 'a shambles,' and *calamity* are alike because…."

Teacher Note

If the students struggle to answer the question, think aloud about ways you think the words are alike. (You might say, "I think *discourteous* and *thoughtless* are alike because they both have to do with how a person acts or behaves. I also think they are alike because it is hurtful to be discourteous or thoughtless.") Alternatively, you might stimulate the students' thinking by asking questions such as, "How do you feel when someone is discourteous to you or thoughtless?" or "What might someone do that is discourteous and thoughtless?" Then discuss how *jumble*, "a shambles," and *calamity* are alike as a class, rather than in pairs.

Teacher Note

Support struggling students by thinking aloud about how you think the words are alike or by asking questions such as, "When might you use the words *jumble*, 'a shambles,' and *calamity*?" "What do you picture in your mind when you think of these words?" and "What does a jumble look like? A shambles? A calamity?"

Making Meaning® Vocabulary

Week 16

Overview

Articles

"Copycats: Why Clone?"

"The Debate on Banning Junk Food Ads"

Words Taught

ethical

unethical

desirable

regulate

influence

consume/consumer

Word-learning Strategies

- Recognizing antonyms (review)
- Using context to determine word meanings (review)
- Using the suffix *-er* to determine word meanings (review)

Words Reviewed: desert/deserter, flourish, revive, spectacle, topple

DO AHEAD

- Prior to Day 3, write the context sentence from "The Debate on Banning Junk Food Ads" on the board or a sheet of chart paper or make a transparency of the sentence (BLM13). (See Step 1 on page 355.)

- Prior to Day 3, review More Strategy Practice on page 362. Write the "Use the Clues" sentences on the board or a sheet of chart paper or make a transparency of the sentences (BLM14).

- Prior to Day 4, review "More Strategy Practice" on pages 365–366.

- Prior to Day 5, write the "What's the Missing Word?" sentences on the board or a sheet of chart paper or make a transparency of the sentences (BLM15). (See Step 2 on page 368.)

- Prior to Day 5, collect these word cards for Ongoing Review: 60, 66, 82, 83, and 85.

Week 16 ▶ Day 1

Day 1

Introduce *Ethical, Unethical,* and *Desirable*

Materials
- "Copycats" (see pages 370–371)
- Chart paper
- A marker
- (Optional) *Making Meaning Student Response Book*

Words Taught

ethical (p. 370)
Ethical means "right according to a society's beliefs." When people think something is ethical, they believe it is the right thing to do.

unethical
Unethical means "wrong according to a society's beliefs." When people think something is unethical, they believe it is the wrong thing to do.

desirable (p. 371)
Desirable means "worth having or wishing for."

INTRODUCE AND PRACTICE USING *ETHICAL*

1 Introduce and Define *Ethical*

Briefly review "Copycats: Why Clone?"

Remind the students that the article discusses cloning, or creating one living thing that is an exact copy of another. Read the following sentences from the second paragraph of the article on page 370 aloud, emphasizing the word *ethical*: "In 1997, scientists succeeded in cloning the first mammal. Since then, debate has raged about whether it is necessary or ethical to clone animals—including humans."

Teacher Note
You might have the students bring their *Making Meaning Student Response Books* to the rug and follow along as you read from the article.

Tell the students that the first word they will learn today is *ethical* and that *ethical* means "right according to a society's beliefs." Explain that a society is a group of people who live in the same country and share

348 | Making Meaning® Vocabulary

the same laws and customs. Explain that, when people in a society think something is ethical, they believe it is the right thing to do.

Explain that people in American society have differing opinions about whether or not cloning is ethical, or right.

Discuss as a class:

Q *Do you think that cloning is ethical? Why?*

PROMPT: "I [do/do not] think cloning is ethical because...."

Have the students say the word *ethical*, and write it on the chart.

◀ **Teacher Note**
If the students struggle to answer the question, you might review some of the pros and cons of cloning and ask questions such as, "Do you think that cloning [plants/animals/people] is ethical? Why?" "Do you think that cloning is ethical if it helps to save people's lives? Why?" and "Do you think that cloning is ethical if it is used to create a 'super human'? Why?"

INTRODUCE AND PRACTICE USING *UNETHICAL*

2 **Introduce and Define *Unethical* and Review Antonyms**

Tell the students that the next word they will learn today is *unethical*. Have the students say *unethical*, and then write it on the chart.

Explain that *unethical* and *ethical* are antonyms, or words with opposite meanings. Then discuss as a class:

Q *If* ethical *means "right according to a society's beliefs" and* ethical *and* unethical *are antonyms, what do you think* unethical *means?*

PROMPT: "I think *unethical* means ['wrong according to a society's beliefs']."

If necessary, explain that *unethical* means "wrong according to a society's beliefs." Explain that, when people think something is unethical, they believe it is the wrong thing to do.

Have the students say the word *unethical*, and write it on the chart.

Teacher Note
You might point to the prefix *un-* in *unethical* and explain that *un-* is a prefix that means "not."
◀ For practice using the prefix *un-*, see the Extension on page 352.

◀ **Teacher Note**
If you started an antonym chart, add *ethical* and *unethical* to it.

Week 16 ▶ Day 1

3 ▶ Discuss Whether Tulip's Behavior Is Ethical or Unethical

Explain that we often use the words *ethical* and *unethical* to describe a person's conduct or behavior. If a person behaves in a way that people believe is right or good, we say that the person's behavior is ethical. If a person behaves in a way that people believe is wrong or bad, we say that the person's behavior is unethical.

Explain that you will describe something our friend Tulip does. Partners will discuss whether Tulip's behavior is ethical or unethical and why they think so.

Begin with:

- *On the playground, Tulip finds a 5-dollar bill. She puts the bill into her pocket and does not tell anyone that she found it.*

Ask:

Q *Is Tulip's behavior ethical or unethical? Why? Turn to your partner.*

PROMPT: "Tulip's behavior is [ethical/unethical] because…."

In the same way, discuss:

- *During a math test, Tulip notices that a girl at her table is copying answers from another student's paper. Tulip does not want the girl to get into trouble, so she does not tell the teacher what she sees.*

- *Tulip's friend Hank gives Tulip a picture he drew of her. Tulip does not like the drawing at all. She thinks it makes her look silly. But Tulip tells Hank she likes the drawing and thanks him for giving it to her.*

Review the pronunciation and meaning of the words *ethical* and *unethical*.

INTRODUCE AND PRACTICE USING *DESIRABLE*

4 Introduce and Define *Desirable*

Remind the students that some farmers support cloning animals because they hope that it will help them breed better livestock. Read "Building a Better Breed" on page 371 of the article aloud, emphasizing the word *desirable*.

Tell the students that the last word they will learn today is *desirable* and that *desirable* means "worth having or wishing for." Explain that, when farmers breed animals, they want the offspring to have desirable traits like thick wool and high-quality meat—traits that make their animals more desirable, or more worth having.

Have the students say the word *desirable*, and write it on the chart.

◀ **Teacher Note**

You might explain that the word *desirable* is related to the word *desire*, which means "want, wish for, or long for something." The word *desire* is taught in grade 4 of *Making Meaning Vocabulary*.

5 Discuss Desirable Things

Remind the students that *desirable* means "worth having or wishing for."

Ask:

Q *Which of these animals do you think is more desirable, or worth having, as a pet: a cat or a dog? Why? Turn to your partner.*

PROMPT: "I think a [cat/dog] is more desirable as a pet because…."

Then ask:

Q *If you could have any job you wanted when you grew up, what job would be most desirable? Why? Turn to your partner.*

PROMPT: "I think [being a police officer] would be the most desirable job because…."

Review the pronunciation and meaning of the word.

Week 16 ▸ Day 1

EXTENSION

Discuss Other Words with the Prefix *un-*

Point to the prefix *un-* in *unethical* on the chart, and explain that *un-* is a prefix that means "not." Explain that, when you add the prefix *un-* to the word *ethical*, you make *unethical*, which means "not ethical, or wrong according to a society's beliefs." Review that *ethical* and *unethical* are antonyms.

Have the students use what they know about the prefix *un-* to discuss the meanings of these words: *unbundled*, *uncomfortable*, *unconcerned*, *undesirable*, and *undignified*.

Invite the students to listen and watch for other words that use the prefix *un-*, and discuss the words the students find.

Teacher Note

You might remind the students that they learned the meaning of these vocabulary words earlier: *bundle* (wrap or tie things together), *desirable* (worth having or wishing for), and *dignified* (confident, calm, and in control).

Teacher Note

The prefix *un-* is formally taught in grade 3 of *Making Meaning Vocabulary*. For a list of words that use the prefix *un-* and other word lists, visit Developmental Studies Center's website at www.devstu.org.

Day 2

Review *Ethical, Unethical,* and *Desirable*

Words Reviewed

ethical
Ethical means "right according to a society's beliefs." When people think something is ethical, they believe it is the right thing to do.

unethical
Unethical means "wrong according to a society's beliefs." When people think something is unethical, they believe it is the wrong thing to do.

desirable
Desirable means "worth having or wishing for."

Materials
- Word chart from Day 1

REVIEW THE WORDS

1 Briefly Review the Words

Review the pronunciation and meaning of each word.

Use "Think, Pair, Share" to discuss:

Q *Which of the words might you use if you were writing a report about the pros and cons of hunting animals for sport? How might you use the word?* [pause] *Turn to your partner.*

PROMPT: "I might use the word [*desirable*]. I might write…."

Week 16 ▸ Day 2

PRACTICE USING THE WORDS

2 Play "Does That Make Sense?"

Explain that partners will play the game "Does That Make Sense?" Explain that you will read a scenario that includes one of the vocabulary words. Partners will decide whether or not the word makes sense in the scenario and why they think so.

Point to the word *ethical*, and explain that the first scenario includes the word *ethical*.

Then read the following scenario aloud twice:

- *The Centerville city council wants to build a zoo in the town park. Mrs. Torres is against the zoo project. She thinks it is ethical to keep wild animals penned up in zoos.*

Ask:

Q *Does the word* ethical *make sense in the scenario? Why do you think that? Turn to your partner.*

PROMPT: "The word *ethical* [does/does not] make sense because…."

In the same way, discuss:

[unethical]

- *Margo's soccer teammates plan to trip their opponents on purpose in their next game. Margo refuses to do it because she thinks tripping a player on purpose is unethical.*

[desirable]

- *Mr. Lee is watching a TV show about life in a big city. When it is over, he says, "For me living in a big city would be desirable, because I hate noise, traffic, and crowds."*

Teacher Note

If the students struggle to answer the questions, call for attention. Reread the scenario aloud, and explain that *ethical* does not make sense. If Mrs. Torres thinks it is ethical, or right, to keep animals in zoos, then she will be *for* the zoo project, rather than *against* it. Then read the scenario that uses the word *unethical*, and discuss it in pairs.

354 | Making Meaning® Vocabulary

Day 3

Introduce *Regulate, Influence,* and *Consume/Consumer*

Words Taught

regulate (p. 372)
Regulate means "control or manage, usually through rules or laws."

influence (p. 372)
Influence means "affect the way someone develops, behaves, or thinks."

consume/consumer (p. 373)
Consume means "buy and use products and services." A *consumer* is "a person who consumes."

Materials

- "The Debate on Banning Junk Food Ads" (see pages 372–373)
- Word chart from Day 1
- A marker
- (Optional) *Making Meaning Student Response Book*
- Context sentence or transparency (BLM13; see Step 1 below)
- (Optional) "Use the Clues" sentences or transparency (BLM14; see More Strategy Practice on page 362)
- (Optional) Overhead projector and marker

INTRODUCE AND PRACTICE USING *REGULATE*

1 Introduce *Regulate* and Use Context Clues to Figure Out Its Meaning

Briefly review "The Debate on Banning Junk Food Ads."

Display the transparency, or write the following sentence from "What's Junk?" on the board or a sheet of chart paper and underline the word *regulate*:

> Many people argue that one way to help people, especially children, to choose more nutritious foods is to <u>regulate</u>, or control, the messages they receive about food from advertising.

Grade Five | 355

Week 16 ▶ Day 3

Remind the students that on average children and teenagers see between 40 and 50 hours of junk food ads on TV each year. Then read "What's Junk?" on page 372 of the article aloud, emphasizing the word *regulate*.

> **Teacher Note** ▶
>
> You might have the students bring their *Making Meaning Student Response Books* to the rug and follow along as you read from the article.

Tell the students that the first word they will learn today is *regulate*. Remind them that sometimes you can figure out the meaning of a word by rereading the sentence that includes the word, or the sentence before or after it, looking for clues.

Direct the students' attention to the context sentence, and explain that, as you reread the sentence that includes the word *regulate*, you want them to think about what the word might mean and what words in the sentence are clues to its meaning.

Read the sentence aloud twice, slowly and clearly. Then point to the word *regulate* and discuss as a class:

Q Based on what you just heard, what do you think the word *regulate* might mean? What words in the sentence are clues to the meaning of *regulate*?

> **Teacher Note** ▶
>
> If the students do not immediately determine the meaning of *regulate* from the context, give them the definition, rather than have them guess.

PROMPTS: "I think *regulate* might mean ['control or manage']" and "The words ['or control'] are clues that tell you that *regulate* means 'control or manage.'"

If necessary, explain that *regulate* means "control or manage." Explain that some people want the government to regulate, or control, junk food ads on TV to help people choose more nutritious foods. Point out that the words "or control" are clues to the meaning of *regulate*.

> **Teacher Note** ▶
>
> You might explain that *regulate*, *control*, and *manage* are synonyms. If you started a synonym chart, add *regulate* and its synonyms to it.
>
> You might underline the context clue and explain that a writer sometimes provides the definition of a word immediately after the word to make the word's meaning clear to readers. For more practice with context clues, see More Strategy Practice on page 362.

Have the students say the word *regulate*, and write it on the chart.

▶ 2 Discuss Things That Might Be Regulated

Explain that something that is regulated is controlled or managed, usually through rules or laws set up by the government or a person with authority or power. For example, as the article tells us, some people want the United States government to regulate junk food ads. A city government regulates traffic in the city by putting up signs and signals that control how fast people can drive and when they

356 | Making Meaning® Vocabulary

must stop or slow down. Our school librarian regulates, or controls or manages, the movement of books in and out of our library by setting rules for how books are checked in and checked out.

Tell the students that you will describe a situation and partners will discuss whether or not the situation should be regulated, or controlled or managed, and why they think so.

Begin with the following scenario:

- *Mr. Kim's children watch 4 or 5 hours of TV every school night. Often, they stay up late watching TV. Recently, Mr. Kim's children have been falling asleep in class, and they have not been turning in their homework.*

Use "Think, Pair, Share" to discuss:

Q *Do you think Mr. Kim should regulate the amount of TV his children watch? Why?* [pause] *Turn to your partner.*

PROMPT: "I [do/do not] think Mr. Kim should regulate the amount of TV his children watch because…."

Have volunteers share their thinking.

Follow up by discussing as a class:

Q *What might Mr. Kim do to regulate the amount of TV his children watch?*

PROMPT: "To regulate the amount of TV his children watch, Mr. Kim might [tell them they can't watch TV until their homework is done]."

In the same way, discuss:

- *A severe drought is causing a water shortage in the town of Dryville. If people do not conserve water, the water supply will run out.*

Q *Do you think that the town council of Dryville should regulate the amount of water residents can use? Why?* [pause] *Turn to your partner.*

Week 16 ▶ Day 3

PROMPT: "I [do/do not] think that the town council should regulate the use of water because…."

Have volunteers share their thinking.

Follow up by discussing as a class:

Q *What might the Dryville town council do to regulate the use of water?*

PROMPT: "They might regulate the use of water by [telling people they can only use a certain amount of water each month]."

Review the pronunciation and meaning of the word.

INTRODUCE AND PRACTICE USING *INFLUENCE*

▶ 3 Introduce and Define *Influence*

Review that some countries, including England, ban junk food ads during children's TV shows. Then read the first paragraph of "Good Habits Start Young" on page 372 aloud, emphasizing the word *influenced*.

> **Teacher Note** ▶
> You might remind the students that a *ban* is "a rule or law that says people must not do something." Something that is banned is not allowed.

Tell the students that the next word they will learn is *influence* and that *influence* means "affect the way someone develops, behaves, or thinks."

Explain that junk food ads influence, or affect, the way many children think about junk food. Children are especially influenced, or affected, by ads in which a favorite cartoon character or superhero tells them to buy junk food. Often after children see one of these ads, they ask their parents to buy the junk food.

Have the students say the word *influence*, and write it on the chart.

358 | Making Meaning® Vocabulary

Week 16 ▸ Day 3

▶4 Discuss People Who Are Positive Influences

Explain that all of us have people in our lives who have influenced us, or affected the way we think or behave. Explain that we say that a person who has influenced us in positive, or good, ways is a "positive influence" in our life. A person who is a positive influence often influences others by serving as an example of a good person or by giving advice about how to live a good life.

Give a couple of examples of people who have been positive influences in your life. (You might say, "When I was growing up, my sister was a positive influence in my life. I looked up to her and tried to be honest and kind like she was. She encouraged me to work hard in school and gave me a lot of good advice. My friend Jasmin is a positive influence in my life these days. She encourages me to try new things and introduces me to interesting new activities, like playing golf.")

Use "Think, Pair, Share" to discuss:

Q *Who is a positive influence in your life? How does he or she influence you in positive ways?* [pause] *Turn to your partner.*

PROMPT: "[My mom] is a positive influence. She influences me by [talking to me about the golden rule and explaining that I should treat people the way I want to be treated]."

Review the pronunciation and meaning of the word.

INTRODUCE AND PRACTICE USING *CONSUME* AND *CONSUMER*

▶5 Introduce and Define *Consume* and *Consumer* and Review the Suffix *-er*

Remind the students that junk food ads influence the way children think about junk food and that some people think the ads should be regulated. Review that other people, however, believe the ads should not be regulated.

Grade Five | 359

Week 16 ▶ Day 3

Read the last paragraph of the article aloud, emphasizing the word *consumer*.

Explain that the last words the students will learn today are *consume* and *consumer*. Explain that *consume* means "buy and use products and services." Explain that a *consumer* is "a person who consumes."

Explain that food is one of the products that consumers consume, or buy and use. Explain that some people believe that it is their right as consumers of food to have as much information about the food as possible. These people believe that, if the government regulates junk food ads, then consumers will not have the information they need to make their own choices about buying this kind of food.

Have the students say the words *consume* and *consumer*, and add them to the chart.

Teacher Note

You might remind the students that they discussed the suffix *-er* earlier when they learned the words *moocher* (a person who tries to get something without paying or working for it) and *deserter* (a person who deserts). If you started a chart of *-er* words, add *consumer* to it.

Point to the suffix *-er* in the word *consumer* on the chart, and review that *-er* is a suffix that means "a person who." Explain that when you add *-er* to *consume*, you make the word *consumer*, which means "a person who consumes, or a person who buys and uses products and services."

6 ▶ Discuss *Consume* and *Consumer*

Tell the students that all of us are consumers. Explain that we consume, or buy and use products and services, every day.

Explain that, in addition to foods, consumers consume products such as clothing, computers, pencils and pens, cars, bikes, and toys. Remind the students that consumers also buy and use services, and explain that a service is something you pay someone to do or provide for you. For example, as consumers we pay for services such as getting our hair cut, having pizza or other food delivered to our houses, or receiving treatment from a doctor.

Ask:

Q *What is a product or service you consumed, or bought and used, recently? Turn to your partner.*

PROMPT: "A [product/service] I consumed is…."

7 Discuss Being a Smart Consumer

Tell the students that companies try to influence consumers through advertising—they try to affect the way consumers think about their products and get them to buy them. Explain that sometimes advertisements cannot be trusted. For that reason, consumers have to be smart when they are deciding which products to buy. For example, they need to think carefully about what they want before they buy anything. They also need to think about how much they can spend. Explain that a smart consumer might ask someone with more experience for advice before he buys a product, or he might try a product out before he spends his money on it.

Discuss as a class:

Q *If you were going to buy a new bicycle, what might you do to be a smart consumer? What might you need to do or think about before you bought the bicycle?*

PROMPT: "To be a smart consumer, I might [ride the bicycle before I bought it]."

In the same way, discuss:

Q *If you were going to buy a new kite, what might you do to be a smart consumer?*

Review the pronunciation and meaning of the words.

◀ **Teacher Note**

If the students struggle to answer the question, think aloud about things you might do to be a smart consumer. (You might say, "To be a smart consumer, I might check to see how much the bike costs, I might ride the bike to see if I liked it, and I might ride other bikes so that I could compare them to each other.") Then discuss the next question as a class.

Week 16 ▶ Day 3

MORE STRATEGY PRACTICE

Play "Use the Clues"

Display the transparency, or write the following sentences on the board or a sheet of chart paper, leaving blanks as shown:

> Vanden was _____ before the doctor's appointment. His palms were sweaty and his stomach was upset.
>
> "I don't want to go!" _____ Vanden. His sobs could be heard from one end of the house to the other as his mother hurried him toward the door.

Explain that partners will play the game "Use the Clues," in which they use clues to figure out a word that is missing from a sentence. Direct the students' attention to the sentences, and review that, as you read the sentences aloud, you want them to think about what the missing word might be and what words in the sentences are clues to the missing word. Remind them that more than one word might make sense as the missing word and that the word does not have to be a vocabulary word.

Read the first sentence aloud twice, slowly and clearly, saying "blank" for the missing word.

Use "Think, Pair, Share" to discuss:

Q *What's the missing word? What words are clues to the missing word?* [pause] *Turn to your partner.*

Have a few pairs share their ideas with the class.

If necessary, explain that the missing word might be *nervous* or *scared* and that the words "his palms were sweaty" and "his stomach was upset" are clues that Vanden was nervous or scared.

Discuss the second example the same way.

Teacher Note

Listen as partners share. If the students suggest words that are not supported by the context, call for attention. Provide a word and point out the context clues.

Teacher Note

Although *nervous* or *scared* are logical responses, the students may reasonably argue that *upset*, *sick*, or another word is also supported by the clues in the sentence. What is important is that the students explain their thinking.

Teacher Note

Possible responses include *screamed*, *yelled*, *shouted*, *cried*, and *exclaimed*.

362 | Making Meaning® Vocabulary

Day 4

Review *Regulate, Influence,* and *Consume/Consumer*

Words Reviewed

regulate
Regulate means "control or manage, usually through rules or laws."

influence
Influence means "affect the way someone develops, behaves, or thinks."

consume/consumer
Consume means "buy and use products and services." A *consumer* is "a person who consumes."

Materials
- Word chart from Day 3
- A marker

REVIEW THE WORDS

1 Briefly Review the Words

Review the pronunciation and meaning of each word.

Discuss as a class:

Q *Do you think that parents should regulate their children's bedtimes? Why?*

PROMPT: "I [do/do not] think that parents should regulate their children's bedtimes because…."

Week 16 ▶ Day 4

Ask:

Q *Do you think that your friends influence you? Why? Turn to your partner.*

PROMPT: "I think that my friends [do/do not] influence me because…."

In the same way, discuss:

Q *As a consumer, are you influenced by what your friends buy? Why? Turn to your partner.*

PROMPT: "As a consumer, I [am/am not] influenced by what my friends buy because…."

PRACTICE USING THE WORDS

▶ 2 Do the Activity "Tell Me a Story"

Explain that partners will do the activity "Tell Me a Story." Review that you will tell the beginning of a story that includes one of the vocabulary words. The students will use what they know about the word and their imaginations to make up an ending for the story.

Begin by reading the following story aloud twice, slowly and clearly:

- "We are wasting too much paper," Mr. Paulson told his students. "To stop the waste, I plan to regulate our use of paper by…."

Use "Think, Pair, Share" to discuss:

Q *How might you finish the story? What might Mr. Paulson do to regulate the students' use of paper? [pause] Turn to your partner.*

PROMPT: "To stop the waste, I plan to regulate our use of paper by…."

Week 16 ▶ Day 4

In the same way, discuss:

- *Buckley's mother wants him to be a good influence on his little brother. She is always telling him, "To be a good influence on your brother, you need to…."*

Q *How might you finish the story? What might Buckley do to be a good influence on his little brother?* [pause] *Turn to your partner.*

PROMPT: "To be a good influence on your brother, you need to…."

- *Claire's father looked around her bedroom. "Wow!" he said to Claire. "From now on I'm going to call you Claire the Consumer because…."*

Q *How might you finish the story? Why might Claire's father call her Claire the Consumer?* [pause] *Turn to your partner.*

PROMPT: "From now on I'm going to call you Claire the Consumer because…."

Teacher Note

For a crossword puzzle you can use to review words taught during weeks 15 and 16, visit Developmental Studies Center's website at www.devstu.org.

MORE STRATEGY PRACTICE

Discuss Other Words with the Suffix -er

Remind the students that a *suffix* is "a group of letters that is added to the end of a word and changes the meaning of the word." Point to the word *consumer* on the word chart, and review that the suffix -er means "a person who." Review that when -er is added to the word *consume*, which means "buy and use products and services," it makes the word *consumer*, which means "a person who consumes, or a person who buys and uses products and services."

continues

◀ Teacher Note

You might explain that when you add -er to the word *consume*, you take away the *e* before you add the suffix. For a comprehensive grade 5 spelling program, see Developmental Studies Center's *Guided Spelling*.

Week 16 ▶ Day 4

Teacher Note

You might explain that when you add -*er* to the word *rap*, you double the letter *p* to spell *rapper*. ▶

ELL Note

You might explain that when you rap a song, you chant or speak the words of the song in time with music.

Teacher Note ▶

You might explain that the suffix -*or* also means "a person who" and is used in words such as *inventor*, *narrator*, and *visitor*.

Teacher Note

For a list of words that use the suffixes -*er* and -*or* and other word lists, visit Developmental Studies Center's website at www.devstu.org.

MORE STRATEGY PRACTICE *continued*

Write the word *rapper* on the board, and explain that this is another word that uses the suffix -*er*. Point to the word *rapper* and discuss as a class:

Q *Based on what you know about the word* rap *and the suffix* -er, *what do you think the word* rapper *means? What is a rapper?*

Have volunteers share their thinking. If necessary, explain that a *rapper* is "a person who raps, or chants or speaks the words of a song in time with music." Discuss the words *learner*, *skier*, *tickler*, and *wanderer* the same way.

If you started a chart of -*er* words, add *rapper*, *learner*, *skier*, *tickler*, and *wanderer* to it. Invite the students to think of other words that use the suffix -*er*, and add them to the chart. You might stimulate their thinking by asking questions such as, "What do you call a person who observes? advises? mourns?"

---

366 | Making Meaning® Vocabulary

Day 5

Ongoing Review

Words Reviewed

desert/deserter
Desert means "abandon, or leave someone or something that should not be left behind." A *deserter* is "a person who deserts."

flourish
Flourish means "grow well or be successful."

revive
Revive means "bring back to a healthy, active condition or give new strength or freshness to."

spectacle
A *spectacle* is "an unusual or remarkable sight."

topple
Topple means "fall over or make something fall over."

Materials

- Pocket chart
- Word cards 60, 66, 82, 83, 85
- Sentences or transparency (BLM15) for "What's the Missing Word?" (see Step 2 on page 368)
- (Optional) Overhead projector and marker

REVIEW THE WORDS

1 Display the Word Cards and Briefly Review the Words

Review the pronunciation and meaning of the words.

Week 16 ▶ Day 5

PRACTICE USING THE WORDS

2 Play "What's the Missing Word?"

Display the transparency or write the following sentences (without the answers) on the board or a sheet of chart paper, leaving blank spaces as shown:

> Lots of sunshine and rain caused the crops to _____. (flourish)
>
> Little Leon worried that one sneeze would cause his tower of blocks to _____. (topple)
>
> After being sick in bed for weeks, Alicia took long walks outside to _____. (revive)
>
> Ike had to leave his puppy at home when he went to school. Ike felt like a _____. (deserter)
>
> Hundreds of people dancing in the streets created quite a _____. (spectacle)

> **Teacher Note**
> For a fully written-out example of the activity, see page 263.

Explain that partners will play the game "What's the Missing Word?" Direct the students' attention to the sentences, and point out that a word is missing from each sentence. Explain that you will read each sentence aloud and partners will discuss which vocabulary word could replace the missing word and why they think so.

Begin by pointing to this sentence and reading it aloud twice:

- Lots of sunshine and rain caused the crops to _____.

Ask:

Q *What's the missing word? Why do you think so? Turn to your partner.*

PROMPT: "I think [*flourish*] is the missing word because…."

Reread the sentence using the word *flourish*.

Have volunteers share their thinking with the class. Then reread the sentence, replacing the blank with the vocabulary word.

Discuss the remaining sentences the same way.

> **Teacher Note**
> You might invite partners to write a "What's the Missing Word?" sentence of their own and share it with the class.

CLASS VOCABULARY PROGRESS ASSESSMENT

As you observe the students, ask yourself:

- Are the students able to identify the word that completes each sentence?
- Do their explanations show that they know what each word means?
- Are they showing a growing appreciation for learning new words?

For more information about reviewing and practicing the words, see "Retaining the Words" on pages xviii–xix.

INDIVIDUAL VOCABULARY PROGRESS ASSESSMENT

Before continuing with week 17, take this opportunity to assess individual students' understanding of the words taught in weeks 13–16 by administering "Word Check 4" (BLM26). Please refer to pages 626–627 for instructions on administering the assessment.

STUDENT SELF-ASSESSMENT

In addition to or in place of the Individual Vocabulary Progress Assessment, have the students evaluate their understanding of the words taught in weeks 13–16 through this self-assessment (BLM30). For instructions on administering the assessment, see pages 634–635.

COPYCATS

WHY CLONE?

Cloning is a hi-tech way to create a living thing that is an exact copy of another. Why would we want to create identical living things? For farmers, there are many reasons. Farmers already use cloning techniques to produce desired varieties of plants, such as apple trees that grow crisp, juicy fruit. One technique is to grow plants from cuttings taken from other plants. A plant that grows from a cutting is a clone because it has the same genetic makeup as the original plant.

In 1997, scientists succeeded in cloning the first mammal. Since then, debate has raged about whether it is ethical or necessary to clone animals—including humans. Although the idea is controversial, many scientists believe that cloned human beings will one day become a reality. Other technologies, such as organ transplants, once faced the same kinds of debate, and today they are widely used.

In 2006, the Food and Drug Administration approved the eating of meat from animals that have been cloned. In 2008, the FDA approved the sale of cloned animals in supermarkets without being labeled as such.

PRO

Building a Better Breed

Since the first mammal was cloned, scientists have cloned many other creatures, including cows, cats, and fruit flies. Today, farmers pair a male animal with a female and hope that they'll get offspring with desirable traits, such as animals that have thick wool or high-quality meat. In the future, they might use cloning as a quicker way to get that same result.

Protection from Extinction

Cloning might also be a way to protect endangered species from extinction. In 2005, scientists created clones of the gray wolf, a species once hunted to near extinction. Today, gray wolves are thriving in several states, including Minnesota and Wisconsin.

Human Health

There are many potential advantages of cloning human beings. It might give infertile couples a chance to have children of their own. Additionally, people who are likely to have a child with a genetic disorder might use cloning for the chance to produce a healthy child. Cloning could also be used to create healthy organs for people who are sick.

Cloning might help us to understand how human genes work. This could lead to the discovery of treatments for genetic disorders such as cystic fibrosis. Discoveries like these have the potential to make many people's lives easier. These discoveries might even save lives.

CON

Cloning for the Wrong Reasons

Where do we draw the line between the right reasons and the wrong reasons for using cloning? If human cloning is allowed in a few specific cases, people might begin to use it in other ways. For example, cloning might be used to create children who have specialized talents—such as amazing mathematical or athletic abilities—much like animals might be cloned for specific desirable traits. From there, cloning could lead to the creation of groups of people for specific purposes, such as fighting in war. Many people argue that it is wrong to experiment with human life in this way.

Health Risks

Studying human cloning has big complications. Real human cells must be used, so if a particular experiment did not work out, the result could be a flawed copy of a human being—and that person would never have a normal life.

So far, scientists have found it difficult to produce healthy clones of mammals. For example, studies done in Japan have shown that cloned mice have poor health and die early. About a third of the cloned calves born in the United States have died young, and many of them were too large. Many cloned animals appear healthy at a young age but die suddenly. We should expect the same problems in human clones.

Even if scientists were able to produce human clones that were physically healthy, other important parts of human development might be affected. For example, a person's mood, intelligence, and sense of individuality might not develop normally.

Legal Roadblocks

In most countries, it is against the law to clone a human being, because of the many ethical and safety concerns. The United States Congress is currently considering passing a law to ban human cloning.

The Debate on Banning Junk Food Ads

Advertising Works

Food companies spend millions of dollars on TV advertising each year. The reason is simple: advertising works. It's especially effective with children. A 2006 study found that each year, children between the ages of eight and twelve see 50 hours of junk food ads on TV, and teenagers see 40 hours. About 90 percent of all food ads during children's viewing times are devoted to junk food—none are for fruit and vegetables.

What's Junk?

Junk food may taste good, but it's low in nutritional value. For example, a sugary donut doesn't have as many nutrients as an apple. Many people argue that one way to help people, especially children, to choose more nutritious foods is to regulate, or control, the messages they receive about food from advertising. Others argue that regulating advertising will simply create more problems.

Pros

Good Habits Start Young

Some countries already regulate TV advertising for junk food. England introduced the Children's Food Bill in 2006, which bans junk food advertising during children's TV shows. They say that TV advertising encourages bad eating habits among young people, because young people are more easily influenced than adults by advertising. One study found that children aged twelve and younger who watched junk food ads often asked their parents to buy the foods they had seen advertised. Young people are especially affected by junk food ads when their favorite cartoon characters, celebrities, or superheroes are telling them to buy it.

Junk food is a slang term for food with little nutritional value. It includes food that is high in fat, sugar, or salt (or all three). These foods make up a large portion of foods we see advertised on TV.

A child who develops unhealthy habits is also likely to keep on making unhealthy choices as an adult. So it makes sense to control the messages that young people receive. This gives them a better chance at having a healthy future.

Good health is a big concern to many people today. Worldwide, hundreds of millions of people have serious problems related to an unhealthy diet, such as diabetes and heart disease. A common problem in the United States is obesity. It's estimated that nearly 200 million adults and 7 million children are overweight or obese. Limiting junk food ads may be one way to help people make choices that will prevent obesity and other health problems.

"In England foods such as olive oil, honey, and cheese are labeled as junk food."

England's Children's Food Bill bans junk food ads during children's TV shows and on children's channels.

Cons

Giving Food a Bad Name

There are some big problems with creating rules about junk food advertising. For example, how do we decide exactly what is junk food and what is not? In England, foods such as olive oil, honey, and cheese have been banned from advertising during certain hours because they are labeled "junk food." These foods have nutritional value, but they are also high in fat, salt, or sugar. Calling these foods "junk food" makes it more difficult for people to understand what makes up a healthy, balanced diet.

To make things even more complicated, some ads for fast food now emphasize more nutritious choices—for example, fruit and milk with children's meals. Some promote health and fitness, too. If all fast food ads were banned from children's TV, these healthy messages would be, as well.

Some parents feel that they have the right to decide what is best for their children, and that regulating TV ads takes away that right. It is up to the parent to say "yes" or "no" when a child asks for something he or she has seen advertised on TV. What the parent says helps the child to learn about how advertising affects the people who see it.

Regulating TV ads takes away some of the information parents and children have access to. They need that information in order to make their own decisions. Making decisions is the consumer's right, not the right of the government.

Week 17 Overview

Articles

"All-girls' and All-boys' Schools: Better for Kids"

"Do Kids Really Need Cell Phones?"

Words Taught

interact

academic

get on board

dependent

device

preteen

Word-learning Strategies

- Recognizing idioms (review)
- Using the prefix pre- to determine word meanings (review)

Words Reviewed: apprehensive, ethical, frugal, hospitable, unethical

DO AHEAD

- Prior to Day 3, review More Strategy Practice on pages 389–390.
- Prior to Day 5, collect these word cards for Ongoing Review: 9, 73, 75, 91, and 92.

Week 17 ▶ Day 1

Day 1

Introduce *Interact*, *Academic*, and "Get on Board"

Materials

- "All-girls' and All-boys' Schools" (see pages 396–397)
- Chart paper
- A marker
- (Optional) *Making Meaning Student Response Book*

Words Taught

interact (p. 396)
Interact means "talk or work with people."

academic (p. 397)
Academic means "having to do with school, studying, and learning."

get on board (p. 397)
"Get on board" means "accept or go along with something."

INTRODUCE AND PRACTICE USING *INTERACT*

1 Introduce and Define *Interact*

Briefly review "All-girls' and All-boys' Schools: Better for Kids."

Teacher Note ▶

You might have the students bring their *Making Meaning Student Response Books* to the rug and follow along as you read from the article.

Review that the introduction to the article points out that all-girls' and all-boys' schools are becoming more common. Then read the introduction on page 396 aloud, emphasizing the word *interact* in the first sentence.

Tell the students that the first word they will learn today is *interact* and that *interact* means "talk or work with people." Explain that outside of school, boys and girls often interact, or talk or work with one another. But in all-girls' and all-boys' schools, boys and girls do not interact because they are not in school together.

Have the students say the word *interact*, and write it on the chart.

376 | Making Meaning® Vocabulary

2 Discuss People with Whom We Interact

Explain that we interact, or talk or work, with many different people during the day. Give examples of people with whom you interacted today, and describe how you interacted with them. (You might say, "This morning I interacted with my husband and children before I left for school. I talked with each of them, and I helped my son pack his lunch. On the way to work, I interacted with the crossing guard at the end of my street by waving and saying hello. When I got to school, I interacted with Mr. Carpenter in the teacher's lounge by saying, 'Good morning,' and discussing our plans for the day. This morning I've interacted with many of you by talking or joking with you and helping you with your work.")

Ask:

Q *Who are some people with whom you have interacted today? How did you interact with them? Turn to your partner.*

PROMPT: "I interacted with [Jason] by [talking to him and playing basketball with him before school]."

Explain that we often interact with a person we know differently than with a stranger. For example, when you interact with family members, you feel very comfortable. You can talk and joke easily with them because you know them well. But when you interact with a stranger, you might feel shy and have little to say, or you might be careful about what you say.

Discuss as a class:

Q *How might you interact differently with an adult than with a friend your own age? Why?*

PROMPT: "When I interact with an adult, I [might not joke around or talk about personal things the way I do with a friend] because…."

Review the pronunciation and meaning of the word.

Week 17 ▶ Day 1

INTRODUCE AND PRACTICE USING *ACADEMIC*

▶ 3 Introduce and Define *Academic*

Review that one method people use to measure the success of all-boys' and all-girls' classrooms is to compare the test scores of the students in them with the scores of students in coeducational classes (classes with boys and girls).

Read "Positive Proof in Test Results" on page 397 aloud, emphasizing the word *academic* in the sentence, "Not only did behavior improve, but academic results did, too."

Tell the students that the next word they will learn today is *academic* and that *academic* means "having to do with school, studying, and learning."

Explain that administrators of all-boys' and all-girls' schools saw an improvement in both the students' behavior and their academic work, or work related to studying and learning, in subjects such as reading and writing. Academic results on tests—or results that measure how much the students learned—improved in both reading and writing.

Have the students say the word *academic*, and write it on the chart.

▶ 4 Discuss Academic Subjects

Explain that academic subjects, or subjects we study in school, include reading, writing, math, science, and social studies.

Ask:

Q *What is your favorite academic subject? Why? Turn to your partner.*

PROMPT: "My favorite academic subject is [math] because…"

378 | Making Meaning® Vocabulary

Week 17 ▶ Day 1

Discuss as a class:

Q *Do you think being in an all-boys' or all-girls' class would help you to do better in your academic work? Why?*

PROMPT: "I [do/do not] think being in an all-girls' or all boys' class would help me do better in my academic work because…."

Review the pronunciation and meaning of the word.

INTRODUCE AND PRACTICE USING "GET ON BOARD"

▶ **5** **Introduce and Define "Get on Board" and Review Idioms**

Review that all-girls' and all-boys' schools are becoming more popular throughout the United States. Read "An Increasingly Popular Option" on page 397 aloud, emphasizing the words "getting on board."

Explain that "get on board" means "accept or go along with something." Explain that more and more people are getting on board with, or accepting or going along with, the idea that all-boys' and all-girls' schools are a way to improve students' academic test scores and confidence.

Have the students say "get on board," and write it on the chart.

Point to the words "get on board" on the word chart, and explain that "get on board" is an idiom. Review that an *idiom* is "an expression or phrase that means something different from what it appears to mean." Explain that "get on board" is a phrase we often use to talk about getting onto a bus or train to go somewhere. Explain that, when we say school districts, parents, and students are "getting on board" with all-girls' and all-boys' schools, we do not mean they are taking a train or bus somewhere. Instead, we mean that they are joining others in accepting or going along with these types of schools.

Teacher Note

◀ If you started an idiom chart, add "get on board" to it.

Grade Five | 379

Week 17 ▶ Day 1

6 Discuss "Get on Board"

Explain that people "get on board" with an idea or activity, or accept or go along with it, because they think it is a good idea or because it sounds like a fun or interesting activity. Tell the students that you will describe an activity or idea and partners will discuss whether or not they would get on board with it and why.

Begin with:

- *The music teacher in our school wants to put on a play. He is looking for students who are interested in singing, dancing, and acting.*

Ask:

Q *Would you get on board with being in the school play? Why? Turn to your partner.*

PROMPT: "I [would/would not] get on board with being in the school play because…."

In the same way, discuss:

- *The principal wants to add an hour to the school day so that students can complete their homework assignments at school and get extra help if they need it.*

Q *Would you get on board with the principal's idea? Why? Turn to your partner.*

PROMPT: "I [would/would not] get on board with the principal's idea because…."

Review the pronunciation and meaning of the word.

EXTENSION

Introduce and Discuss the Prefix *inter-*

Point to the prefix *inter-* in *interact* on the chart, and explain that *inter-* is a prefix that means "between or among." Explain that when *inter-* is added to the word *act* it makes the word *interact*, which means "act between or among people, or talk or work with people."

Explain that knowing that the prefix *inter-* means "between or among" can help the students figure out the meaning of other words that use the prefix. For example, an interstate highway is a highway that runs between (connects) two states. An international conference is a conference between or among nations.

Have the students discuss the meaning of other words that use the prefix *inter-*, such as *interchangeable*, *intergalactic*, and *interplanetary*.

◀ **Teacher Note**

For a list of words that use the prefix *inter-* and other word lists, visit Developmental Studies Center's website at www.devstu.org.

Week 17 ▶ Day 2

Day 2

Review *Interact, Academic,* and "Get on Board"

Materials
- Word chart from Day 1

Words Reviewed

interact
Interact means "talk or work with people."

academic
Academic means "having to do with school, studying, and learning."

get on board
"Get on board" means "accept or go along with something."

REVIEW THE WORDS

1 Briefly Review the Words

Review the pronunciation and meaning of each word.

Ask:

Q *Which of the words we learned yesterday do you think was interesting or fun to talk about? Why? Turn to your partner.*

PROMPT: "I think the word [*academic*] was [interesting/fun] to talk about because…."

382 | Making Meaning® Vocabulary

PRACTICE USING THE WORDS

2 Discuss What You Might Say or Do

Explain that you will describe a situation and partners will discuss what they might say or do in that situation.

Begin with:

- It is your first day at a new school. You interact with your new classmates.

Ask:

Q *What might you say or do when you interact with your new classmates? Turn to your partner.*

PROMPT: "When I interact with my new classmates, I might…."

In the same way, discuss:

- You decide you want to do better in all your academic subjects.

Q *What might you say or do if you want to do better in your academic subjects? Turn to your partner.*

PROMPT: "If I want to do better in my academic subjects, I might…."

- A group of friends asks if you'll get on board with their idea of starting a gardening club.

Q *What might you do or say if your friends asked you to get on board with their idea of starting a gardening club? Turn to your partner.*

PROMPT: "If my friends asked me to get on board with their idea of starting a gardening club, I might…."

Week 17 ▶ Day 3

Day 3

Introduce *Dependent*, *Device*, and *Preteen*

Materials

- "Do Kids Really Need Cell Phones?" (see pages 398–399)
- Word chart from Day 1
- A marker
- (Optional) *Making Meaning Student Response Book*

Words Taught

dependent (p. 399)
Dependent means "relying on or needing someone or something for help or support."

device (p. 399)
A *device* is "a tool, machine, or piece of equipment that does a particular job."

preteen (p. 399)
A *preteen* is "a boy or girl before he or she becomes a teenager." A preteen is between the ages of 8 and 12.

INTRODUCE AND PRACTICE USING *DEPENDENT*

1 Introduce and Define *Dependent*

Teacher Note

You might have the students bring their *Making Meaning Student Response Books* to the rug and follow along as you read from the article.

Briefly review "Do Kids Really Need Cell Phones?"

▶ Review that the article discusses the benefits of allowing children to have cell phones. Read the first paragraph of "Preparing for Working with Technology" on page 399 aloud, emphasizing the word *dependent* in the first sentence.

Teacher Note

You might explain that *dependent* is related to the word *depend*, which means "rely on or need."

▶ Tell the students that the first word they will learn today is *dependent* and that *dependent* means "relying on or needing someone or something for help or support."

384 | Making Meaning® Vocabulary

Explain that one argument for allowing children to have cell phones is that giving children experience with cell phones now will help them in their jobs as adults, because in the future, people will be more dependent on, or will rely on or need, cell phones to do their jobs.

Have the students say the word *dependent*, and write it on the chart.

2 Discuss Things and People We Are Dependent On

Review that, according to the article, people in the future will be dependent on, or need, cell phones to do their jobs, and explain that even now many people are dependent on cell phones for their work. For example, salespeople need their cell phones to call their offices and stay in touch with customers when they are traveling.

Give a few more examples of things people are dependent on to do their jobs. (You might say, "I'm dependent on my lesson plans and my computer to do my job. A farmer is dependent on his tractor to plant and tend his crops. An airplane pilot is dependent on her gauges to make sure she is flying at the right altitude.")

Ask:

Q *What are you dependent on to get your class work done? Turn to your partner.*

PROMPT: "To get my class work done, I am dependent on…."

Explain that we are dependent not only on things, but also on people, and give a couple of examples of people you are dependent on. (You might say, "I am dependent on our parent volunteers. I rely on them to create your homework packets and to be reading buddies. I am dependent on my doctor. When I am sick, I rely on her to give me the correct medicine or advice so that I can get better.")

Discuss as a class:

Q *In what ways are children dependent on their parents? In what ways do children rely on or need their parents?*

Week 17 ▶ Day 3

PROMPT: "Children are dependent on their parents to [feed them and give them a place to live]."

Review the pronunciation and meaning of the word.

INTRODUCE AND PRACTICE USING *DEVICE*

3 ▶ Introduce and Define *Device*

Review that cell phones are just one type of technology people are becoming dependent on to do their jobs. Reread the first two sentences from "Preparing for Working with Technology" aloud, emphasizing the word *devices*.

Tell the students that the next word they will learn is *device* and that a *device* is "a tool, machine, or piece of equipment that does a particular job." Explain that a cell phone is a device, or piece of equipment, that does several jobs. It allows people to talk to one another, connect to the Internet, send text messages, and take pictures.

Have the students say the word *device*, and write it on the chart.

4 ▶ Discuss Devices We Use

Remind the students that some devices, such as cell phones, are used to help people complete tasks or do jobs. Explain that other devices, such as TVs and video game players, are used for entertainment.

Give a few examples of devices you or someone you know uses, and explain how each device is used. (You might say, "My dad has a device that automatically sorts his change. My friend Evan has a device on his key chain that stores 50 digital pictures. Our custodian Mr. Phelps uses a device he calls 'the waxer' to wax and polish the floors. My favorite device is my portable headphones. I use my headphones to listen to music when I jog.")

Week 17 ▶ Day 3

Explain that you will give the students a few moments to look around the classroom for devices, or tools, machines, or other pieces of equipment, they might use during the day. Then they will discuss what they noticed.

Give the students a few moments to look around for devices. Then discuss as a class:

Q *What devices do we have in the classroom? What do the devices do?*

PROMPT: "One device we have is [an overhead projector]. It is a device that…."

Then use "Think, Pair, Share" to discuss:

Q *What device at home do you consider especially useful or important? Why?* [pause] *Turn to your partner.*

PROMPT: "[The smoke detector] is an especially useful device because…."

Review the pronunciation and meaning of the word.

◀ **Teacher Note**

Students might mention devices such as an overhead projector, pencil sharpener, three-hole punch, stapler, microscope, loudspeaker, tape dispenser, floor heater, fan, calculator, telephone, printer, photocopier, or computer.

INTRODUCE AND PRACTICE USING *PRETEEN*

5 **Introduce and Define *Preteen* and Review the Prefix *pre-***

Review that the number of children who have cell phones is increasing every day. Read the following sentences from "An Unstoppable Trend" on page 399 aloud, emphasizing the word *preteen*: "Researchers say that about 6 million of the 20 million American children between eight and twelve years old had cell phones by the end of 2006. Researchers also predict that, by 2010, there will be 10.5 million preteen cell phone users."

Grade Five | 387

Week 17 ▶ Day 3

Explain that the last word the students will learn today is *preteen* and that a *preteen* is "a boy or girl before he or she becomes a teenager." Explain that a preteen is between the ages of 8 and 12. Point out that the students are preteens.

Have the students say the word *preteen*, and write it on the chart.

Point to the prefix *pre-* in *preteen* on the chart, and review that *pre-* is a prefix that means "before." Explain that when you add the prefix *pre-* to the word *teen*, which means "a teenager," you make the word *preteen*, which means "before a teenager, or a boy or girl before he or she becomes a teenager."

Teacher Note

Remind the students that earlier they learned these words that use the prefix *pre-*: *prearrange* (arrange or plan something before it happens) and *prejudice* (an unfair opinion of someone based on the person's race, religion, or other characteristic). If you started a chart of *pre-* words, add *preteen* to it.

6 ▶ Discuss the Privileges of Being a Preteen

Explain that now that the students are preteens, or boys and girls between the ages of 8 and 12, they have more privileges than when they were 5, 6, or 7 years old. For example, as preteens they can probably stay up later than they used to.

Use "Think, Pair, Share" to discuss:

Q *What are other privileges you have as a preteen that you did not have when you were younger?* [pause] *Turn to your partner.*

PROMPT: "As a preteen, I am allowed to…."

Explain that in a few years the students will no longer be preteens. They will be teenagers, or boys and girls who are 13 years old or older.

Discuss as a class:

Q *Do you think being a teenager will be more fun than being a preteen? Why?*

PROMPT: "I [do/do not] think being a teenager will be more fun than being a preteen, because…."

Review the pronunciation and meaning of the word.

Making Meaning® Vocabulary

MORE STRATEGY PRACTICE

Discuss Other Words with the Prefix *pre-*

Review that a *prefix* is "a group of letters that is added to the beginning of a word and changes the meaning of the word." Point to the word *preteen* on the word chart, and review that the prefix *pre-* means "before." Review that when you add *pre-* to the word *teen*, you make the word *preteen*, which means "a boy or girl before he or she becomes a teenager."

Remind the students that one part of the article "Do Kids Really Need Cell Phones?" suggests things parents can do to prevent their children from going over the cell phone spending limit. Explain that, as you read a sentence from that part of the article aloud, you want the students to listen for a word that begins with the prefix *pre-*. Then read the following sentence from "Easy to Set Controls and Limits" on page 399 aloud twice, "Parents can also opt for a prepaid plan so that their child can't go over spending limits."

Discuss as a class:

Q *What word did you hear that begins with the prefix* pre-?

Q *Based on what you know about the prefix* pre- *and the word* paid, *what do you think the word* prepaid *means? What would a prepaid phone plan be?*

If necessary, explain that *prepaid* means "paid for before it is needed or used." Explain that parents who choose a prepaid phone plan pay for a certain number of minutes of phone use before the minutes are used. Children using the phone can only use the number of minutes that have been paid for ahead of time. After the minutes are used, the phone stops working.

continues

Week 17 ▶ Day 3

Teacher Note ▶

For a list of words that use the prefix *pre-* and other word lists, visit Developmental Studies Center's website at www.devstu.org.

> **MORE STRATEGY PRACTICE** *continued*
>
> If you started a chart of *pre-* words, add *prepaid* to it. Invite the students to think of other words that use the prefix *pre-*, and add them to the chart. If they struggle to think of words, stimulate the students' thinking by asking questions such as, "What word means 'mix beforehand' (*premix*)? 'record before' (*prerecord*)? 'cook beforehand' (*precook*)?" Other *pre-* words you might discuss are *pretest*, *preshrink*, and *presoak*.

Day 4

Week 17 ▶ Day 4

Review *Dependent, Device,* and *Preteen*

Words Reviewed

dependent
Dependent means "relying on or needing someone or something for help or support."

device
A *device* is "a tool, machine, or piece of equipment that does a particular job."

preteen
A *preteen* is "a boy or girl before he or she becomes a teenager." A preteen is between the ages of 8 and 12.

Materials
- Word chart from Day 3
- A marker

REVIEW THE WORDS

▶ **1 Briefly Review the Words**

Review the pronunciation and meaning of each word.

Ask:

Q *In what way is a pet dependent on its owner? Turn to your partner.*

PROMPT: "A pet is dependent on its owner [to feed it and take it to the animal hospital if it's sick]."

Grade Five | 391

Week 17 ▶ Day 4

In the same way, discuss:

Q *Do you think a computer is a necessary device for a preteen to have? Why? Turn to your partner.*

PROMPT: "I [do/do not] think a computer is a necessary device for a preteen to have because…."

PRACTICE USING THE WORDS

2 Do the Activity "Create a Sentence"

Explain that partners will do the activity "Create a Sentence." Review that partners will work together to create sentences that use the vocabulary words.

Point to the word *dependent* on the chart, and review that *dependent* means "relying on or needing someone or something for help or support."

Use "Think, Pair, Share" to discuss:

Q *How might you use the word* dependent *in a sentence?* [pause] *Turn to your partner.*

Have a few pairs share their sentences.

Follow up by asking:

Q *Does it make sense to say, ["I am dependent on my friends because I need people to have fun with"]? Why?*

In the same way, have partners work together to use *device* and *preteen* in sentences.

Teacher Note

Support struggling students by asking questions such as, "Who or what are you dependent on?" If they continue to struggle, provide a sentence starter such as, "I am dependent on my friends because…" or "I am dependent on my computer because…."

Teacher Note

[*device*] Support struggling students by asking questions such as, "What is a device you wish you had? Why?" and "What is a device you would like to invent? Why?" If they continue to struggle, provide a sentence starter.

[*preteen*] Support struggling students by asking questions such as, "What do you [like/dislike] about being a preteen?" and "What is something your parents let you do because you are a preteen?" If they continue to struggle, provide a sentence starter.

Day 5

Ongoing Review

Words Reviewed

apprehensive
Apprehensive means "uneasy or worried and slightly afraid."

ethical
Ethical means "right according to a society's beliefs." When people think something is ethical, they believe it is the right thing to do.

frugal
Frugal means "careful in spending money or not wasteful."

hospitable
Hospitable means "friendly, welcoming, and generous to visitors."

unethical
Unethical means "wrong according to a society's beliefs." When people think something is unethical, they believe it is the wrong thing to do.

Materials
- Pocket chart
- Word cards 9, 73, 75, 91, 92

REVIEW THE WORDS

1 Display the Word Cards and Briefly Review the Words

Review the pronunciation and meaning of the words.

Week 17 ▶ Day 5

PRACTICE USING THE WORDS

▶2 Review the Activity "Describe the Character"

Explain that partners will do the activity "Describe the Character." Explain that you will read a scenario aloud and partners will discuss which vocabulary word best describes the main character of the scenario and why they think so. Tell the students that, before they do the activity in pairs, they will practice as a class.

Explain that the main character of the first scenario is Wally. Then read the following scenario aloud twice:

- *Wally works for a trash company called We'll Recycle Your Junk. Instead of taking the trash he collects to the recycling center, he dumps it into the town lake.* (unethical)

Point to the vocabulary words and ask:

Q *Which vocabulary word best describes Wally? Why?*

PROMPT: "The word [*unethical*] best describes Wally because…."

▶3 Do the Activity "Describe the Character" in Pairs

Continue the activity in pairs using the scenarios that follow.

Explain that the main character of the next scenario is a girl named Sue. Then read the following scenario aloud twice:

- *Sue decides to try out for a TV talent show. A few days before the tryout, she starts to feel uncertain about her decision. She worries that she is not talented enough to impress the judges.* (apprehensive)

Ask:

Q *Which vocabulary word best describes Sue? Why? Turn to your partner.*

Have one or two pairs share their thinking with the class.

Teacher Note

If the students struggle to answer the questions, call for attention, reread the scenario, and think aloud about which word best describes Wally. (You might say, "I think the word *unethical* best describes Wally, because if something is unethical it is the wrong thing to do. Wally is dumping garbage into a lake, and that is wrong or unethical.") Then read the next scenario.

394 | Making Meaning® Vocabulary

In the same way, discuss:

- *Solomon is hosting a pumpkin-picking party at his grandfather's pumpkin patch. He greets his guests at the door, takes their jackets, and offers them something to drink.* (hospitable)

- *Lucy strives to find ways to save money. She buys used books, eats at home, and uses coupons at the grocery store.* (frugal)

- *Theo went to the store to buy a bottle of orange juice. When he was ready to pay for the juice, the clerk was not at the counter. Theo left the money for the juice on the counter with a note that said, "This money is for a bottle of orange juice. Yours truly, Theo."* (ethical)

◀ **Teacher Note**
You might review that *strive* means "try very hard."

All-girls' and

Better for Kids

Out in the world, males and females live, work, and interact with one another. But at an increasing number of schools, the classrooms are filled with all boys or all girls. Life isn't separated into male and female sides, so why should schools be?

TOGETHER OR APART?

Because male and female students think, learn, and behave differently from one another, it makes sense that they would do better at schools that understand these differences. Research has shown that students at all-boys' or all-girls' schools are more confident, more willing to try new things, and might even perform better academically than students at coeducational schools.

DIFFERENT BRAINS, DIFFERENT GAINS

You might not realize it, but your brain develops differently from the brain of a classmate of the opposite sex. For example, the area of a girl's brain that understands language is one of the first areas to develop. In a boy's brain, other areas develop first, such as the part that makes sense of math. Because of differences like these, males and females learn different subjects in different ways.

An all-boys' or all-girls' school can focus its instruction to meet the needs of either male or female students, not both at the same time. This helps students to make quicker, stronger progress. For example, one Michigan study compared graduates of all-boys' and all-girls' high schools with

In 1972, a new law came into effect stating that all U.S. public schools should be coeducational. However, the law was changed in 2002 to allow all-boys' and all-girls' public schools.

All-boys' Schools

graduates of coeducational schools. The researchers found that male students in all-boys' schools scored better in reading and writing than male graduates of coeducational schools. Likewise, female students in all-girls' schools scored better in math and science than did their female peers in coed classrooms.

Shy students may feel happier about participating in an all-boys' or all-girls' class. Taking part in classroom discussions helps them get more out of the lesson.

POSITIVE PROOF IN TEST RESULTS

In 2000, the principal of Thurgood Marshall Elementary School in Seattle, Washington, decided to separate the students at his school into all-boys' or all-girls' classrooms. He hoped that this would improve the behavior of students. Not only did behavior improve, but academic results did, too. Boys increased their average scores in reading from about 20 percent to 66 percent. In writing, they scored the highest in their state. An inner-city high school in Montreal, Canada, also made the switch from coed to all-boys' and all-girls' classrooms in 2000. Before then, an average of only about 65 percent of students would pass final exams each year. Since the switch, the average has soared to 80 percent.

BUILDING CONFIDENCE

Supporters of all-boys' and all-girls' classrooms argue that in those environments, the students are less distracted. This makes it easier for all students to focus on the lesson.

Students who feel shy around people of the opposite sex could benefit the most from all-boys' or all-girls' schools. Without the pressure of worrying about how they might look to members of the opposite sex, they can feel free to be themselves. For example, they might explore subjects they wouldn't normally explore and join clubs or sports teams. Shy students are more likely to feel more comfortable in an all-boys' or all-girls' class, so they're more likely to feel enthusiastic about speaking up in class, asking questions, and joining in class discussions.

Many people argue that an all-boys' or all-girls' education could make it more difficult for young people to learn how to relate to members of the opposite sex. It's true that we live in a world where males and females live and work with one another, not segregated as in boys' or girls' schools. But many graduates of these schools say that they feel confident not only about their academic abilities, but they're also more confident in their personalities. And this confidence can give graduates a head start in building friendships with the opposite sex.

AN INCREASINGLY POPULAR OPTION

All-boys' and all-girls' classes and schools are gaining favor across the United States. In 1995, only three public schools in the United States offered this option. Today, there are more than 250. School districts, parents, and students are increasingly getting on board with all-boys' and all-girls' education as a great way to boost students' scores and confidence.

Grade Five

Do Kids Really Need Cell Phones?

Benefits Beyond the Cool Factor

There are more than 2 billion cell phone users worldwide—and the trend is catching on among eight- to twelve-year-olds. With bright colors and catchy ringtones, cell phones are hard for young people to resist.

But why does a person as young as eight years old need a cell phone? He or she is likely to come up with a list of reasons why, including, "All my friends have them." However, for very young kids, there are many benefits to having cell phones, beyond the obvious "cool" factor.

A Cell Phone Is a Lifeline

In an emergency, a cell phone can be a lifeline. Cell phones allow children to dial 911 or call their parents if there is an accident or emergency. Cell phones allow children to stay in contact with family. Children, parents, and other caregivers are often in different places throughout the day, and things often don't go as expected. For example, if soccer practice ends early or a parent is stuck in traffic, a cell phone can let everyone know how plans have changed.

As our lives become busier, the number of students at home alone after school is increasing. Between 1970 and 2002, the number of children in the United States with mothers in the labor force increased from about 39 percent to 63 percent. Today, about 40 percent of twelve-year-old students are alone at home after school.* This means that it is more important than ever to have a way of keeping in touch with family—and a way of getting help in an emergency.

*Source: U.S. Dept. of Commerce, U.S. Census Bureau, 2002.

Cell phones can help the day run smoothly by keeping family members in touch with one another.

Easy to Set Controls and Limits

Many people worry that cell phones put young children in danger. Bullies or even criminals might use the phones to contact children, and the Internet features of cell phones put children even more at risk. There is also the chance that children can run up high cell phone charges.

However, many cell phones now have parental controls. For example, it's possible to place limits on who can call and be called with some phones. Many cell phones don't have Internet access or text messaging. Some have Global Positioning System (GPS) tracking so that parents can find their child easily, using another cell phone or a website.

Parents can also opt for a prepaid plan so that their child can't go over spending limits. So, it's possible for children to get the benefits of cell phone use without the risks.

Workplaces around the world are becoming more and more reliant on technology.

Preparing for Working with Technology

In the near future, many jobs will be dependent on cell phones and similar devices. Many people predict that mobile devices such as cell phones will be as important in the future as the computer has been in the last twenty years. One way to ensure that young people are familiar with this technology is to allow them to use cell phones now.

Using a cell phone isn't limited to text messaging and talking any more. For example, cell phones can be helpful when doing schoolwork. On a standard cell phone, students can check the Internet for definitions and spellings of tricky words, take photos and make short videos for school projects, and listen to audio books using an MP3 player. Carrying out a variety of tasks using cell phones can help boost young people's confidence around technology—and, in turn, help them feel confident when they grow up and begin working.

Cell Phones Teach Responsibility

Owning a tool such as a cell phone can be a great way for a child to learn responsibility. Because cell phones are valuable and can be used in different ways, children must learn to use them wisely—for example, making sure they don't lose them, keeping them charged, and using them only when they are not in school. These things help young people learn to treat personal possessions with care. Learning responsibility in this way helps children to respect other people's belongings, too.

An Unstoppable Trend

Researchers say that about 6 million of the 20 million American children between eight and twelve years old had cell phones by the end of 2006. Researchers also predict that, by 2010, there will be 10.5 million preteen cell phone users. If young children don't already own cell phones, it's likely that they will in the future. The best way for young people to benefit from this technology is to learn to use it responsibly today.

Week 18

Overview

Functional Texts

"How to Make an Origami Cup"

"Ashton Hammerheads Schedule for July, 2008"

"Frontier Fun Park" Ticket Prices

Words Taught

procedure

sequence

indicate

supreme

hair-raising

priority

Word-learning Strategies

- Recognizing words with multiple meanings (review)
- Recognizing synonyms (review)
- Recognizing idioms (review)

Words Reviewed: device, hunger, regulate, strive, thrust

DO AHEAD

- Prior to Day 1, collect a map of the United States. You will use the map to discuss the word *indicate*.

- Prior to Day 5, write the "Find Another Word" sentences on the board or a sheet of chart paper or make a transparency of the sentences (BLM16). (See Step 2 on page 419.)

- Prior to Day 5, collect these word cards for Ongoing Review: 64, 74, 87, 94, and 101.

Grade Five | 401

Week 18 ▶ Day 1

Day 1

Introduce *Procedure, Sequence,* and *Indicate*

Materials

- "How to Make an Origami Cup" (see page 421)
- "Ashton Hammerheads Schedule for July, 2008" (see page 422)
- Chart paper
- A marker
- A map of the United States
- (Optional) *Making Meaning Student Response Book*

Words Taught

procedure
A *procedure* is "a way to do something, or method of doing it, especially by a series of steps."

sequence
A *sequence* is "a series of events or objects in a particular order."

indicate (p. 422)
Indicate means "point out or show." *Indicate* also means "be a sign of."

INTRODUCE AND PRACTICE USING *PROCEDURE*

▶ **1 Introduce and Define *Procedure***

Briefly review "How to Make an Origami Cup."

Tell the students that the first word they will learn today is *procedure* and that a *procedure* is "a way to do something, or method of doing it, especially by a series of steps."

Teacher Note ▶

You might have the students bring their *Making Meaning Student Response Books* to the rug to refer to as you discuss the functional texts used in today's lesson.

Show "How to Make an Origami Cup." Explain that these instructions tell you the procedure, or the way to make, an origami cup in a series of steps. If you follow the procedure step-by-step, you will be able to make the cup.

Have the students say the word *procedure*, and write it on the chart.

402 | Making Meaning® Vocabulary

Week 18 ▶ Day 1

2 ▶ Discuss Procedures

Explain that we have certain procedures, or ways to do things, that we follow in our classroom. Explain that these procedures keep our classroom running smoothly. Give an example of a classroom procedure. (You might say, "We have a procedure, or way, for starting our day. First, I check attendance and a volunteer puts the attendance slip outside the door. Then, I call everyone to the rug for our morning meeting. We begin the meeting by going through the daily schedule, which is written on the board. Then, I answer any questions you have about what we will be learning or doing.")

Explain that the school also has procedures. Discuss as a class:

Q *What is our school's procedure for evacuating the building during a fire drill?*

PROMPT: "Our procedure for evacuating the building during a fire drill is…."

Follow up by discussing as a class:

Q *Why do you think we have a procedure for evacuating the building in case of a fire? What might happen if we did not have a procedure?*

PROMPTS: "We have a procedure for evacuating the building because…" or "If we did not have a procedure for evacuating the building…."

3 ▶ Do the Activity "Imagine That!"

Have the students imagine the following scene:

- *Space aliens have landed in our town. You have been selected by the Society for Clean Teeth to teach the aliens a procedure for brushing their teeth.*

Q *What step-by-step procedure for brushing teeth will you teach the aliens? Turn to your partner.*

PROMPT: "The step-by-step procedure I will teach the aliens is…."

Grade Five | 403

Week 18 ▸ Day 1

In the same way, discuss:

- *You did a great job for the Society for Clean Teeth. Now the Pedestrian Safety Committee wants you to teach the aliens a step-by-step procedure for crossing the street safely.*

Review the pronunciation and meaning of the word.

INTRODUCE AND PRACTICE USING *SEQUENCE*

4 ▸ Introduce and Define *Sequence*

Tell the students that the next word they will learn is *sequence* and that a *sequence* is "a series of events or objects in a particular order."

Show "How to Make an Origami Cup" again. Point out that the instructions include a sequence, or series, of steps. Explain that the first step in the sequence is step 1. The second step in the sequence is step 2.

Discuss as a class:

Q *Which step in the sequence is the last step?*

PROMPT: "[Step 5] is the last step in the sequence."

Follow up by discussing as a class:

Q *What might happen if you do not follow the steps in the sequence as you are making the cup?*

PROMPT: "If you do not follow the steps in the sequence…."

Have the students say the word *sequence*, and write it on the chart.

5 ▸ Discuss *Sequence*

Explain that books, TV shows, movies, and people's lives are all made up of sequences of events, or series of events, one event following another.

Ask:

Q *What is the sequence of events that has made up your day so far? Turn to your partner.*

PROMPT: "The sequence of events that has made up my day is…."

Tell the students that a sequence is often important when you are carrying out a procedure. Remind them that, if we do not follow the sequence of steps for making the origami cup, the cup will not look the way it should or it will not hold water.

Discuss as a class:

Q *What is something you do every day that has a sequence of steps? Why do you do the steps in sequence?*

PROMPT: "I use a sequence of steps to [get ready for school] because…."

Follow up by asking each volunteer:

Q *What sequence do you follow when you [get ready for school]?*

PROMPT: "The sequence I follow when I [get ready for school] is…."

Review the pronunciation and meaning of the word.

◀ **Teacher Note**

Support struggling students by asking questions such as, "What is the first thing you did or that happened to you today? What did you do or what happened after that? Then what did you do or what happened?"

◀ **Teacher Note**

If the students struggle to answer the questions, give an example of something you do that has a sequence of steps, or ask questions such as, "What are some things you do in sequence in the morning to get ready for school?" "What are some things you do in sequence when you are doing school work or playing a game?" and "What is something you make by following a sequence of steps?"

INTRODUCE AND PRACTICE USING *INDICATE*

6 **Introduce and Define** *Indicate*

Briefly review "Ashton Hammerheads Schedule for July, 2008."

Show "Ashton Hammerheads Schedule for July, 2008," and review that the schedule provides information such as when the Hammerheads will be playing, what teams they will be playing, and what time each game begins.

Grade Five | 405

Week 18 ▶ Day 1

Read the following sentence from the legend aloud, emphasizing the word *indicated*, "All games begin at 6:00 p.m. unless otherwise indicated."

Tell the students that the last word they will learn today is *indicate* and that *indicate* means "point out or show."

Explain that the sentence "All games begin at 6:00 p.m. unless otherwise indicated" means that every game begins at 6:00 p.m. unless another time is indicated, or shown. Show the schedule again, and point out that no time is indicated, or shown, for July 1, so that day's game will start at 6:00. Point out that a time is indicated, or shown, for July 2, so that day's game will start at a different time, 12:30.

Have the students say the word *indicate*, and write it on the chart.

7 ▶ Act Out and Discuss Indicating

Explain that you are going to ask a volunteer to indicate, or point out or show, where our state is on the map of the United States. Ask the students to watch carefully. Then have a volunteer indicate where the state is on the map.

Discuss as a class:

Q *What did you see [Caitlin] do when [she] indicated where our state is?*

PROMPT: "When [Caitlin] indicated where our state is, [she]...."

Then ask:

Q *If your backpack looks like other backpacks in our class, what might you do to indicate, or show, that your backpack belongs to you? Turn to your partner.*

PROMPT: "To indicate that my backpack belongs to me, I might...."

8 ▶ Discuss Another Meaning of *Indicate*

Remind the students that words often have more than one meaning. Point to the word *indicate* on the chart, and review that *indicate* means "point out or show." Explain that *indicate* can also mean "be a sign of." For example, a high fever indicates, or is a sign, that someone is sick. Dark clouds indicate, or are a sign, that a storm is coming. Smoke indicates, or is a sign, that something is on fire.

Ask:

Q *What might a ringing bell indicate? Turn to your partner.*

PROMPT: "A ringing bell might indicate…."

In the same way, discuss:

Q *What might tears on a person's face indicate? Turn to your partner.*

PROMPT: "Tears might indicate that…."

Review the pronunciation and meanings of the word.

EXTENSION

Explore the Suffix *-tion*

Write the word *indication* on the board. Point to *-tion* and explain that *-tion* is a suffix that means "the act, state, or result of doing something." Explain that when you add *-tion* to a verb, you turn the verb into a noun. When *-tion* is added to the verb *indicate*, it makes the noun *indication*, which means "something that indicates, or is a sign of."

Remind the students that earlier they learned the words *regulate* and *interact*. Review the words' meanings; then write the words *regulation* and *interaction* on the board. Discuss the way each word is made and what it means. (A *regulation* is "a rule or law that controls or manages how people behave or what they can do." An *interaction* is "an activity in which people talk or work with one another.")

Week 18 ▶ Day 1

Teacher Note

You might explain that the suffix *-sion* also means "the act, state, or result of doing something" and is used in words such as *decision*, *collision*, *explosion*, and *confusion*. ▶

Ask the students for other examples of *-tion* words, and discuss them, or have the students discuss words you provide (for example, *population*, *education*, and *reaction*). During the next few days, have the students watch and listen for other *-tion* words, and discuss each one.

Teacher Note

For a list of words with the suffix *-tion* and other word lists, visit Developmental Studies Center's website at www.devstu.org.

Day 2

Week 18 ▸ Day 2

Review *Procedure, Sequence,* and *Indicate*

Words Reviewed

procedure
A *procedure* is "a way to do something, or method of doing it, especially by a series of steps."

sequence
A *sequence* is "a series of events or objects in a particular order."

indicate
Indicate means "point out or show." *Indicate* also means "be a sign of."

Materials
- Word chart from Day 1

REVIEW THE WORDS

1 Briefly Review the Words

Review the pronunciation and meaning of each word.

Ask:

Q *Which of the words we learned yesterday might you use when you are talking with your friends or family? How might you use the word?*

PROMPT: "I might use the word [*procedure*] when I'm talking with [my little brother]. I might say…."

Grade Five | 409

Week 18 ▶ Day 2

PRACTICE USING THE WORDS

Teacher Note

If the students struggle to answer the questions, think aloud about associations you might make and why. (You might say, "I think *procedure* goes with *recipe*, because a recipe is a procedure, or way to prepare something to eat. I think *sequence* goes with *recipe*, too, because the steps of a recipe are listed in sequence. I think *indicate* can go with *recipe* also, because the measurements in a recipe indicate, or show, how much of each ingredient to use.") Then discuss the word *number* as a class, rather than in pairs.

2 ▶ Do the Activity "Which Word Goes With?"

Tell the students that partners will do the activity "Which Word Goes With?" Review that you will write a word on the board and partners will discuss which of the vocabulary words they learned yesterday goes with the word. Then you will ask some pairs to share their thinking with the class.

Write the word *recipe* on the board and read the word aloud. Use "Think, Pair, Share" to discuss:

Q *Which of yesterday's words do you think goes with* recipe? *Why do you think that?* [pause] *Turn to your partner.*

PROMPT: "I think [*procedure*] goes with *recipe* because…."

Write the word *number* on the board and read the word aloud.

Use "Think, Pair, Share" to discuss:

Q *Which of yesterday's words do you think goes with* number? *Why do you think that?* [pause] *Turn to your partner.*

PROMPT: "I think [*procedure*] goes with *number* because…."

When most pairs have finished talking, ask one or two pairs to share their thinking with the class.

Teacher Note

If the students have trouble making associations, think aloud about associations you might make or ask questions such as, "How might the word *procedure* go with *number*? When might a procedure be numbered? Where might you see a procedure organized by numbered steps?" "How might the word *sequence* go with *number*? Where might you see a sequence of numbers?" and "How might the word *indicate* go with *number*? What do the numbers on a [thermometer/clock] indicate?"

410 | Making Meaning® Vocabulary

Day 3

Week 18 ▶ Day 3

Introduce *Supreme, Hair-raising,* and *Priority*

Words Taught

supreme
Supreme means "the best or the highest in quality, power, or rank."

hair-raising
Hair-raising means "exciting, thrilling, or terrifying."

priority (p. 423)
A *priority* is "something that is more important or more urgent than other things."

Materials
- "Frontier Fun Park" ticket prices (see page 423)
- Word chart from Day 1
- A marker
- (Optional) *Making Meaning Student Response Book*

INTRODUCE AND PRACTICE USING *SUPREME*

1 Introduce and Define *Supreme*

Briefly review "Frontier Fun Park" ticket prices.

Remind the students that, in addition to giving ticket prices, the price list tells about Pine Mountain, the park's roller coaster. Read the description of Pine Mountain, beginning with the sentence, "At 460 feet, Pine Mountain is the nation's highest roller coaster!"

Tell the students that the first word they will learn today is *supreme*. Explain that *supreme* means "the best or the highest in quality, power, or rank."

Explain that the owners of the amusement park believe that Pine Mountain is the supreme, or best, roller coaster in the nation. They think it is supreme, or highest in quality, because it is the highest

◀ **Teacher Note**
You might have the students bring their *Making Meaning Student Response Books* to the rug to refer to as you discuss the functional text used in today's lesson.

◀ **Teacher Note**
You might explain that *supreme*, *best*, and *greatest* are synonyms. If you started a synonym chart, add *supreme* and its synonyms to it.

Grade Five | 411

Week 18 ▶ Day 3

roller coaster in the country and the "greatest, most thrilling roller coaster ever."

Have the students say the word *supreme*, and write it on the chart.

▶2 Imagine Creating Supreme Products

Remind the students that we use the word *supreme* to describe something that is the best of its kind or the highest in quality, power, or rank. For example, we call the highest, most powerful court in the United States the Supreme Court. We describe the highest-ranking general in an army as the supreme commander. Kings, emperors, or other rulers with great power are sometimes called supreme rulers.

Explain that businesses sometimes use the word *supreme* to describe a product because they want customers to think the product is the best of its kind or the highest in quality. For example, a restaurant that makes hamburgers might call their best hamburger the "Supreme Burger" or the "Burger Supreme."

Have the students imagine the following scene:

- *You work in a sandwich shop. The owner asks you to create a new sandwich called "The Supreme Sandwich."*

Use "Think, Pair, Share" to discuss:

Q *What ingredients might you use to create The Supreme Sandwich? Why would those ingredients make the sandwich supreme?* [pause] *Turn to your partner.*

PROMPT: "The ingredients in The Supreme Sandwich might be [chicken, cheese, and tomatoes]. The ingredients would make the sandwich supreme because…."

In the same way, discuss:

- *You are an expert who knows what preteens think is fun and exciting. The owners of a summer camp ask you to design the best summer camp for preteens ever. It will be called "Camp Supreme."*

Teacher Note

You might review that a *preteen* is "a boy or girl before he or she becomes a teenager." A preteen is between the ages of 8 and 12.

412 | Making Meaning® Vocabulary

Q *What will Camp Supreme look like? What kind of activities will there be?* [pause] *Turn to your partner.*

PROMPT: "Camp Supreme…."

Review the pronunciation and meaning of the word.

INTRODUCE AND PRACTICE USING *HAIR-RAISING*

3 **Introduce and Define *Hair-raising* and Review Synonyms and Idioms**

Show "Frontier Fun Park" ticket prices again, and review that the Pine Mountain roller coaster is described as the "most thrilling roller coaster ever."

Explain that the next word the students will learn is *hair-raising*. Explain that *hair-raising* means "exciting, thrilling, or terrifying" and that *hair-raising*, *exciting*, *thrilling*, and *terrifying* are synonyms. Explain that the owners of Pine Mountain think that riding their roller coaster is a hair-raising, or thrilling, experience.

◀ **Teacher Note**

If you started a synonym chart, add *hair-raising* and its synonyms to it.

Have the students say *hair-raising*, and write it on the chart.

Point to the word *hair-raising* on the chart, and explain that *hair-raising* is an idiom. Remind the students that an *idiom* is "an expression or phrase that means something different from what it appears to mean." Explain that when we say a roller coaster ride is hair-raising, we do not mean that your hair actually stands on end from fear or excitement when you ride it. Instead, we mean that the ride is so exciting or thrilling that your skin tingles, and it feels like your hair is standing on end. Explain that scary movies and stories are sometimes described as hair-raising because they can be thrilling or terrifying.

◀ **Teacher Note**

If you started an idiom chart, add *hair-raising* to it.

Week 18 ▶ Day 3

▶4 Discuss a Hair-raising Experience

Tell the students about a time you or someone you know had a hair-raising experience. (You might say, "When I was young, I was chased by a stray dog. It was a hair-raising experience because I was terrified that the dog was going to bite me. A friend told me that, when she parachuted out of an airplane for the first time, it was a hair-raising experience because it was so exciting. She said it was thrilling to fall and float through the air.")

Use "Think, Pair, Share" to discuss:

Q *When have you had a hair-raising experience? What made it hair-raising?* [pause] *Turn to your partner.*

PROMPT: "I had a hair-raising experience when I [went skiing for the first time] because…."

Review the pronunciation and meaning of the word.

Teacher Note

Support struggling students by asking questions such as, "What is the most exciting or thrilling thing you have ever done?" "What is the scariest thing that has ever happened to you?" and "When have you seen a movie or read a book that was hair-raising? Why was it hair-raising?" If the students cannot think of a hair-raising experience, ask alternative questions such as, "What is something that might happen to you that would be hair-raising?" or "Who do you know who has had a hair-raising experience?"

INTRODUCE AND PRACTICE USING *PRIORITY*

▶5 Introduce and Define *Priority*

Direct the students' attention to the disclaimer at the bottom of "Frontier Fun Park" ticket prices and explain that this part of the text gives information about park safety. Read the following sentence aloud, emphasizing the word *priority*, "The safety of our guests is Frontier Fun Park's highest priority."

Tell the students that the last word they will learn today is *priority* and that a *priority* is "something that is more important or more urgent than other things." Explain that the owners of the amusement park want guests to know that their safety is the park's highest priority. Safety is more important than anything else.

414 | Making Meaning® Vocabulary

Discuss as a class:

Q *Why do you think safety is the park's highest priority, or more important than anything else?*

PROMPT: "I think safety is the park's highest priority because…."

Have the students say the word *priority*, and write it on the chart.

6 Discuss Tulip's Priorities

Tell the students that you will describe two things that Tulip needs to do and partners will discuss which one should be Tulip's priority and why.

Begin with:

- *Tulip gets home late from school and finds a note from her mom. The note says, "Please study for your math test and clean your room before I get home." Tulip realizes she has time to do only one thing before her mother gets home.*

Ask:

Q *Which of these should be Tulip's priority: studying for her math test or cleaning her room? Why? Turn to your partner.*

PROMPT: "[Studying for her math test] should be Tulip's priority because…."

In the same way, discuss:

- *Tulip tells her friend Iris that she will help her with her homework after school. Then she remembers that she told her little sister Angela she would play with her after school.*

Q *Which of these should be Tulip's priority: helping her friend Iris with her homework or playing with her little sister Angela? Why? Turn to your partner.*

Review the pronunciation and meaning of the word.

Week 18 ▶ Day 4

Day 4

Review *Supreme, Hair-raising,* and *Priority*

Materials
- Word chart from Day 3
- A marker

Words Reviewed

supreme
Supreme means "the best or the highest in quality, power, or rank."

hair-raising
Hair-raising means "exciting, thrilling, or terrifying."

priority
A *priority* is "something that is more important or more urgent than other things."

REVIEW THE WORDS

1 Briefly Review the Words

Review the pronunciation and meaning of each word.

Ask:

Q *Which of these words might you use if you were writing a story about the most frightening creature in the world? How might you use the word? Turn to your partner.*

PROMPT: "I might use the word [*supreme*]. I might write…."

416 | Making Meaning® Vocabulary

Week 18 ▶ Day 4

PRACTICE USING THE WORDS

2 **Do the Activity "What Do You Think About?"**

Explain that partners will do the activity "What Do You Think About?" Point to the words on the chart, and explain that you want the students to notice what they think about, or what picture comes into their minds, when they hear each of the words.

Have the students close their eyes. Then use "Think, Pair, Share" to discuss:

Q *What do you think about when you hear the word* supreme? *Why?* [pause] *Open your eyes and turn to your partner.*

PROMPT: "When I hear the word *supreme*, I think of [a king] because…."

Discuss the remaining words the same way.

Teacher Note

If the students struggle to make associations, call for attention and think aloud about what comes into your mind when you hear the word *supreme*. (You might say, "When I hear the word *supreme*, I think about the Supreme Court because it is the most powerful court in the United States.")

If the students continue to struggle, support them by asking questions such as, "What makes something supreme?" and "What [foods/activities] do you think are supreme?"

Teacher Note

Support struggling students by thinking aloud about what you picture in your mind when you hear the word or by asking questions such as,
[*hair-raising*] "When have you had a hair-raising experience?" and "What kind of experience would be hair-raising?"
[*priority*] "What priorities do you have at school?" and "What might your first priority be if you want to do well in school?"

Teacher Note

For a crossword puzzle you can use to review words taught during weeks 17 and 18, visit Developmental Studies Center's website at www.devstu.org.

Grade Five | 417

Week 18 ▶ Day 5

Day 5

Ongoing Review

Materials
- Pocket chart
- Word cards 64, 74, 87, 94, 101
- Charted sentences or transparency (BLM16) for "Find Another Word" (see Step 2 on page 419)
- (Optional) Overhead projector and marker

Words Reviewed

device
A *device* is "a tool, machine, or piece of equipment that does a particular job."

hunger
Hunger is "a strong desire or want."

regulate
Regulate means "control or manage, usually through rules or laws."

strive
Strive means "try very hard."

thrust
Thrust means "push or shove suddenly or with force."

REVIEW THE WORDS

▶ **1 Display the Word Cards and Briefly Review the Words**
Review the pronunciation and meaning of the words.

PRACTICE USING THE WORDS

2 Play "Find Another Word"

Display the transparency or write the following sentences (without the answers) on the board or a sheet of chart paper and underline the words shown:

> Hillary always <u>works very hard</u> to make sure her customers are satisfied. (strives)
>
> One day, Greg found a strange little <u>machine</u> on the floor of his shop. (device)
>
> Every morning Josie <u>has a strong desire</u> to take a long walk around her neighborhood. (hungers)
>
> Moments after the alarm went off, police officers <u>forcefully pushed</u> the door open. (thrust)
>
> The newspaper article said we can reduce pollution by <u>controlling</u> the number of cars on the road. (regulating)

Explain that partners will play "Find Another Word." Direct the students' attention to the sentences, and review that you will read each sentence aloud. Partners will discuss which vocabulary word could replace the underlined words.

Begin by pointing to this sentence and reading it aloud:

- *Hillary always works very hard to make sure her customers are satisfied.*

Ask:

Q *Which word could replace "works very hard" in the sentence? Why? Turn to your partner.*

◀ **Teacher Note**

You might explain that the students may need to change the form of a word to complete the sentence by adding an ending such as *-s*, *-ing*, or *-ed*.

Week 18 ▶ Day 5

PROMPT: "I think the word [*strives*] could replace 'works very hard' because…."

Teacher Note

You might invite partners to work together to create their own "Find Another Word" sentences and have them share their sentences with the class. ▶

Have volunteers share their thinking.

Reread the sentence, replacing the underlined words with the vocabulary word.

Discuss the remaining sentences the same way.

CLASS VOCABULARY PROGRESS ASSESSMENT

As you observe the students, ask yourself:

- Can the students identify the vocabulary word that replaces the underlined words?
- Do their explanations show that they understand the words' meanings?
- Are they using the synonyms they are learning in their writing?

For more information about reviewing and practicing the words, see "Retaining the Words" on pages xviii–xix.

How to Make an Origami Cup

Now you can learn to make a handy cup using only a sheet of paper!
Begin with a square piece of paper and follow the instructions below:

Step 1:

Fold your square on the diagonal, matching up corners **A** and **B**.

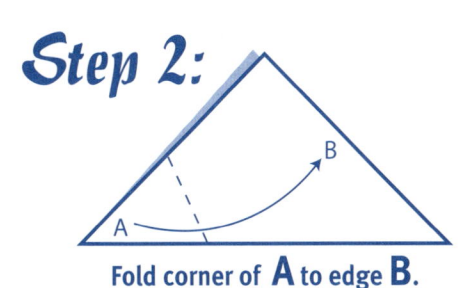

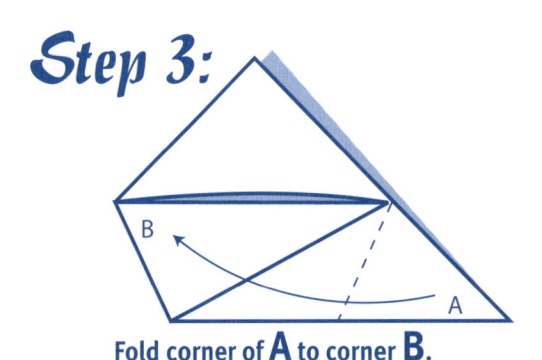

Step 2:

Fold corner of **A** to edge **B**.

Step 3:

Fold corner of **A** to corner **B**.

Step 4:

Take the top flap (flap **A**) and fold down toward you. Turn the cup over and repeat the step with the other remaining flap.

Step 5:

Gently push sides in to form your cup. If you followed the instructions above, your cup should look like this and be able to hold water. Enjoy your cup!

Grade Five | 421

Hammerheads
ASHTON, CALIF

Ashton Hammerheads Schedule
for July, 2008

Sunday	Monday	Tuesday	Wednesday	Thursday	Friday	Saturday
		1 vs Glen Hill @ Bank Park	**2** vs Flourbell @ Fair Stad 12:30 p.m.	**3**	**4** vs Ardmore	**5** vs Plymouth 12:15 p.m.
6 vs Plymouth	**7** vs Paulsboro	**8** vs Paulsboro	**9** vs Paulsboro 12:30 p.m.	**10**	**11** vs Mt Holly @ Holly Stad 9:00 p.m.	**12** vs Mt Holly @ Holly Stad
13 vs Mt Holly @ Holly Stad 3:00 p.m.	**14** vs Beverley @ Bev Stad 9:00 p.m.	**15** vs Beverley @ Bev Stad 9:00 p.m.	**16** vs Springfield @ Spring Bank 1:30 p.m.	**17**	**18** vs Bridgeport @ Broomall	**19** vs Bridgeport @ Broomall 2:30 p.m.
20 vs Ridley Crew @ Broomall 1:30 p.m.	**21**	**22** vs Wishton	**23** vs Wishton	**24** vs Oreland 12:15 p.m.	**25** vs Oreland 9:00 p.m.	**26** vs Chester
27 vs Chester 1:15 p.m.	**28** vs Glenolden @ Wales Park	**29** vs Paulsboro @ Wales Park 2:00 p.m.	**30** vs Paulsboro @ Wales Park	**31** vs Paulsboro @ Wales Park		

Hammerheads t-shirt day
(free t-shirt for first 1500 fans)

Hammerheads cap day
(free baseball cap for all fans under fifteen)

League Championship ticket raffle
(all fans entered into a drawing for 4 free tickets to the League Championship game)

☐ = Hammerheads Home Game   ■ = Hammerheads Away Game

All games begin at 6:00 p.m. unless otherwise indicated.

Tickets $25

422 | Making Meaning® Vocabulary

FRONTIER FUN PARK

Home of the Legendary PINE MOUNTAIN

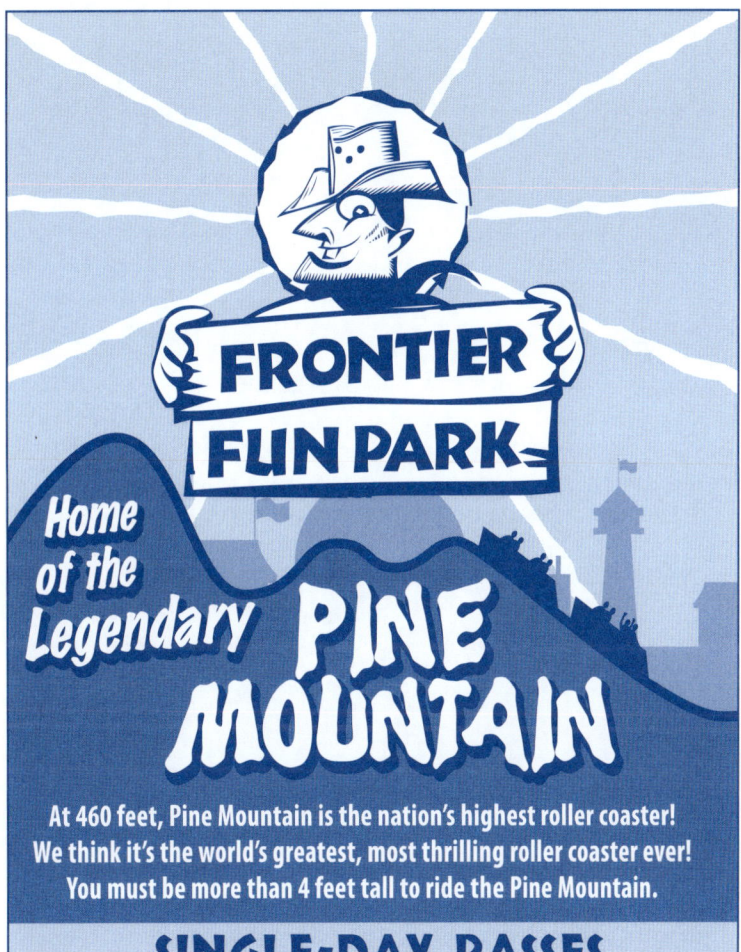

At 460 feet, Pine Mountain is the nation's highest roller coaster! We think it's the world's greatest, most thrilling roller coaster ever! You must be more than 4 feet tall to ride the Pine Mountain.

SINGLE-DAY PASSES

	Adults (Age 10+)	Children (Ages 3–9)
1-DAY BASIC PASS	$40.00	$30.00

Includes entry to all main attractions (does not include Pine Mountain roller coaster)

	Adults (Age 10+)	Children (Ages 3–9)
1-DAY PINE MOUNTAIN PASS	$50.00	$40.00

Includes entry to all main attractions, including Pine Mountain roller coaster

1-DAY PINE MOUNTAIN FAMILY PASS — $140.00
(Up to 2 adults and 2 children aged 3–9)
Includes entry to all main attractions, including Pine Mountain roller coaster

1-DAY PINE MOUNTAIN PLUS FAMILY PASS — $160.00
(Up to 2 adults and 2 children aged 3–9)
Includes entry to all main attractions, including Pine Mountain roller coaster, plus a 20% discount on all purchases from the Frontier Cabin Outdoor Superstore

ONE-WEEK PASSES

1-WEEK PINE MOUNTAIN FAMILY PASS — $320.00
(Up to 2 adults and 2 children aged 3–9)
Includes entry to all main attractions, including Pine Mountain roller coaster, for 7 consecutive days

Disclaimer
The safety of our guests is Frontier Fun Park's highest priority. However, the Frontier Fun Park will not be liable for any injuries, damages, or losses that occur in connection with the Fun Park's activities.

Week 19 Overview

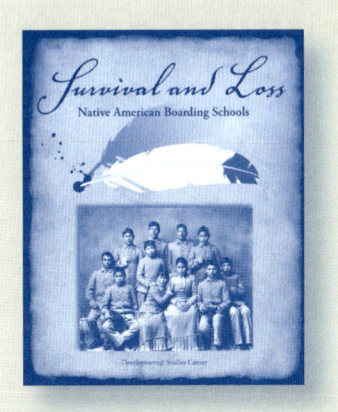

Survival and Loss: Native American Boarding Schools
(Developmental Studies Center, 2008)

Words Taught

resolve

compel

comply

squander

clash

defenseless

Word-learning Strategies

- Recognizing synonyms (review)
- Using the suffix *-less* to determine word meanings (review)

Words Reviewed: deprive, episode, fanciful, prejudice, solitary

DO AHEAD

- Prior to Day 3, review More Strategy Practice on page 438.

- Prior to Day 5, write the "What's the Missing Word?" sentences on the board or a sheet of chart paper or make a transparency of the sentences (BLM17). (See Step 2 on page 443.)

- Prior to Day 5, collect these word cards for Ongoing Review: 32, 71, 77, 78, and 84.

Grade Five | 425

Week 19 ▸ Day 1

Day 1

Introduce *Resolve, Compel,* and *Comply*

Materials

- *Survival and Loss*
- Chart paper
- A marker

Words Taught

resolve (p. 3)
Resolve means "find an answer or solution to a problem."

compel
Compel means "force."

comply
Comply means "do what you are asked to do or what a law or rule requires you to do."

INTRODUCE AND PRACTICE USING *RESOLVE*

▶ **1 Introduce and Define *Resolve***

Briefly review *Survival and Loss*.

Show pages 2–3 and review that, as the number of European settlers increased, the settlers began to compete with Native Americans for land. Read the following sentence from the second paragraph of page 3 aloud, emphasizing the word *resolve*, "In 1836, the U.S. government tried to resolve its 'Indian problem' by giving the eastern Native American tribes two years to move westward from their homelands."

Explain that the first word the students will learn today is *resolve* and that *resolve* means "find an answer or solution to a problem."

Explain that the U.S. government had a problem: settlers wanted land that Indians were living on. The government tried to resolve the problem, or find an answer or solution, by requiring that eastern Native American tribes give up their land and move west.

Have the students say the word *resolve*, and then write it on a sheet of chart paper.

2 Discuss Ways We Might Resolve a Problem

Tell the students that people resolve, or find answers or solutions to, problems every day, and give an example of a problem you or someone you know resolved. (You might say, "When I got to school this morning, I realized I had left my house key at home. I resolved the problem by calling my son and having him bring me the key. The other day my son wanted to go for a bike ride with a friend, but he didn't have his bike because it was at the bike shop being repaired. He resolved the problem by borrowing his brother's bike.")

Discuss as a class:

Q *What is a problem you have resolved recently? How did you resolve the problem?*

PROMPT: "This morning [my shoelace broke]. I resolved the problem by…."

Tell the students you will describe a problem and partners will discuss how they might resolve it.

Begin with:

- *You are locked out of your house.*

Ask:

Q *How might you resolve the problem? Turn to your partner.*

PROMPT: "I might resolve the problem by…."

Week 19 ▶ Day 1

In the same way, discuss:

- *When you get home from school, you find that your cat is stuck in a tree.*

Review the pronunciation and meaning of the word.

INTRODUCE AND PRACTICE USING *COMPEL*

▶ 3 Introduce and Define *Compel* and Review Synonyms

Show pages 2–3 again, and review that the U.S. government gave eastern Native American tribes two years to move westward. Read the following sentence from the second paragraph of page 3 aloud, "If these tribes didn't move within the two-year period, they would be forced to leave."

Teacher Note ▶

If you started a synonym chart, add *compel* and *force* to it.

Explain that the next word the students will learn is *compel*. Explain that *compel* means "force" and that *compel* and *force* are synonyms. Explain that the government told the Native Americans that, if they did not move westward within two years, they would be compelled, or forced, to leave.

Have the students say the word *compel*, and write it on the chart.

▶ 4 Discuss *Compel*

Explain that we usually use the word *compel* to talk about situations in which people are forced to do things they do not want to do. For example, if you are sick, you might feel compelled, or forced, to go to the doctor, even though you do not want to. If you are very hungry, but the cafeteria is not serving anything you like to eat, you might feel compelled, or forced, to eat something you do not want to eat. If a hurricane is heading toward the town where you live, you might feel compelled to leave your home to be safe.

Discuss as a class:

Q *What else might compel you to leave your home to be safe?*

428 | Making Meaning® Vocabulary

Week 19 ▸ Day 1

PROMPT: "A [fire or flood] might compel me to leave my home."

Explain that in most communities recycling bottles, cans, and other trash is voluntary. That means that people do not have to recycle if they do not want to.

Ask:

Q *Do you think the government should compel people to recycle? Why? Turn to your partner.*

PROMPT: "I [do/do not] think the government should compel people to recycle because…."

Review the pronunciation and meaning of the word.

INTRODUCE AND PRACTICE USING *COMPLY*

5 Introduce and Define *Comply*

Tell the students that the last word they will learn today is *comply* and that *comply* means "do what you are asked to do or what a law or rule requires you to do."

Show pages 2–3 again, and read the following sentence from the second paragraph of page 3 aloud, "While many tribes had little choice but to go, some tribes fought against removal."

Explain that, when the government told the tribes they must move westward, many tribes complied, or did what they were required to do. But other tribes did not comply—they did not do what the government told them to do. Those tribes fought against being removed from their land.

Have the students say the word *comply*, and write it on the chart.

Grade Five | 429

Week 19 ▶ Day 1

6 ▶ Discuss Times We Comply

Tell the students that we comply with many rules and requests at school, and give a few examples. (You might say, "When our PE teacher Mrs. King asks you to put away basketballs and other equipment after class, you comply, or do what you are asked to do, by putting the equipment where it belongs. When the principal announces that we will have indoor recess, we comply by staying in the classroom. When I ask you to gather on the rug for a vocabulary lesson, you comply by coming to the rug.")

Discuss as a class:

Q *In what other ways do you comply at school?*

PROMPT: "We comply by [cleaning up our table area when you ask us to]."

Point out that the students also comply with the rules and requests of their parents at home.

Ask:

Q *In what ways do you comply with your parents? Turn to your partner.*

PROMPT: "I comply with my parents by [doing my chores when they ask me to]."

Review the pronunciation and meaning of the word.

430 | Making Meaning® Vocabulary

Day 2

Review *Resolve, Compel,* and *Comply*

Words Reviewed

resolve
Resolve means "find an answer or solution to a problem."

compel
Compel means "force."

comply
Comply means "do what you are asked to do or what a law or rule requires you to do."

Materials

- Word chart from Day 1

REVIEW THE WORDS

1 Briefly Review the Words

Review the pronunciation and meaning of each word.

Ask:

Q *Which of the words we learned yesterday do you think was interesting or fun to talk about? Why? Turn to your partner.*

PROMPT: "I think the word [*comply*] was [interesting/fun] to talk about because…."

Week 19 ▸ Day 2

PRACTICE USING THE WORDS

2 Think More About the Words

Tell the students that you will describe a situation and partners will use vocabulary words to discuss it. Explain that partners may not always agree about a situation and that is fine. What is important is that they explain their thinking.

Read the following scenario aloud twice:

- *Mrs. Gilbert has a problem. Her children are not eating enough fruits and vegetables. To resolve the problem, Mrs. Gilbert compels her children to eat at least one fruit and one vegetable at dinner. Until they do, they cannot leave the table.*

Use "Think, Pair, Share" to discuss:

Q *Do you think compelling the children to eat at least one fruit and one vegetable before they can leave the table is a good way for Mrs. Gilbert to resolve the problem? Why?* [pause] *Turn to your partner.*

PROMPT: "I [do/do not] think compelling the children to eat at least one fruit and one vegetable before they can leave the table is a good way to resolve the problem because…."

In the same way, discuss:

- *Mrs. Gilbert has another problem. Her children do not keep their bedroom tidy. She has asked the children several times to clean up their room, but they do not comply.*

Q *What might Mrs. Gilbert do to get the children to comply with her request to clean up their room?* [pause] *Turn to your partner.*

PROMPT: "To get the children to comply with her request, Mrs. Gilbert might…."

Day 3

Introduce *Squander, Clash,* and *Defenseless*

Words Taught

squander
Squander means "carelessly waste something such as money, time, or opportunities."

clash
Clash means "fight or argue."

defenseless (p. 13)
Defenseless means "without defense, helpless, or unprotected."

Materials

- *Survival and Loss*
- Word chart from Day 1
- A marker

INTRODUCE AND PRACTICE USING *SQUANDER*

1 Introduce and Define *Squander*

Show pages 4–5 of *Survival and Loss*, and review that settlers passed through Native American hunting grounds as they moved west to find gold. Read the following sentences from the second paragraph of "The Reservations" aloud: "Unlike Native Americans, the settlers were not respectful of the land. They cut down many trees and hunted too many animals."

Tell the students that the first word they will learn today is *squander* and that *squander* means "carelessly waste something such as money, time, or opportunities."

Explain that, when the settlers cut down many trees and hunted too many animals, they were squandering, or carelessly wasting,

Teacher Note
You might review that an *opportunity* is "a chance to do something."

Grade Five | 433

Teacher Note ▶
You might explain that a *resource* is "something that is valuable or useful to people."

resources that were important to Native Americans. Explain that, when the Native Americans saw that the settlers were squandering trees and animals that were a source of food, they fought with the settlers.

Have the students say the word *squander*, and write it on the chart.

▶2 Play "Is Tulip Squandering?"

Tell the students that you will describe something that Tulip is doing and partners will discuss whether or not she is squandering something and why they think so.

Begin with:

- *Tulip wants to be an artist, so she takes an art class. When her instructor tells her what she might do to be a better painter, Tulip ignores the suggestions.*

Ask:

Q *Do you think Tulip is squandering the opportunity to become a better painter? Why? Turn to your partner.*

PROMPT: "I [do/do not] think Tulip is squandering the opportunity to become a better painter because…."

In the same way, discuss:

- *Tulip is eating dinner. She takes a few bites and then feeds the rest of her meal to her dog.*

Q *Do you think Tulip is squandering her food? Why? Turn to your partner.*

PROMPT: "I [do/do not] think Tulip is squandering her food because…."

- *Each week Tulip's parents give her 5 dollars as an allowance. Tulip usually spends the money on candy.*

Q *Do you think Tulip is squandering her allowance? Why? Turn to your partner.*

Week 19 ▶ Day 3

PROMPT: "I [do/do not] think Tulip is squandering her allowance because…."

Review the pronunciation and meaning of the word.

INTRODUCE AND PRACTICE USING *CLASH*

▶3 Introduce and Define *Clash* and Review Synonyms

Show pages 4–5 again. Review that the U.S. government passed a law that required Native Americans to live on areas of land known as reservations. Read the following sentence from the last paragraph on page 5 aloud, "In some cases, the U.S. government had promised the same land to more than one tribe, and fights broke out between the tribes as they competed for water, game, and land."

Explain that the next word the students will learn is *clash*. Explain that *clash* means "fight or argue" and that *clash, fight,* and *argue* are synonyms. Explain that, because many tribes lived on the same land, they clashed, or fought with one another, over the land and its water and animals.

◀ **Teacher Note**

If you started a synonym chart, add the words *clash*, *fight,* and *argue* to it.

Have the students say the word *clash*, and write it on the chart.

▶4 Discuss Times We Have Clashed with Others

Explain that individuals sometimes clash, or fight or argue, and give examples of times you have clashed with someone. (You might say, "My sister and I used to clash, or argue, over who would sit in the front seat of the car. We would also clash about whose turn it was to take out the garbage.")

Ask:

Q *When have you clashed with someone? Turn to your partner.*

PROMPT: "[My brother] and I clashed when…."

Week 19 ▶ Day 3

In the same way, discuss:

Q *What might you do to avoid clashing with someone who has made you angry? Turn to your partner.*

PROMPT: "To avoid clashing with someone who has made me angry, I might…."

Review the pronunciation and meaning of the word.

INTRODUCE AND PRACTICE USING *DEFENSELESS*

5 Introduce and Define *Defenseless* and Review the Suffix *-less*

Show pages 12–13. Remind the students that Captain Richard Henry Pratt wanted to "Americanize" Native American children by educating them in boarding schools. In 1879, Pratt built a boarding school in Pennsylvania. Then read page 13 aloud, emphasizing the word *defenseless* in the second paragraph.

Tell the students that *defenseless* is the last word they will learn today, and explain that *defenseless* means "helpless or unprotected."

Explain that Captain Pratt persuaded Spotted Tail to send his children to the boarding school by telling him that his people were defenseless, or helpless or unprotected, because they could not read and write in English. Pratt argued that, if Native Americans learned to speak, read, and write English, they would be able to defend themselves against unfair treatment by European Americans. They would no longer be defenseless.

Have the students say *defenseless*, and then write the word on the chart.

Point to the suffix *-less* in *defenseless* on the chart, and review that *-less* is a suffix that means "without." Explain that when you add the suffix *-less* to the word *defense*, you make the word *defenseless*, which means "without defense, helpless, or unprotected."

Teacher Note

You might remind the students that earlier they learned these words that use the suffix *-less*: *selfless* (unselfish, or without thought for yourself), *thoughtless* (without thought for the feelings or needs of others), and *motionless* (without motion, still, or not moving). If you started a chart of *-less* words, add *defenseless* to it.

6 Play "Defenseless or Not Defenseless?"

Remind the students that a person or animal that is defenseless is helpless or unprotected. Explain that you will describe a situation and partners will decide whether or not the person or animal in the situation is defenseless and why they think so.

Begin with:

- *A hunter with a gun spots a deer a few yards away. The deer raises its ears and sniffs the air.*

Ask:

Q *Is the deer defenseless, or helpless, against the hunter? Why? Turn to your partner.*

PROMPT: "The deer [is/is not] defenseless against the hunter because…."

In the same way, discuss:

- *A hungry fox creeps up on a baby chick asleep in its nest. The chick's mother is nowhere in sight.*

Q *Is the baby chick defenseless against the fox? Why? Turn to your partner.*

PROMPT: "The baby chick [is/is not] defenseless against the fox because…."

- *A bully is teasing a little boy on the playground. A teacher and other students are standing nearby.*

Q *Is the little boy defenseless against the bully? Why? Turn to your partner.*

PROMPT: "The little boy [is/is not] defenseless against the bully because…."

Review the pronunciation and meaning of the word.

Week 19 ▶ Day 3

MORE STRATEGY PRACTICE

Play "Synonym Match"

Write these words in two columns on a sheet of chart paper:

1	2
clash	nervous
devour	best
motionless	fight
supreme	still
uneasy	eat

Explain that partners will play "Synonym Match." Point to the words in column 1, and explain that these are vocabulary words the students have learned. Point to the words in column 2, and explain that these are synonyms of the words in column 1, or words that mean the same thing or almost the same thing. Explain that partners will match each vocabulary word to its synonym.

Point to the word *clash*, pronounce it, and have the students pronounce it.

Then point to the words in column 2, and ask:

Q *Which word in column 2 is the synonym of* clash? *Turn to your partner.*

PROMPT: "[*Fight*] is the synonym of *clash*."

Have volunteers share their thinking. Then have a volunteer draw a line from the word *clash* to the word *fight*.

Discuss the remaining words the same way. When you get to the final two words, have the students discuss them together by asking:

Q *Which word in column 2 is the synonym of* supreme *and which word is the synonym of* uneasy? *Turn to your partner.*

Making Meaning® Vocabulary

Day 4

Week 19 ▶ Day 4

Review *Squander, Clash,* and *Defenseless*

Words Reviewed

squander
Squander means "carelessly waste something such as money, time, or opportunities."

clash
Clash means "fight or argue."

defenseless
Defenseless means "without defense, helpless, or unprotected."

Materials
- Word chart from Day 3
- A marker

REVIEW THE WORDS

1 Briefly Review the Words

Review the pronunciation and meaning of each word.

Ask:

Q *Would a frugal person be likely to squander money? Why? Turn to your partner.*

PROMPT: "A frugal person [would/would not] be likely to squander money because…."

In the same way, discuss:

Q *Would an irate customer be likely to clash with a rude store clerk? Why? Turn to your partner.*

◀ **Teacher Note**
You might review that *frugal* means "careful in spending money or not wasteful."

◀ **Teacher Note**
You might review that *irate* means "furious, or extremely angry."

Grade Five | 439

Week 19 ▶ Day 4

PROMPT: "An irate customer [would/would not] be likely to clash with a rude store clerk because…."

Q *Would a solitary seal be defenseless against a group of sharks? Why? Turn to your partner.*

Teacher Note ▶
You might review that *solitary* means "living or being alone."

PROMPT: "A solitary seal [would/would not] be defenseless against a group of sharks because…."

PRACTICE USING THE WORDS

2 Do the Activity "Tell Me a Story"

Explain that partners will do the activity "Tell Me a Story." Review that you will tell the beginning of a story that includes one of the vocabulary words. The students will use what they know about the word and their imaginations to make up an ending for the story.

Begin by reading the following story aloud twice, slowly and clearly:

- *Alicia's mother told her it was time for bed. "Can I stay up another hour?" Alicia asked. "I need to do my homework." "No, Alicia, you cannot stay up," answered her mother. "You shouldn't have squandered so much time this evening by…."*

Use "Think, Pair, Share" to discuss:

Q *How might you finish the story? What might Alicia have been doing to squander time? [pause] Turn to your partner.*

PROMPT: "You should not have squandered so much time by…."

In the same way, discuss:

- *Cory and Tory are twins. Most of the time they get along, but there are some days when they clash over things like….*

Q *How might you finish the story? What things might Cory and Tory clash over? [pause] Turn to your partner.*

PROMPT: "There are some days when they clash over things like…."

440 | Making Meaning® Vocabulary

- *While his mother dozed in the sun, a bear cub searched for berries. When his belly was full, he looked around and realized he had wandered far from his mother. He was alone in the forest, defenseless against….*

Q *How might you finish the story? What might the bear cub be defenseless against?* [pause] *Turn to your partner.*

PROMPT: "He was alone in the forest, defenseless against…."

Week 19 ▶ Day 5

Day 5

Ongoing Review

Materials

- Pocket chart
- Word cards 32, 71, 77, 78, 84
- Sentences or transparency (BLM17) for "What's the Missing Word?" (see Step 2 on page 443)
- (Optional) Overhead projector and marker

Words Reviewed

deprive
Deprive means "prevent from having something or take something away."

episode
An *episode* is "an event or series of events in a person's life."

fanciful
Fanciful means "imaginary, or not real."

prejudice
Prejudice is "an unfair opinion of someone based on the person's race, religion, or other characteristic."

solitary
Solitary means "living or being alone."

REVIEW THE WORDS

▶ **1 Display the Word Cards and Briefly Review the Words**

Review the pronunciation and meaning of the words.

Week 19 ▶ Day 5

PRACTICE USING THE WORDS

2 Play "What's the Missing Word?"

Display the transparency or write the following sentences (without the answers) on the board or a sheet of chart paper, leaving blanks as shown:

> If people or animals are _____ of food and water, they may become weak or ill. (deprived)
>
> Mr. Winters has a _____ against teenagers. He thinks all teenagers are immature and should not be allowed to drive. (prejudice)
>
> Ralph regrets arguing with his sister. He wants to forget that the _____ ever happened. (episode)
>
> Trudy helps her mother decorate for the party by placing a _____ rose in a vase on each table. (solitary)
>
> No one believes what my brother says because he is always making up _____ stories. (fanciful)

Explain that partners will play the game "What's the Missing Word?" Direct the students' attention to the sentences, and point out that a word is missing from each sentence. Explain that you will read each sentence aloud and partners will discuss which vocabulary word could replace the missing word and why they think so.

Begin by pointing to this sentence and reading it aloud twice:

- *If people or animals are _____ of food and water, they may become weak or ill.*

Ask:

Q *What's the missing word? Why do you think so? Turn to your partner.*

◀ **Teacher Note**

You might explain that the students may need to change the form of a word to complete the sentence by adding an ending such as *-s*, *-ing*, or *-ed*.

Grade Five | 443

Week 19 ▶ Day 5

PROMPT: "I think [*deprived*] is the missing word because…."

Have volunteers share their thinking with the class. Then reread the sentence, replacing the blank with the vocabulary word.

Teacher Note ▶

You might invite partners to work together to create their own "What's the Missing Word?" sentences and have them share their sentences with the class.

Discuss the remaining sentences the same way.

Week 20 Overview

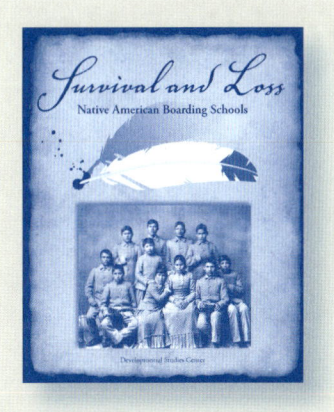

Survival and Loss: Native American Boarding Schools
(Developmental Studies Center, 2008)

Words Taught

befuddled

heartless

quality

deliberately

drastic

injustice

Word-learning Strategies

- Recognizing synonyms (review)
- Using the suffix -less to determine word meanings (review)
- Recognizing antonyms (review)

Words Reviewed: befuddled, hair-raising, indicate, squander, trample

DO AHEAD

- Prior to Day 5, collect these word cards for Ongoing Review: 45, 105, 107, 112, and 115.

Week 20 ▶ Day 1

Day 1

Introduce *Befuddled*, *Heartless*, and *Quality*

Materials
- *Survival and Loss*
- Chart paper
- A marker

Words Taught

befuddled
Befuddled means "completely confused."

heartless
Heartless means "without heart (kindness or compassion), unkind, or cruel."

quality (p. 16)
A *quality* is "a special characteristic, or feature, of a person's personality or character." Friendliness and honesty are examples of qualities a person might have.

INTRODUCE AND PRACTICE USING *BEFUDDLED*

▶ 1 Introduce and Define *Befuddled* and Review Synonyms

Briefly review *Survival and Loss*.

Show pages 14–15. Review that Captain Pratt persuaded the Sioux chief Spotted Tail to send his tribe's children to Carlisle Indian Industrial School. Read "The Journey" on page 14 aloud.

Teacher Note
If you started a synonym chart, add the words *befuddled* and *confused* to it. ▶

Tell the students that the first word they will learn today is *befuddled*. Explain that *befuddled* means "completely confused" and that *befuddled* and *confused* are synonyms.

446 | Making Meaning® Vocabulary

Week 20 ▶ Day 1

Explain that the children were befuddled, or completely confused, about where they were going and why they had to leave their families and homes. They were also befuddled, or confused, by the crowds of people that stared at them curiously whenever they stopped.

Have the students say the word *befuddled*, and then write it on a sheet of chart paper.

2 Discuss Being Befuddled

Explain that new or strange situations can befuddle people. Give examples of times you or someone you know was befuddled. (You might say, "My husband got a new computer recently, and the directions for setting it up befuddled, or completely confused, him. He finally had to call the computer company for help. Recently, I was driving in an unfamiliar city, and I took a wrong turn. I was befuddled. I didn't know where I was, and I didn't have a map. I finally stopped at a gas station and got directions. When I was your age, some math problems befuddled me. I would become confused and had trouble solving them.")

Use "Think, Pair, Share" to discuss:

Q *When have you been befuddled? Why were you befuddled?* [pause] *Turn to your partner.*

PROMPT: "I was befuddled by [a question on our social studies quiz the other day]. I was befuddled because…."

Review the pronunciation and meaning of the word.

◀ **Teacher Note**

Support struggling students by asking questions such as, "When have you been befuddled, or confused, by something someone said to you or asked you to do?" "When have you been befuddled by something at school?" and "When have you been befuddled by instructions or directions you were following?"

INTRODUCE AND PRACTICE USING *HEARTLESS*

3 Introduce and Define *Heartless* and Review Synonyms and the Suffix *-less*

Show pages 14–15 again. Review that, when the children arrived at the boarding school, the process of westernizing them began immediately. Read "'Before' and 'After'" on page 14 aloud.

Grade Five | 447

Week 20 ▶ Day 1

Teacher Note ▶

If you started a synonym chart, add *heartless*, *unkind*, and *cruel* to it.

If you started a chart of *-less* words, add *heartless* to it.

Tell the students that the next word they will learn is *heartless*. Explain that *heartless* means "unkind or cruel" and that *heartless*, *unkind*, and *cruel* are synonyms.

Explain that the treatment the Indian children received at Carlisle was heartless, or unkind and cruel. Review that the children were stripped of their traditional clothing and beaded necklaces and that the clothing was burned. They were scrubbed in hot baths and given uncomfortable clothing and shoes to wear. The boys' hair was cut, which caused the boys to wail, or cry. Explain that all of these are examples of the heartless, or cruel, way the children were treated.

Have the students say *heartless*, and then write the word on the chart.

Point to the suffix *-less* in *heartless* on the chart, and review that *-less* is a suffix that means "without." Point to the word *heart* and explain that people consider the heart to be the part of the body that feels emotions such as kindness or compassion. Explain that when you add the suffix *-less* to the word *heart*, you make the word *heartless*, which means "without heart, or without kindness or compassion." Review that heartless behavior is unkind or cruel.

▶ 4 Review Antonyms and Discuss *Heartless* and *Kind*

Tell the students that the antonym, or opposite, of the word *heartless* is the word *kind*.

Explain that you will describe a situation involving our friend Tulip. Partners will first discuss what Tulip might do or say in the situation if she were heartless. Then they will discuss what she might do or say if she were kind.

Begin with:

- *Tulip's friend is upset because she lost a necklace she got for her birthday.*

448 | Making Meaning® Vocabulary

Ask:

Q *If Tulip were heartless, what might she do or say? Turn to your partner.*

PROMPT: "If Tulip were heartless, she might…."

Then ask:

Q *If Tulip were kind, what might she do or say? Turn to your partner.*

PROMPT: "If Tulip were kind, she might…."

In the same way, discuss:

- *A stray dog follows Tulip home.*

Review the pronunciation and meaning of the word.

INTRODUCE AND PRACTICE USING *QUALITY*

5▶ Introduce and Define *Quality*

Show pages 16–17. Review that Native American children were forbidden to speak their native languages or use their Native American names at school. Explain that names are very important to Native Americans and that, without their names, the children no longer felt like themselves. Then read "What's in a Name?" on page 16 aloud, emphasizing the word *qualities*.

Tell the students that the last word they will learn today is *quality* and that a *quality* is "a special characteristic, or feature, of a person's personality or character."

Explain that friendliness is an example of a quality, or feature, that we might admire in a person's personality or character. Honesty is another quality that we might admire in people.

Week 20 ▶ Day 1

Explain that Native American names sometimes honor a quality, or feature of a person's personality. For example, a Cherokee who possessed the quality of faithfulness (loyalty) might be named Hantaywee, which means "faithful."

Have the students say the word *quality*, and write it on the chart.

▶6 Discuss Qualities

Explain that we sometimes refer to qualities we admire or like in people, such as friendliness and honesty, as "good qualities" or "positive qualities." Explain that other good or positive qualities are loyalty, sense of humor, kindness, compassion, gentleness, generosity, courage, and wisdom.

Teacher Note ▶
You might list positive qualities on the board or a sheet of chart paper.

Tell the students that we often choose as friends people who have qualities we like or admire, and give examples of qualities you look for in a friend. (You might say, "One quality I look for in my friends is kindness. I want my friends to be people who treat other people with kindness rather than cruelty. I also think a good sense of humor is an important quality in a friend, because I really enjoy laughing and being around funny people.")

Use "Think, Pair, Share" to discuss:

Q *What is a quality you look for in a friend? Why?* [pause] *Turn to your partner.*

PROMPT: "A quality I look for in a friend is [courage] because...."

Have volunteers share their thinking.

Follow up by asking:

Q *What is a positive quality you think you possess (have)? Why do you think that? Turn to your partner.*

PROMPT: "A positive quality I think I possess is [a sense of humor], because...."

Review the pronunciation and meaning of the word.

EXTENSION

Give Your Best Friend a New Name

Review that Native Americans are sometimes given names that honor or recognize positive qualities. They are also given names that honor things they can do or have done. For example, the Cherokee name Ayita means "first to dance."

Tell the students that you want them to think of a name they might give to their best friend that honors a positive quality or something the friend can do or has done. Give a couple of examples of names you might give to a friend. (You might say, "I would give my friend Eric the name "Eric the Friendly" because he is one of the friendliest people I know. My sister Kelly is my best friend. I would give Kelly the name Caring Kelly because she is a very caring person. She cares about her family and about the other people in her life.")

Use "Think, Pair, Share" to discuss:

Q *What is a name you would give to your best friend that would honor one of his or her positive qualities? Why?* [pause] *Turn to your partner.*

PROMPT: "I would give my friend the name [Gary the Brave] because…."

Have a few students share their thinking with the class.

Tell the students that all names have meanings and that the study of names is called "onomastics." If the students are interested in learning about the meaning of their names, you might have them search the Internet, using the keyword search "name meanings."

Week 20 ▶ Day 2

Day 2

Review *Befuddled*, *Heartless*, and *Quality*

Materials
- Word chart from Day 1

Words Reviewed

befuddled
Befuddled means "completely confused."

heartless
Heartless means "without heart (kindness or compassion), unkind, or cruel."

quality
A *quality* is "a special characteristic, or feature, of a person's personality or character." Friendliness and honesty are examples of qualities a person might have.

REVIEW THE WORDS

▶1 Briefly Review the Words

Review the pronunciation and meaning of each word.

Ask:

Q *Which of the words we learned yesterday do you think was especially fun or interesting to talk about? Why? Turn to your partner.*

PROMPT: "I think the word [*befuddled*] was especially [fun/interesting] to talk about because…."

452 | Making Meaning® Vocabulary

PRACTICE USING THE WORDS

2 Discuss "Would You?" Questions

Explain that you will ask questions that include one of yesterday's words and a word they learned earlier in the year.

Point to the word *befuddled* and ask:

Q *If you went home and found your bedroom in a shambles, would you be befuddled? Why? Turn to your partner.*

PROMPT: "If I found my bedroom in a shambles, I [would/would not] be befuddled because…."

◀ **Teacher Note**

You might review that when a place is a shambles, it is very messy or in complete disorder or ruin.

In the same way, discuss:

[heartless]

Q *Would it be heartless to desert a friend on a hike? Why? Turn to your partner.*

PROMPT: "It [would/would not] be heartless to desert a friend on a hike because…."

◀ **Teacher Note**

You might review that *desert* means "abandon, or leave someone or something that should not be left behind."

[quality]

Q *If a person possessed qualities that you did not like, would you be his or her comrade? Why? Turn to your partner.*

PROMPT: "If a person possessed qualities that I did not like, I [would/would not] be his or her comrade because…."

◀ **Teacher Note**

You might review that a *comrade* is "a good friend or companion."

Week 20 ▶ Day 3

Day 3

Introduce *Deliberately, Drastic,* and *Injustice*

Materials
- *Survival and Loss*
- Word chart from Day 1
- A marker

Words Taught

deliberately (p. 17)
Deliberately means "intentionally or on purpose."

drastic (p. 26)
Drastic means "harsh, extreme, or very severe."

injustice (p. 28)
An *injustice* is "a situation in which people are treated very unfairly."

INTRODUCE AND PRACTICE USING *DELIBERATELY*

1 Introduce and Define *Deliberately*

Show pages 16–17 of *Survival and Loss*.

Review that many restrictions were placed on Native American children in boarding schools, but that some students found ways to fight back. Read the following sentences from the first paragraph of "Keeping Culture Alive" on page 17 aloud, emphasizing the word *deliberately*: "Many refused to respond to their teachers. If a teacher asked a question, a student might stare into space, blank faced and silent. Some students would deliberately do their work very slowly."

Teacher Note
You might explain that *deliberately* and *intentionally* are synonyms and add them to the synonym chart. ▶

Tell the students that the first word they will learn today is *deliberately* and that *deliberately* means "intentionally or on purpose." Explain that some of the children rebelled against their teachers by deliberately, or intentionally, doing their work slowly.

454 | Making Meaning® Vocabulary

Week 20 ▶ Day 3

Have the students say the word *deliberately*, and write it on the chart.

2 Discuss Things We Have Done Deliberately

Tell the students that, when something is done deliberately, it is done with a plan and a result in mind, and give a few examples of things you do deliberately in the classroom or elsewhere. (You might say, "I deliberately, or intentionally, arranged the desks in our classroom this way so that we would have a place to meet as a group on the rug. I deliberately schedule our independent reading time after math so that students who finish their math work early can begin reading right away. At home last night, I deliberately put my briefcase next to the front door so that I would not forget it this morning.")

Use "Think, Pair, Share" to discuss:

Q *When have you deliberately done something? Why did you do it deliberately?* [pause] *Turn to your partner.*

PROMPT: "I deliberately [put my homework in my backpack] because…."

Review the pronunciation and meaning of the word.

INTRODUCE AND PRACTICE USING *DRASTIC*

3 Introduce and Define *Drastic*

Show pages 24–25. Review that by the 1930s most Native American boarding schools were closed, because the U.S. government determined that the children should not be taken away from their families to be educated. Read the first paragraph of page 24 aloud, emphasizing the word *drastic*.

Tell the students that the next word they will learn today is *drastic*. Explain that *drastic* means "harsh, extreme, or very severe."

Teacher Note

You might explain that *drastic*, *harsh*, *extreme*, and *severe* are synonyms and add the words to the synonym chart.

Grade Five | 455

Week 20 ▶ Day 3

Explain that the boarding schools used drastic, or harsh or very severe, measures to westernize Native American children and stop them from living the life they had known before school. Review that the children were forbidden to wear their native clothing or speak their native languages. They were not allowed to eat traditional foods. Even their names were changed. The schools' drastic efforts to give the children a western-style education damaged many of them forever by destroying their connection to their traditional way of life.

Have the students say the word *drastic*, and write it on the chart.

4 Discuss Drastic Actions

Remind the students that *drastic* means "harsh, extreme, or very severe," and explain that something that is drastic is beyond what is normally or usually done. Give a few examples of drastic things you or someone you know has done. (You might say, "My cousin takes drastic, or extreme, steps to make sure he doesn't get sick. He always wears gloves, he never touches doorknobs because of germs, and he will not go near a hospital. A friend of mine wanted to lose weight so she took drastic action—she decided not to eat anything at all on Mondays, Wednesdays, or Fridays. She quickly found out that it was unhealthy and even dangerous to go without food, so she ended her drastic weight loss plan.")

Have the students imagine the following scenario:

- *A museum wants to prevent people from touching the art, so they place a guard next to each painting.*

Ask:

Q *Do you think the museum's action is drastic? Why? Turn to your partner.*

PROMPT: "I think the museum's action [is/is not] drastic because…."

Have volunteers share their thinking.

456 | Making Meaning® Vocabulary

Follow up by asking:

Q *What might the museum do that would be less drastic? More drastic?*

PROMPT: "A [less] drastic action might be…."

In the same way, discuss:

- *There have been a few skateboarding accidents at the park, so the city council bans people from riding skateboards, in-line skates, bicycles, and scooters in the park.*

Review the pronunciation and meaning of the word.

◀ **Teacher Note**

You might review that a *ban* is "a rule or law that says people must not do something." Something that is banned is not allowed.

INTRODUCE AND PRACTICE USING *INJUSTICE*

5 **Introduce and Define *Injustice***

Show pages 26–27. Review that a few Native Americans were able to use what they learned in the boarding schools to help them work for the rights of all Native Americans.

Read the following sentences from "Hope for the Future" on page 26 aloud, emphasizing the word *injustice*: "They knew enough about the European American world to be able to reason with the government and to inform all Americans about the damage that had been done to Native American culture. It was the first step in bringing to light centuries of injustice and the first step toward healing the wounds."

Tell the students that *injustice* is the last word they will learn today and that an *injustice* is "a situation in which people are treated very unfairly." Explain that Native Americans who worked for the rights of their people informed other Americans of the injustices, or unfair treatment, that Native Americans faced.

Have the students say the word *injustice*, and write it on the chart.

◀ **Teacher Note**

You might explain that the word *injustice* is the antonym of the word *justice*, which means "fair treatment or behavior."

6 Discuss Native American Injustices

Explain that you will read an example from *Survival and Loss* of an injustice, or very unfair situation, faced by Native Americans, and partners will discuss why they think the situation is an injustice.

Begin with:

- *"When the United States was formed in 1776, Native Americans were not included as citizens."*

Ask:

Q *Why was not including the Native Americans as citizens an injustice? Turn to your partner.*

PROMPT: *"Not including the Native Americans as citizens was an injustice because…."*

Have volunteers share their thinking.

Follow up by asking:

Q *What could have been done to treat the Native Americans more fairly?*

In the same way, discuss:

- *"Present-day Oklahoma was set aside as Native American territory. However, this land was different from the land the eastern tribes were used to. The crops they had grown in the East didn't grow on the new land, there were few wild animals to hunt, and the plants and geography were unfamiliar."*

- *"The (Native American) children were taken away from their families and the lives they knew and sent to boarding schools."*

Review the pronunciation and meaning of the word.

Day 4

Review *Deliberately, Drastic,* and *Injustice*

Words Reviewed

deliberately
Deliberately means "intentionally or on purpose."

drastic
Drastic means "harsh, extreme, or very severe."

injustice
An *injustice* is "a situation in which people are treated very unfairly."

Materials
- Word chart from Day 3
- A marker

REVIEW THE WORDS

1 Briefly Review the Words

Review the pronunciation and meaning of each word.

Discuss as a class:

Q *Which of the words we learned yesterday might you use in a conversation with your family or friends? How might you use the word?*

PROMPT: "I might use the word [*drastic*] when I talk with [my mom]. I might say…."

Week 20 ▶ Day 4

PRACTICE USING THE WORDS

2 **Do the Activity "Imagine That!"**

Have the students imagine the following scene:

- *You are leaving your house to go to school, and you deliberately leave the front door open.*

Use "Think, Pair, Share" to discuss:

Q *Why might you deliberately leave the front door open?* [pause] *Turn to your partner.*

PROMPT: "I might deliberately leave the front door open because [my little sister is following right behind me]."

In the same way, discuss:

- *Your dad tells you it's time to go to bed. You throw yourself on the floor, grab his leg, and scream, "I don't want to go to bed! I'll die if I have to go to bed!"*

Q *Is your response drastic? Why?* [pause] *Turn to your partner.*

PROMPT: "My response [is/is not] drastic because…."

- *You go to a movie with your friends. The ticket seller won't sell you a ticket because you must be 17 years old to see the movie without your parents.*

Q *Is this an injustice? Why?* [pause] *Turn to your partner.*

PROMPT: "This [is/is not] an injustice because…."

Teacher Note

For a crossword puzzle you can use to review words taught during weeks 19 and 20, visit Developmental Studies Center's website at www.devstu.org.

Day 5

Ongoing Review

Words Reviewed

befuddled
Befuddled means "completely confused."

indicate
Indicate means "point out or show." *Indicate* also means "be a sign of."

hair-raising
Hair-raising means "exciting, thrilling, or terrifying."

squander
Squander means "carelessly waste something such as money, time, or opportunities."

trample
Trample means "damage or crush by walking or stepping on something heavily."

Materials
- Pocket chart
- Word cards 45, 105, 107, 112, 115

REVIEW THE WORDS

1 Display the Word Cards and Briefly Review the Words

Review the pronunciation and meaning of the words.

PRACTICE USING THE WORDS

2 Discuss What You Might Say or Do

Explain that you will describe a situation and partners will discuss what they might say or do in that situation.

Begin with:

- Your friend tells you how to get to his house. You are befuddled by his directions.

Ask:

Q *What might you say or do if you are befuddled by your friend's directions? Turn to your partner.*

PROMPT: "If I am befuddled by my friend's directions, I might…."

In the same way, discuss:

- You are watching a hair-raising movie.

Q *What might you say or do if you are watching a hair-raising movie? Turn to your partner.*

PROMPT: "If I am watching a hair-raising movie, I might…."

- You've just had your tonsils removed and you cannot speak. You want to indicate to your mother that you would like something to drink.

Q *What will you do to indicate that you would like something to drink? Turn to your partner.*

PROMPT: "To indicate that I would like something to drink, I might…."

Week 20 ▶ Day 5

- You are working with a partner on a project. You have 1 hour to get it done, and your partner is squandering her time writing notes to a friend.

Q What might you say or do if your partner is squandering her time? Turn to your partner.

PROMPT: "If my partner is squandering time, I might…."

- You are walking home from school. You see someone deliberately trample your neighbor's flowers.

Q What might you say or do when you see the person trample the flowers? Turn to your partner.

PROMPT: "When I see the person trample the flowers, I might…."

CLASS VOCABULARY PROGRESS ASSESSMENT

As you observe the students, ask yourself:

- Do the students' responses indicate that they understand the words' meanings?

- Are they using the words they are learning in their writing and in conversations outside of vocabulary time?

For more information about reviewing and practicing the words, see "Retaining the Words" on pages xviii–xix.

Grade Five | 463

Week 20 ▶ Day 5

INDIVIDUAL VOCABULARY PROGRESS ASSESSMENT

Before continuing with week 21, take this opportunity to assess individual students' understanding of the words taught in weeks 17–20 by administering "Word Check 5" (BLM27). Please refer to pages 628–629 for instructions on administering the assessment.

STUDENT SELF-ASSESSMENT

In addition to or in place of the Individual Vocabulary Progress Assessment, have the students evaluate their understanding of the words taught in weeks 17–20 through this self-assessment (BLM30). For instructions on administering the assessment, see pages 634–635.

Week 21

Overview

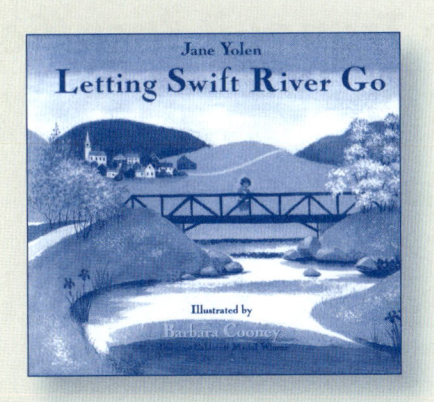

Letting Swift River Go
by Jane Yolen,
illustrated by Barbara Cooney
(Little, Brown, 1992)

Words Taught

tranquil

insufficient

sufficient

disperse

ascend

inundate

Word-learning Strategies

- Recognizing synonyms (review)
- Recognizing antonyms (review)
- Recognizing words with multiple meanings (review)

Words Reviewed: clash, devastate, get on board, preserve, sympathize

DO AHEAD

- Prior to Day 3, review More Strategy Practice on pages 477–478.
- Prior to Day 5, collect these word cards for Ongoing Review: 14, 17, 65, 99, and 113.

Grade Five | 465

Week 21 ▶ Day 1

Day 1

Introduce *Tranquil, Insufficient,* and *Sufficient*

Materials
- *Letting Swift River Go*
- Chart paper
- A marker

Words Taught

tranquil
Tranquil means "calm or peaceful."

insufficient
Insufficient means "not enough or not adequate."

sufficient
Sufficient means "enough or adequate."

INTRODUCE AND PRACTICE USING *TRANQUIL*

▶ **1 Introduce and Define *Tranquil* and Review Synonyms**

Briefly review *Letting Swift River Go*.

Show pages 4–5 and review that Sally Jane lives in the Swift River Valley. Read page 4 aloud.

Tell the students that the first word they will learn today is *tranquil* and that *tranquil* means "calm or peaceful." Explain that *tranquil*, *calm*, and *peaceful* are synonyms.

> **Teacher Note** ▶
> If you started a synonym chart, add *tranquil*, *calm*, and *peaceful* to it.

Point to the illustration on page 5, and explain that life in the Swift River Valley is tranquil, or calm and peaceful. Point out that there are no crowds of people or cars whizzing by. Instead, the valley is quiet, and life moves at a slow pace. Explain that Sally Jane has nothing to fear in her tranquil valley. It is so calm and peaceful that she can

466 | Making Meaning® Vocabulary

Week 21 ▶ Day 1

walk to school alone without fear and without encountering anyone until she meets her friends.

Have the students say the word *tranquil*, and then write it on a sheet of chart paper.

◀ **Teacher Note**

For further practice with the word *tranquil*, show pages 6–7, read page 6 aloud, and discuss ways life in the summer is tranquil.

2 Discuss a Tranquil Place

Show the illustration on page 5 again, and review that a tranquil place is calm or peaceful. Explain that a tranquil place is a good place to rest or relax.

Have the students close their eyes and picture in their minds a tranquil place where they might rest or relax. Explain that it might be a familiar place, such as their room at home, a place they have visited, or an imaginary place.

Then use "Think, Pair, Share" to discuss:

Q *What is your tranquil place? Why is it tranquil?* [pause] *Open your eyes and turn to your partner.*

PROMPT: "[My bedroom] is my tranquil place. [My bedroom] is tranquil because…."

Review the pronunciation and meaning of the word.

◀ **Teacher Note**

Have a few students share their thinking with the class. Hearing from only a few students keeps the lesson moving.

INTRODUCE AND PRACTICE USING *INSUFFICIENT*

3 Introduce and Define *Insufficient*

Show pages 14–15 and review that men from Boston come to the valley to talk to the residents about Boston's need for water. Read page 14 aloud.

Tell the students that the next word they will learn today is *insufficient* and that *insufficient* means "not enough or not adequate." Explain that Boston's water supply is insufficient; there is not enough water to support the growing city.

Grade Five | 467

Week 21 ▶ Day 1

Discuss as a class:

Q *Why might people worry about having an insufficient supply of water?*

PROMPT: "People might worry about having an insufficient supply of water because…."

Teacher Note ▶

You might explain that *insufficient* begins with the prefix *in-*, which means "not." For more about the prefix *in-*, see the Extension on page 470.

Have the students say the word *insufficient*, and write it on the chart.

INTRODUCE AND PRACTICE USING *SUFFICIENT*

▶ **4 Introduce and Define *Sufficient* and Review Antonyms**

Tell the students that the last word they will learn today is *sufficient*. Have the students say the word *sufficient*, and then write it on the chart.

Explain that *sufficient* and *insufficient* are antonyms, or words with opposite meanings.

Then discuss as a class:

Q *If* sufficient *and* insufficient *are antonyms and* insufficient *means "not enough or not adequate," what do you think* sufficient *means?*

If necessary, explain that *sufficient* means "enough or adequate."

Explain that the Swift River Valley will be flooded so that Boston will have a sufficient, or adequate, supply of water. When the valley is flooded, there will be enough water to quench Boston's "mighty long thirst."

Teacher Note ▶

If you started an antonym chart, add *sufficient* and *insufficient* to it.

468 | Making Meaning® Vocabulary

Week 21 ▶ Day 1

5 ▶ Play "Insufficient or Sufficient?"

Tell the students that you will describe something they are provided with (given) at school. Partners will discuss whether what is provided is sufficient or insufficient and why they think so.

Begin with:

- *You are given [40 minutes] for lunch.*

Ask:

Q *Is [40 minutes] a sufficient or an insufficient amount of time for lunch? Why? Turn to your partner.*

PROMPT: "[Forty minutes] is [a sufficient/an insufficient] amount of time for lunch because…."

In the same way, discuss:

- *You are allowed to check out [two books] from the library every week.*

Q *Is [two books] a sufficient or an insufficient number of books? Why? Turn to your partner.*

- *There are [two kickballs] available to play with at recess.*

Q *Is [two kickballs] a sufficient or an insufficient number of balls? Why? Turn to your partner.*

Review the pronunciation and meaning of the words *insufficient* and *sufficient*.

Grade Five | 469

Week 21 ▶ Day 1

EXTENSION

Discuss Other Words with the Prefix *in-*

Point to the prefix *in-* in *insufficient* on the chart, and explain that *in-* is a prefix that means "not or the opposite." Review that, when you add *in-* to the word *sufficient*, you make the word *insufficient*, which is the opposite of *sufficient* and means "not sufficient, or not enough or not adequate."

Have the students discuss the meanings of these words that use the prefix *in-*: *inaccurate, inactive, inconsiderate, inconspicuous,* and *inhospitable.*

Invite the students to listen and watch for other words that use the prefix *in-*, and discuss the words they find.

Teacher Note

You might review that *conspicuous* means "obvious or noticeable" and *hospitable* means "friendly, welcoming, and generous to visitors." ▶

Teacher Note ▶

The prefix *in-* is formally taught in grade 4 of *Making Meaning Vocabulary.* For a list of words that use the prefix *in-* and other word lists, visit Developmental Studies Center's website at www.devstu.org.

Day 2

Review *Tranquil, Insufficient,* and *Sufficient*

Words Reviewed

tranquil
Tranquil means "calm or peaceful."

insufficient
Insufficient means "not enough or not adequate."

sufficient
Sufficient means "enough or adequate."

Materials
- Word chart from Day 1

REVIEW THE WORDS

1 Briefly Review the Words

Review the pronunciation and meaning of each word.

Discuss as a class:

Q *Which of the words we learned yesterday might you use to describe your lunchtime? How might you use the word?*

PROMPT: "I might use the word [*tranquil*] to describe my lunchtime. I might say, ['Sitting on the grass during lunchtime was very tranquil.']"

Week 21 ▶ Day 2

PRACTICE USING THE WORDS

▶ 2 Discuss "Would You?" Questions

Explain that you will ask questions that include one of yesterday's words and a word they learned earlier in the year.

Point to the word *tranquil* and ask:

Q *Would you be likely to see pandemonium in a tranquil place? Why? Turn to your partner.*

Teacher Note ▶ You might review that *pandemonium* is "chaos or confusion."

PROMPT: "You [would/would not] be likely to see pandemonium in a tranquil place because…."

In the same way, discuss:

[sufficient]

Q *Would you be dissatisfied if you had a sufficient amount of food? Why? Turn to your partner.*

Teacher Note ▶ You might review that *dissatisfied* means "not satisfied or happy with the way things are." When you are dissatisfied, you want something more or something different.

PROMPT: "I [would/would not] be dissatisfied if I had a sufficient amount of food because…."

[insufficient]

Q *Would getting an insufficient amount of sleep improve your stamina? Why? Turn to your partner.*

Teacher Note ▶ You might review that *stamina* is "the energy and strength to keep doing something for a long time."

PROMPT: "Getting an insufficient amount of sleep [would/would not] improve my stamina because…."

472 | Making Meaning® Vocabulary

Day 3

Introduce *Disperse, Ascend,* and *Inundate*

Words Taught

disperse
Disperse means "scatter in different directions."

ascend
Ascend means "go up, move up, or climb."

inundate
Inundate means "fill or cover completely with water." *Inundate* also means "overwhelm with a large amount of something."

Materials
- *Letting Swift River Go*
- Word chart from Day 1
- A marker

INTRODUCE AND PRACTICE USING *DISPERSE*

1 Introduce and Define *Disperse*

Show pages 22–23 of *Letting Swift River Go*. Review that, when Boston votes to flood the valley, all of the people and buildings must be moved. Read page 23 aloud.

Tell the students that the first word they will learn today is *disperse* and that *disperse* means "scatter in different directions." Explain that when the residents of Swift River find new places to live, they disperse, or scatter in different directions, to nearby towns.

Have the students say the word *disperse*, and write it on the chart.

Week 21 ▸ Day 3

▶ 2 Do the Activity "Imagine That!"

Have the students close their eyes and imagine:

- *You pick a dandelion and blow on it. The seeds are dispersed by the wind.*

Use "Think, Pair, Share" to discuss:

Q *What does it look like when the seeds are dispersed by the wind?* [pause] *Open your eyes and turn to your partner.*

PROMPT: "When the seeds are dispersed by the wind, they…."

In the same way, discuss:

- *You walk outside after school. You see children dispersing from the building.*
- *You are walking in the park. You see a man dispersing seeds for the birds.*

Review the pronunciation and meaning of the word.

INTRODUCE AND PRACTICE USING *ASCEND*

▶ 3 Introduce and Define *Ascend*

Show pages 26–27 and review that, when the buildings and houses are gone, dams are built across the rivers, and water floods the valley. Read pages 26–27 aloud.

Tell the students that the next word they will learn is *ascend* and that *ascend* means "go up, move up, or climb." Explain that, when the rivers are dammed, the water slowly ascends, or moves up the sides of the hills.

Have the students say the word *ascend*, and write it on the chart.

Teacher Note ▶

You might explain that the antonym of *ascend* is *descend*, which means "go down, move down, or come down." If you started an antonym chart, add *ascend* and *descend* to it.

4 ▶ Discuss *Ascend*

Tell the students that things other than water ascend, or go up, move up, or climb. For example, airplanes and hot air balloons ascend.

Ask:

Q *What other things ascend? Turn to your partner.*

PROMPT: "[Birds, smoke, and rockets] ascend."

Explain that people can also ascend. For example, people ascend, or go up, hills and mountains. They also ascend, or climb, ladders.

Use "Think, Pair, Share" to discuss:

Q *When have you ascended something?* [pause] *Turn to your partner.*

PROMPT: "I ascended [the steps in front of the school building this morning]."

Review the pronunciation and meaning of the word.

◀ **Teacher Note**

You might challenge pairs to think of at least three things that ascend.

INTRODUCE AND PRACTICE USING *INUNDATE*

5 ▶ Introduce and Define *Inundate*

Show pages 26–27 again.

Tell the students that the last word they will learn today is *inundate* and that *inundate* means "fill or cover completely with water."

Point to the illustration on pages 26–27. Explain that, after the water from the rivers ascended for seven years, the valley was inundated, or filled or covered completely with water.

Grade Five | 475

Week 21 ▶ Day 3

Discuss as a class:

Q *How might a basement become inundated with water?*

PROMPT: "A basement might become inundated with water when…."

Have the students say the word *inundate*, and write it on the chart.

▶6 Discuss Another Meaning of *Inundate*

Remind the students that words often have more than one meaning.

Point to the word *inundate* on the chart, and review that *inundate* means "fill or cover completely with water." Tell the students that *inundate* can also mean "overwhelm with a large amount of something." Explain that, if lots of parents call the school office at the same time, the office might be inundated with calls, or overwhelmed by the large number of calls. If a food bank gets lots and lots of donations during the holiday season, it might be inundated, or overwhelmed, with donations. There might be too many donations to handle.

Tell the students that you will read a sentence and partners will discuss whether *inundate* means "fill or cover completely with water" or "overwhelm with a large amount of something" in the sentence and why they think so.

Teacher Note ▶

You might write the two definitions of *inundate* on the board.

Begin with:

- *During the month of December, the post office is inundated with cards and packages.*

Ask:

Q *In the sentence, does* inundate *mean "fill or cover completely with water" or "overwhelm with a large amount of something"? Why do you think so? Turn to your partner.*

PROMPT: "*Inundate* means ['overwhelm with a large amount of something'] because…."

Week 21 ▶ Day 3

In the same way, discuss:

- *The bathroom was inundated with water when the bathtub overflowed.*
- *At the end of the day, the children were inundated with homework.*

Review the pronunciation and meaning of the word.

MORE STRATEGY PRACTICE

Play "Antonym Match"

Write these words in two columns on a sheet of chart paper:

1	2
scarce	sociable
solitary	real
blunt	kind
fanciful	plentiful
heartless	pointed

Explain that partners will play "Antonym Match." Point to the words in column 1, and explain that these are vocabulary words the students have learned. Point to the words in column 2, and explain that these are antonyms of the words in column 1, or words that have opposite meanings. Explain that partners will match each vocabulary word to its antonym.

Point to the word *scarce*, pronounce it, and have the students pronounce it.

Then point to the words in column 2, and ask:

Q *Which word in column 2 is the antonym of* scarce? *Turn to your partner.*

PROMPT: "[*Plentiful*] is the antonym of *scarce*."

continues

Grade Five | 477

Week 21 ▶ Day 3

> **MORE STRATEGY PRACTICE** *continued*
>
> Have volunteers share their thinking. Then have a volunteer draw a line from the word *scarce* to the word *plentiful*.
>
> Discuss the remaining words the same way. When you get to the final two words, have the students discuss them together by asking:
>
> **Q** *Which word in column 2 is the antonym of* fanciful *and which word is the antonym of* heartless? *Turn to your partner.*

Day 4

Review *Disperse*, *Ascend*, and *Inundate*

Words Reviewed

disperse
Disperse means "scatter in different directions."

ascend
Ascend means "go up, move up, or climb."

inundate
Inundate means "fill or cover completely with water." *Inundate* also means "overwhelm with a large amount of something."

Materials
- Word chart from Day 3
- A marker

REVIEW THE WORDS

1 Briefly Review the Words

Review the pronunciation and meaning of each word.

Ask:

Q *Which of the words we learned yesterday might you use if you were writing a story about finding a cave full of bats? Why? Turn to your partner.*

PROMPT: "I might use the word [*disperse*]. I might write…."

Week 21 ▶ Day 4

PRACTICE USING THE WORDS

2 Do the Activity "Create a Sentence"

Explain that partners will do the activity "Create a Sentence." Review that partners will work together to create sentences that use the vocabulary words.

Point to the word *disperse* on the chart, and review that *disperse* means "scatter in different directions."

Use "Think, Pair, Share" to discuss:

Q *How might you use the word* disperse *in a sentence?* [pause] *Turn to your partner.*

Have a few pairs share their sentences.

Follow up by asking:

Q *Does it make sense to say, ["The crowd dispersed after the concert"]? Why?*

In the same way, have partners work together to use *ascend* and *inundate* in sentences.

Teacher Note

Support struggling students by asking questions such as, "When might you see people disperse from a building?" and "What things might be dispersed by the wind?" If they continue to struggle, provide a sentence starter such as, "The crowd dispersed after…" or "The strong winds dispersed…."

Teacher Note

[*ascend*] Support struggling students by asking questions such as, "What is something people ascend?" and "What animals or objects can ascend?" If they continue to struggle, provide a sentence starter such as, "The plane ascended…" or "Jake huffed and puffed as he ascended…."

[*inundate*] Support struggling students by asking questions such as, "When have you been inundated with something?" and "What might cause a yard to be inundated with water?" If they continue to struggle, provide a sentence starter such as, "The village was inundated with water when…" or "I was inundated with…."

480 | Making Meaning® Vocabulary

Day 5

Week 21 ▶ Day 5

Ongoing Review

Words Reviewed

clash
Clash means "fight or argue."

devastate
Devastate means "destroy or badly damage."

get on board
"Get on board" means "accept or go along with something."

preserve
Preserve means "protect from harm or damage."

sympathize
Sympathize means "understand how someone feels."

Materials

- Pocket chart
- Word cards 14, 17, 65, 99, 113

REVIEW THE WORDS

▶1 Display the Word Cards and Briefly Review the Words

Review the pronunciation and meaning of the words.

Grade Five | 481

Week 21 ▶ Day 5

PRACTICE USING THE WORDS

Teacher Note

If the students struggle to answer the question, think aloud about ways you think the words are different. (You might say, "I think *clash* and 'get on board' are different because when you clash with people, you fight or argue with them, but when you get on board with what people are doing, you give your support and help.) Alternatively, you might stimulate the students' thinking by asking questions such as, "How do you feel when you clash with someone? When you get on board with something?" or "Why might you clash with someone? Get on board with someone?" Then discuss how *clash* and *sympathize* are different as a class, rather than in pairs.

2 Play "Alike or Different"

Explain that partners will play the game "Alike or Different." Point to the review words, and explain that today you will ask the students to think about how pairs of vocabulary words are different.

Explain that the words may be different in many ways and that partners may not always agree. Explaining why the words are different is the most important thing.

Tell the students that, before they play the game in pairs, they will practice as a class. Point to the word *clash* and the idiom "get on board." Then discuss as a class:

▶ **Q** *How are the words* clash *and "get on board" different?*

PROMPT: "The words *clash* and 'get on board' are different because...."

Teacher Note

Support struggling students by thinking aloud about ways the words are different or by asking questions such as, "When might you use the words *clash* and *sympathize*?" and "How do you feel when you clash with someone? Sympathize with someone?"

3 Play "Alike or Different" in Pairs

Point to the words *clash* and *sympathize*. Use "Think, Pair, Share" to discuss:

▶ **Q** *How are the words* clash *and* sympathize *different?* [pause] *Turn to your partner.*

PROMPT: "The words *clash* and *sympathize* are different because...."

Point to the words *devastate* and *preserve*. Use "Think, Pair, Share" to discuss:

Teacher Note

Support struggling students by thinking aloud about ways the words are different or by asking questions such as, "When might you use the words *devastate* and *preserve*?" and "What happens when something is devastated? When something is preserved?"

▶ **Q** *How are the words* devastate *and* preserve *different?* [pause] *Turn to your partner.*

PROMPT: "The words *devastate* and *preserve* are different because...."

482 | Making Meaning® Vocabulary

Week 22 Overview

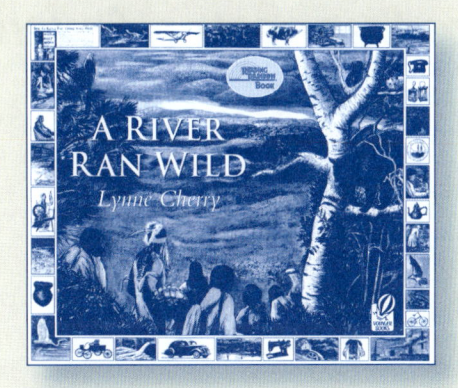

A River Ran Wild
by Lynne Cherry
(Harcourt, 2002)

Words Taught

supporter

dwelling

deteriorate

vivid

wide-eyed

restore

Word-learning Strategies

- Using the suffix *-er* to determine word meanings (review)

- Recognizing words with multiple meanings (review)

Words Reviewed: comply, deliberately, desirable, merge, sequence

DO AHEAD

- Prior to Day 1, preview the "Author's Note" on pages 4–5 of *A River Ran Wild*. (You did not read the note during the *Making Meaning* lesson.) You will read part of the "Author's Note" aloud to the students to introduce the word *supporter*.

- Prior to Day 1, review More Strategy Practice on pages 489–490.

- Prior to Day 5, write the "Find Another Word" sentences on the board or a sheet of chart paper or make a transparency of the sentences (BLM18). (See Step 2 on page 503.)

- Prior to Day 5, collect these word cards for Ongoing Review: 79, 93, 104, 111, and 118.

Grade Five | 483

Week 22 ▸ Day 1

Day 1

Introduce *Supporter, Dwelling,* and *Deteriorate*

Materials
- *A River Ran Wild*
- Chart paper
- A marker

Words Taught

supporter (p. 4)
A *supporter* is "someone who supports, or helps or favors, a particular person, group, or plan."

dwelling (p. 10)
A *dwelling* is "a place where someone lives, such as a house or an apartment."

deteriorate
Deteriorate means "become worse."

INTRODUCE AND PRACTICE USING *SUPPORTER*

▶ **1 Introduce *Supporter***

Briefly review *A River Ran Wild*.

Show the "Author's Note" on pages 4–5, and read the title aloud. Explain that an author sometimes includes a note to readers at the beginning of a book that gives important information about the book. Explain that in this note Lynne Cherry, the author of *A River Ran Wild*, describes the way the Nashua River became polluted and the way a woman named Marion Stoddart and other people helped to save it.

Read the fourth paragraph on page 4 aloud, emphasizing the word *supporters*.

484 | Making Meaning® Vocabulary

Week 22 ▶ Day 1

Explain that Marion Stoddart and her supporters worked hard to clean up the Nashua River and that *supporter* is the first word the students will learn today.

Ask the students to say the word *supporter*, and then write it on a sheet of chart paper.

▶ 2 Use the Suffix *-er* to Determine the Meaning of *Supporter*

Point to the suffix *-er* in *supporter* on the chart, and review that earlier the students learned that *-er* is a suffix that means "a person who." Explain that when you add *-er* to the word *support*, which means "help or favor," you make the word *supporter*.

Discuss as a class:

Q *Based on what you know about the suffix* -er *and the word* support, *what do you think the word* supporter *means? What did Marion's supporters do?*

PROMPTS: "I think *supporter* means…" or "Marion's supporters…."

Explain that a *supporter* is "someone who supports, or helps or favors, a particular person, group, or plan." Point out that Marion's supporters supported her plan to clean up the Nashua River, or helped the plan succeed, by talking to state officials, convincing the paper companies to build a treatment plant, and removing trash from the banks of the river.

◀ **Teacher Note**

You might remind the students that earlier they discussed these words that use the suffix *-er*: *moocher* (a person who mooches), *deserter* (a person who deserts), and *consumer* (a person who consumes). If you started a chart of *-er* words, add *supporter* to it.

▶ 3 Discuss Being a Supporter

Review that a *supporter* is "someone who supports, or helps or favors, a particular person, group, or plan."

Ask:

Q *If a friend wanted to start an after-school homework club, would you be a supporter? Why? Turn to your partner.*

PROMPT: "I [would/would not] be a supporter because…"

Grade Five | 485

Week 22 ▶ Day 1

Discuss as a class:

Q *What might you do to show you are a supporter of your friend's homework club?*

PROMPT: "To show I'm a supporter, I might…."

Review that people, as well as plans and ideas, can have supporters. For example, during a presidential election each candidate for president has supporters, or people who support the candidate and work to see that he or she is elected. Sports teams also have supporters, or people who favor and support the teams.

Ask:

Q *Who do you know who is a supporter of a sports team? What does the person do that shows he or she is a supporter? Turn to your partner.*

PROMPT: "[My mom] is a supporter of [my softball team]. [She] shows [she] is a supporter by [going to the games and cheering for my team]."

Review the pronunciation and meaning of the word.

INTRODUCE AND PRACTICE USING *DWELLING*

▶ 4 Introduce and Define *Dwelling*

Show pages 10–11. Review that Native Americans settled in the Nashua River Valley. Read the first two sentences on page 10 aloud, emphasizing the word *dwelling*.

Tell the students that the next word they will learn today is *dwelling* and that a *dwelling* is "a place where someone lives, such as a house or an apartment."

486 | Making Meaning® Vocabulary

Show the illustration on page 11, and point out the Native American dwellings. Explain that these dwellings are made out of leaves and branches.

Have the students say the word *dwelling*, and write it on the chart.

5 ▶ Discuss Types of Dwellings

Tell the students that there are many different types of dwellings. For example, igloos, huts, teepees, apartments, houses, and cabins are all dwellings, or places where people live.

Ask:

Q *If you could build your own dwelling, what type of dwelling would you build? Why? Turn to your partner.*

PROMPT: "If I could build my own dwelling, I would build [a log cabin] because…."

Have volunteers share their thinking.

Follow up by asking:

Q *Where would you build your dwelling? Why?*

PROMPT: "I would build my dwelling [by the ocean] because…."

Review the pronunciation and meaning of the word.

INTRODUCE AND PRACTICE USING *DETERIORATE*

6 ▶ Introduce and Define *Deteriorate*

Show pages 22–23 and review that in the 1900s people built paper mills and other factories along the Nashua River. Read page 22 aloud.

Week 22 ▶ Day 1

Tell the students that the last word they will learn today is *deteriorate* and that *deteriorate* means "become worse." Explain that, as time passed and factories dumped more and more waste into the water, the health of the river deteriorated, or became worse.

Tell the students that you will reread the last paragraph on page 22 aloud. Ask the students to listen for evidence that the health of the river deteriorated, or became worse. Then reread the paragraph aloud.

Discuss as a class:

Q *What evidence did you hear that the health of the river deteriorated?*

PROMPT: "[No fish in the river] is evidence that the health of the river deteriorated."

If necessary, explain that evidence that the health of the river deteriorated is that no fish lived in the river, no birds stopped on migration, and the water was dark and dirty.

Have the students say the word *deteriorate*, and write it on the chart.

▶ 7 Do the Activity "Imagine That!"

Have the students imagine the following scenario:

- *When you bought your new bicycle, it was in great condition, but now the condition of the bicycle is deteriorating.*

Use "Think, Pair, Share" to discuss:

Q *In what ways might the bicycle change as its condition deteriorates?* [pause] *Turn to your partner.*

PROMPT: "As the condition of the bicycle deteriorates, it might…."

In the same way, discuss:

- *You are on a picnic on a bright, sunny day. Suddenly, the weather begins to deteriorate.*

488 | Making Meaning® Vocabulary

Q *In what ways might the weather change as it deteriorates?* [pause] *Turn to your partner.*

PROMPT: *"As the weather deteriorates, it might…."*

Review the pronunciation and meaning of the word.

MORE STRATEGY PRACTICE

Discuss Other Words with the Suffix *-er*

Point to the word *supporter* on the chart, and review that the suffix *-er* means "a person who." Review that when *-er* is added to *support*, which means "help or favor," it makes the word *supporter*, which means "a person who supports, or helps or favors, a particular person, group, or plan."

Tell the students that you will read a sentence from *A River Ran Wild* and that you want them to listen for a word that ends with the suffix *-er*. Then read the following sentence from page 12 aloud twice, slowly and clearly, "The Nashua had lived for generations by the clear, clean, flowing river when one day a pale-skinned trader came with a boatload full of treasures."

Discuss as a class:

Q *What word did you hear that ends with the suffix -er?*

Q *What do you think the word* trader *means?*

If necessary, explain that a *trader* is "a person who trades or sells goods."

In the same way, discuss the following sentence from page 14, "The settlers worked together to clear land by cutting down the forests, which they thought were full of danger—wilderness that they would conquer."

continues

Week 22 ▶ Day 1

Teacher Note

If you started a chart of *-er* words, add *trader*, *settler*, and *dweller* to it. You might explain that, when you add *-er* to *settle* and *trade*, you drop the final *e* before adding the suffix. For a comprehensive grade 5 spelling program, see Developmental Studies Center's *Guided Spelling*.

For a list of words that end with the suffix *-er* and other word lists, visit Developmental Studies Center's website at www.devstu.org. ▶

> **MORE STRATEGY PRACTICE** *continued*
>
> Discuss as a class:
>
> **Q** *What word did you hear that ends with the suffix -er?*
>
> **Q** *What do you think the word* settler *means?*
>
> If necessary, explain that a *settler* is "a person who settles, or goes to live in a new place."
>
> Remind the students that they learned the word *dwelling* earlier and that a *dwelling* is "a place where someone lives, such as a house or an apartment." Explain that the word *dwelling* comes from the word *dwell*, which means "live in a certain place."
>
> Discuss as a class:
>
> **Q** *What might you call a person or animal who dwells, or lives in a certain place?*
>
> If necessary, explain that a *dweller* is "a person or animal that lives in a certain place." You might explain that the word *dweller* usually follows the type of place where someone lives. For example, people who live in a city are called "city dwellers" and animals who live in caves are "cave dwellers."

490 | Making Meaning® Vocabulary

Day 2

Review *Supporter, Dwelling,* and *Deteriorate*

Words Reviewed

supporter
A *supporter* is "someone who supports, or helps or favors, a particular person, group, or plan."

dwelling
A *dwelling* is "a place where someone lives, such as a house or an apartment."

deteriorate
Deteriorate means "become worse."

Materials
- Word chart from Day 1

REVIEW THE WORDS

1 Briefly Review the Words

Review the pronunciation and meaning of each word.

Ask:

Q *Which of the words we learned yesterday do you think was interesting or fun to talk about? Why? Turn to your partner.*

PROMPT: "I think the word [*deteriorate*] was [interesting/fun] to talk about because…."

Week 22 ▶ Day 2

PRACTICE USING THE WORDS

▶2 Think More About the Words

Tell the students that you will describe a situation and partners will use vocabulary words to discuss it.

Read the following scenario aloud twice:

- *Your neighbor's dwelling is deteriorating.*

Use "Think, Pair, Share" to discuss:

Q *What might cause the dwelling to deteriorate?* [pause] *Turn to your partner.*

PROMPT: "[Not taking care of the dwelling] might cause it to deteriorate."

Have volunteers share their thinking.

Follow up by asking:

Q *What might the dwelling look like after it has deteriorated?*

PROMPT: "After the dwelling has deteriorated, it might…."

In the same way, discuss:

- *You are a supporter of your community's animal shelter.*

Q *What might you do to show you are a supporter of the animal shelter?* [pause] *Turn to your partner*

PROMPT: "To show I am a supporter of the shelter, I might…."

492 | Making Meaning® Vocabulary

Have volunteers share their thinking.

Follow up by asking:

Q *Why might you choose to become a supporter of an animal shelter?*

PROMPT: "I might choose to become a supporter of an animal shelter because…."

Week 22 ▶ Day 3

Day 3

Introduce *Vivid, Wide-eyed,* and *Restore*

Materials

- *A River Ran Wild*
- Word chart from Day 1
- A marker

Words Taught

vivid (p. 24)
Vivid means "sharp and clear." *Vivid* also means "bright and strong."

wide-eyed (p. 24)
Wide-eyed means "with the eyes wide open, especially because you are amazed or surprised."

restore (p. 26)
Restore means "bring something back to its original condition."

INTRODUCE AND PRACTICE USING *VIVID*

▶ **1 Introduce and Define *Vivid***

Show pages 24–25 and remind the students that pollution from factories devastated the Nashua River. Read the first paragraph on page 24 aloud, emphasizing the word *vivid*.

Tell the students that the first word they will learn today is *vivid* and that *vivid* means "sharp and clear." Explain that Oweana's dream is so vivid, or sharp and clear, that he remembers every detail of it when he wakes up.

Have the students say the word *vivid*, and write it on the chart.

▶ **Teacher Note**

Using a previously taught word such as *devastated* when talking about a new word is an excellent way to review the word. You might review that *devastate* means "destroy or badly damage."

494 | Making Meaning® Vocabulary

2 Discuss Vivid Dreams

Explain that all of us have vivid dreams occasionally, or dreams that are very sharp and clear and seem almost real. Explain that you often remember a vivid dream when you wake up. Give examples of vivid dreams you have had. (You might say, "I sometimes have vivid dreams about places I've visited. In the dreams, I can clearly see the sights I saw when I visited. I can even hear the sounds and see the people I met. I sometimes have vivid dreams about my mother. I see her just as I remember her. When I wake up, it's as if I have spent time with her. I can remember our conversations from the dreams.")

Use "Think, Pair, Share" to discuss:

Q *What is a vivid dream you have had?* [pause] *Turn to your partner.*

PROMPT: "I had a vivid dream about…."

3 Discuss Another Meaning of *Vivid*

Remind the students that words often have more than one meaning. Review that *vivid* means "sharp and clear," and tell the students that *vivid* can also mean "bright and strong." Explain that we often use *vivid*, meaning "bright and strong," to describe colors. For example, a vivid blue sky is a sky that is bright blue in color.

Ask the students to look quietly around the room or out the window for vivid colors. Then give them a few moments to look.

Ask:

Q *What do you see that has vivid colors? What are the vivid colors? Turn to your partner.*

PROMPT: "[My partner's shirt] has vivid colors. The vivid colors are [red and yellow]."

Review the pronunciation and meanings of the word.

◀ **Teacher Note**

Support struggling students by asking questions such as, "What dreams have you had that felt like they were real?" "When have you awakened from a dream and thought, 'I'm glad that was just a dream!'" and "When have you awakened from a dream and wished that you could close your eyes and restart the dream where it left off?"

Week 22 ▶ Day 3

INTRODUCE AND PRACTICE USING *WIDE-EYED*

▶4 Introduce and Define *Wide-eyed*

Show pages 24–25 again, and review that Oweana has a vivid dream about the river. Reread the first sentence on page 24 aloud, emphasizing the word *wide-eyed*.

Tell the students that the next word they will learn today is *wide-eyed* and that *wide-eyed* means "with eyes wide open, especially because you are amazed or surprised."

Explain that Oweana's dream seemed so real and made such a powerful impression on him that he woke up wide-eyed, or with his eyes wide open in surprise or amazement. Demonstrate the way someone looks when he is wide-eyed from surprise or amazement.

Have the students say the word *wide-eyed*, and write it on the chart.

▶5 Discuss Being Wide-eyed

Give examples of times you or someone you know was wide-eyed with surprise or amazement, and act out the way you or the person looked. (You might say, "I was wide-eyed with surprise when I saw a family of raccoons run across my yard, because I could not believe what I was seeing. When I saw a news report about scientists finding ice on Mars, I was wide-eyed with amazement. I didn't think there was water on Mars. This morning Adrian was wide-eyed when I invited her to share her poem with the class. She didn't expect that.")

Teacher Note

If the students cannot think of times they were wide-eyed, ask, "What might happen to you that would cause you to be wide-eyed?" or "When have you seen another person who was wide-eyed with amazement or surprise?"

Use "Think, Pair, Share" to discuss:

▶ Q *When have you been wide-eyed with amazement or surprise?* [pause] *Turn to your partner.*

PROMPT: "I was wide-eyed with [amazement/surprise] when…."

Review the pronunciation and meaning of the word.

496 | Making Meaning® Vocabulary

INTRODUCE AND PRACTICE USING *RESTORE*

6 Introduce and Define *Restore*

Show pages 26–27 and review that Oweana and Marion have the same dream about the Nashua River, and together they decide that something needs to be done. Read the first two sentences on page 26 aloud, emphasizing the word *restore*.

Tell the students that the last word they will learn today is *restore* and that *restore* means "bring something back to its original condition." Explain that Marion asks the people living along the river to help restore the river, or bring it back to the way it was before it became polluted.

Have the students say the word *restore*, and write it on the chart.

7 Do the Activity "Imagine That!"

Remind the students that, when you restore something, you bring it back to its original condition, or the way it was. Have the students imagine the following scene:

- *You move into a house that is next to a park. In the park, there is an old, deteriorating tree house.*

Use "Think, Pair, Share" to discuss:

Q *What might you do to restore the old tree house? Why?* [pause] *Turn to your partner.*

PROMPT: "To restore the old tree house, I might [replace the old boards and paint the new boards] because…."

In the same way, discuss:

- *You have been lying in bed, coughing, sneezing, and blowing your nose for a week.*

◀ **Teacher Note**

You might review that *deteriorate* means "become worse."

Week 22 ▸ Day 3

Q *What might you or your parents do to help restore your health? [pause] Turn to your partner.*

PROMPT: "To restore my health, [I/my parents] might…."

Review the pronunciation and meaning of the word.

EXTENSION

Discuss Vivid Language

Point to the word *vivid* on the chart, and review that *vivid* means "sharp and clear." Tell the students that when authors use words that create sharp or clear pictures in readers' minds, we say that they use "vivid language."

Show pages 26–27 of *A River Ran Wild*, and tell the students that you will read a couple of sentences from this part of the story. Explain that you want them to close their eyes and listen for vivid language that helps them create a picture in their minds. Then read the following sentences from the second paragraph on page 26 aloud: "People listened and imagined a sparkling river, full of fish. They imagined pebbles shining up through clear waters."

Discuss as a class:

Q *What vivid language did you hear? What language helped you create a picture of the river in your mind?*

If necessary, tell the students that the words *sparkling*, *shining*, and *clear* are examples of vivid language.

Day 4

Review *Vivid*, *Wide-eyed*, and *Restore*

Words Reviewed

vivid
Vivid means "sharp and clear." *Vivid* also means "bright and strong."

wide-eyed
Wide-eyed means "with the eyes wide open, especially because you are amazed or surprised."

restore
Restore means "bring something back to its original condition."

Materials
- Word chart from Day 3
- A marker

REVIEW THE WORDS

1 Briefly Review the Words

Review the pronunciation and meaning of each word.

Ask:

Q *Which of the words we learned yesterday might you use when you are talking with your friends or family? How might you use the word? Turn to your partner.*

PROMPT: "I might use the word [*wide-eyed*] when I talk with [my grandmother]. I might say…."

Week 22 ▸ Day 4

PRACTICE USING THE WORDS

▶2 Do the Activity "Tell Me a Story"

Explain that partners will do the activity "Tell Me a Story." Review that you will tell the beginning of a story that includes one of the vocabulary words. The students will use what they know about the word and their imaginations to make up an ending for the story.

Begin by reading the following story aloud twice, slowly and clearly:

- Alison awoke with a scream from a nightmare. "That nightmare was horrible," she said trembling. "I vividly remember…."

Use "Think, Pair, Share" to discuss:

Q *How might you finish the story? What did Alison vividly remember from her nightmare?* [pause] *Turn to your partner.*

PROMPT: "Alison vividly remembers…."

In the same way, discuss:

- The burglar turned around, wide-eyed with surprise because….

Q *How might you finish the story? Why might the burglar turn around, wide-eyed with surprise?* [pause] *Turn to your partner.*

PROMPT: "The burglar turned around, wide-eyed with surprise because…."

Teacher Note

You might review that *deteriorate* means "become worse." ▶

- Jenna woke up in a good mood, but at work her mood deteriorated. When she got home, Jenna restored her good mood by….

Q *How might you finish the story? What might Jenna have done to restore her good mood?* [pause] *Turn to your partner.*

PROMPT: "Jenna restored her good mood by…."

Teacher Note

For a crossword puzzle you can use to review words taught during weeks 21 and 22, visit Developmental Studies Center's website at www.devstu.org.

500 | Making Meaning® Vocabulary

Week 22 ▶ Day 4

EXTENSION

Discuss Vivid Verbs

Write the following sentences on the board or a sheet of chart paper:

Jon ate a sandwich.
Jon devoured a sandwich.

Water gushed from the pipe.
Water flowed from the pipe.

Jen walked through the snow.
Jen trudged through the snow.

Tell the students that one way good writers make their writing interesting and fun to read is by replacing overused verbs like *hit*, *run*, and *talk* with vivid verbs like *clobber*, *whiz*, and *chatter*. Explain that vivid verbs are action words that are strong, clear, and specific. They paint a word picture that helps readers visualize, or see in their minds, what is happening in a story.

Direct the students' attention to the first pair of sentences, and read the sentences aloud. If necessary, review that the students learned the word *devour* earlier and that *devour* means "eat something quickly and hungrily."

Point to the words *ate* and *devoured* in the sentences, and discuss as a class:

Q *Which of these verbs is a vivid verb:* ate *or* devoured? *Why do you think that?*

PROMPT: "[*Devoured*] is a vivid verb because…."

If necessary, explain that *devoured* is a vivid verb because it helps readers picture exactly how Jon ate the sandwich—*quickly* and *hungrily*.

Discuss the remaining sentences the same way. If necessary, review the meanings of *gush* (flow or pour out quickly) and *trudge* (walk with slow, heavy steps because you are tired or it is difficult to walk).

Teacher Note

Other vocabulary words you might discuss as vivid verbs are *clamor*, *trample*, *surge*, *stun*, *hunger*, *topple*, *thrust*, *churn*, *clash*, and *disperse*.

Grade Five | 501

Week 22 ▸ Day 5

Day 5

Ongoing Review

Materials

- Pocket chart
- Word cards 79, 93, 104, 111, 118
- Charted sentences or transparency (BLM18) for "Find Another Word" (see Step 2 on page 503)
- (Optional) Overhead projector and marker

Words Reviewed

comply
Comply means "do what you are asked to do or what a law or rule requires you to do."

deliberately
Deliberately means "intentionally or on purpose."

desirable
Desirable means "worth having or wishing for."

merge
Merge means "combine or join together to form one thing."

sequence
A *sequence* is "a series of events or objects in a particular order."

REVIEW THE WORDS

1 **Display the Word Cards and Briefly Review the Words**
Review the pronunciation and meaning of the words.

PRACTICE USING THE WORDS

2 Play "Find Another Word"

Display the transparency or write the following sentences (without the answers) on the board or a sheet of chart paper and underline the words shown:

> The guide says the rapids are stronger where the two rivers <u>join together</u>. (merge)
>
> Hailey is certain that people will think her invention is <u>worth having</u>. (desirable)
>
> My dog is well trained. When I give a command, she <u>does what I tell her to do</u>. (complies)
>
> Terry did the steps out of <u>order</u>, so he could not solve the problem. (sequence)
>
> It's hard to believe that someone would hurt an animal <u>on purpose</u>. (deliberately)

Explain that partners will play "Find Another Word." Direct the students' attention to the sentences, and review that you will read each sentence aloud. Partners will discuss which vocabulary word could replace the underlined words.

Begin by pointing to this sentence and reading it aloud:

- *The guide says the rapids are stronger where the two rivers <u>join together</u>.*

Ask:

Q *Which word could replace "join together" in the sentence? Why? Turn to your partner.*

PROMPT: "I think the word [*merge*] could replace 'join together' because…."

◀ **Teacher Note**

You might explain that the students may need to change the form of the word to complete the sentence by adding an ending such as *-s*, *-ing*, or *-ed*.

Week 22 ▶ Day 5

Teacher Note
You might invite partners to work together to create their own "Find Another Word" sentences and have them share their sentences with the class.

Have volunteers share their thinking.

Reread the sentence, replacing the underlined words with the vocabulary word.

Discuss the remaining sentences the same way.

CLASS VOCABULARY PROGRESS ASSESSMENT

As you observe the students, ask yourself:

- Can the students identify the vocabulary words that replace the underlined words?

- Do their explanations show that they understand the words' meanings?

- Are they using context clues, prefixes and suffixes, and other word-learning strategies to figure out words in their independent reading?

For more information about reviewing and practicing the words, see "Retaining the Words" on pages xviii–xix.

Week 23

Overview

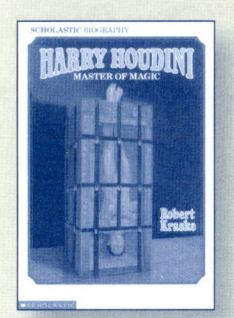

Harry Houdini: Master of Magic
by Robert Kraske
(Scholastic, 1989)

Words Taught

clang

on pins and needles

preposterous

master

mystify

momentous

Word-learning Strategies

- Recognizing idioms (review)
- Recognizing synonyms (review)

Words Reviewed: academic, consume/consumer, dependent, influence, range

DO AHEAD

- Prior to Day 5, write the "What's the Missing Word?" sentences on the board or a sheet of chart paper or make a transparency of the sentences (BLM19). (See Step 2 on page 522.)

- Prior to Day 5, collect these word cards for Ongoing Review: 81, 95, 96, 98, and 100.

Grade Five | 505

Day 1

Introduce *Clang*, "On Pins and Needles," and *Preposterous*

Materials

- *Harry Houdini*
- Chart paper
- A marker

Words Taught

clang (p. 8)
Clang means "make a loud, ringing sound."

on pins and needles
"On pins and needles" means "very nervous or uneasy."

preposterous
Preposterous means "completely ridiculous." If something is preposterous, it is too silly or fantastic to be believed.

INTRODUCE AND PRACTICE USING *CLANG*

▶ **1 Introduce and Define *Clang***

Show pages 6–7 of *Harry Houdini*, and remind the students that they heard the first chapter of the book, "The Great Houdini." Review that the chapter begins by telling about a performance in London in which Houdini escaped from a locked safe.

Turn to page 8, and read the second full paragraph aloud, beginning with, "The heavy steel door clanged shut." Emphasize the word *clang*.

Explain that *clang* is the first word the students will learn today and that *clang* means "make a loud, ringing sound." Explain that, when the metal door on the safe was shut, it clanged, or made a loud ringing sound.

Have the students say the word *clang*, and then write it on the chart.

Week 23 ▶ Day 1

2 Play "Would It Clang?"

Review that, when you slam a steel door shut, the door clangs, or makes a loud ringing sound. Explain that, if you bang two metal pots together, the pots clang.

Tell the students that partners will play "Would It Clang?" You will describe something, and partners will discuss whether the object would clang or not and why they think so.

Begin with:

- *A metal gate closing*

Ask:

Q *Would a metal gate closing clang? Why? Turn to your partner.*

PROMPT: "A metal gate closing [would/would not] clang because…."

In the same way, discuss:

- *A wooden gate closing*
- *Metal spoons, knives, and forks falling on an aluminum table*
- *A bell struck by a hammer*

Review the pronunciation and meaning of the word.

◀ **Teacher Note**

You might explain that aluminum is a kind of metal.

INTRODUCE AND PRACTICE USING "ON PINS AND NEEDLES"

3 Introduce and Define "On Pins and Needles" and Review Idioms

Open the book to page 8 again. Review that, after Houdini was locked in the safe, a screen was placed in front of the safe, and the audience waited for Houdini to reappear. Read pages 8–9 aloud, beginning with, "A half hour passed," and ending with, "'He needs help!'"

Grade Five | 507

Week 23 ▶ Day 1

Tell the students that the audience was on pins and needles as they waited for Houdini to emerge from the safe and that "on pins and needles" is an idiom they will discuss next. Explain that "on pins and needles" means "very nervous or uneasy."

Teacher Note ▶
You might review that *uneasy* means "nervous, worried, or anxious."

Explain that you can tell that the audience was on pins and needles, or uneasy, because they were yelling, "Open the door!" and, "He's dead and can't get out!" One woman even screamed and fainted.

Have the students say "on pins and needles," and write it on the chart.

Remind the students that an *idiom* is "an expression or phrase that means something different from what it appears to mean." Explain that, when we say we are on pins and needles, we do not mean that we are sitting on a seat covered with pins and needles. Instead, we mean that we are nervous or uneasy about something—as nervous or uneasy as we would be if we were actually sitting on pins and needles.

Teacher Note ▶
If you started an idiom chart, add "on pins and needles" to it.

4 ▶ Discuss Being On Pins and Needles

Review that "on pins and needles" means "very nervous and uneasy," and give examples of times you have been on pins and needles. (You might say, "When my dog was sick, I was on pins and needles while I waited to find out what was wrong. I was nervous that it might be something serious. I was on pins and needles while I was watching a movie last night. It was a movie with lots of action and suspense, and I was uneasy because I didn't know what was going to happen next.")

Use "Think, Pair, Share" to discuss:

Q *When have you been on pins and needles? Why were you on pins and needles?* [pause] *Turn to your partner.*

PROMPT: "I was on pins and needles when [I was waiting to find out if I got a part in the school play] because…."

Review the pronunciation and meaning of the word.

508 | Making Meaning® Vocabulary

INTRODUCE AND PRACTICE USING *PREPOSTEROUS*

5 Introduce and Define *Preposterous*

Open to page 8 again, and review that the audience was on pins and needles waiting for Houdini to escape from the safe. Read the last two paragraphs on page 8 and the first two paragraphs on page 9 aloud, beginning with, "'How can he possibly get out?' a woman asked," and ending with, "'Believe me,' the man said turning away. 'It's true!'"

Tell the students that the last word they will learn today is *preposterous* and that *preposterous* means "completely ridiculous." Explain that, if something is preposterous, it is too silly or fantastic to be believed.

Explain that the woman did not believe the man's explanation, because she thought the idea of Houdini changing into a spirit was preposterous, or completely ridiculous.

Have the students say the word *preposterous*, and write it on the chart.

◀ **Teacher Note**

You might explain that *fantastic* means "strange, unusual, or unbelievable."

6 Discuss Preposterous Things Tulip Might Say

Explain that you will describe a situation that Tulip is in. Partners will discuss a preposterous, or completely ridiculous, excuse or explanation Tulip might give to explain the situation. Then partners will discuss an excuse or explanation she might give that would not be preposterous.

Begin with:

- *Tulip comes home late from school. Her mother asks, "Tulip, why are you late?"*

Use "Think, Pair, Share" to discuss:

Q *What preposterous explanation might Tulip give her mother to explain why she is late?* [pause] *Turn to your partner.*

Teacher Note

Support struggling students by asking questions such as, "What is something Tulip might say that is too silly to be believed?" and "What is something that would probably never happen to Tulip on the way home from school?"

Week 23 ▶ Day 1

PROMPT: "A preposterous explanation Tulip might give her mother is [aliens stole her bike and she had to walk home]."

Have volunteers share their thinking.

Then use "Think, Pair, Share" to discuss:

Q *What explanation might Tulip give that is not preposterous?* [pause] *Turn to your partner.*

PROMPT: "An explanation Tulip might give that is not preposterous is…."

In the same way, discuss:

- Tulip is spending the night at her friend Violet's house. During the night, they hear a scratching sound on the roof. Violet asks, "What's making that noise?"

Q *What preposterous explanation might Tulip give to explain the noise?* [pause] *Turn to your partner.*

PROMPT: "A preposterous explanation Tulip might give is…."

Have volunteers share their thinking.

Then use "Think, Pair, Share" to discuss:

Q *What explanation might Tulip give that is not preposterous?* [pause] *Turn to your partner.*

PROMPT: "An explanation Tulip might give that is not preposterous is…."

Review the pronunciation and meaning of the word.

EXTENSION

Discuss Onomatopoeia

Explain that the word *clang* is an example of onomatopoeia and that *onomatopoeia* is "a type of word that sounds like the thing it is describing." Point out that when you say the word *clang*, the word sounds like the noise something makes when it clangs.

Discuss other examples of onomatopoeia, such as *whiz, beep, buzz, crunch, quack, oink, moo, slurp,* and *squish*. Ask the students for additional examples.

◀ **Teacher Note**

For more examples of onomatopoeia and other word lists, visit Developmental Studies Center's website at www.devstu.org.

Week 23 ▶ Day 2

Day 2

Review *Clang*, "On Pins and Needles," and *Preposterous*

Materials

- Word chart from Day 1

Words Reviewed

clang
Clang means "make a loud, ringing sound."

on pins and needles
"On pins and needles" means "very nervous or uneasy."

preposterous
Preposterous means "completely ridiculous." If something is preposterous, it is too silly or fantastic to be believed.

REVIEW THE WORDS

▶ **1 Briefly Review the Words**

Review the pronunciation and meaning of each word.

Ask:

Q *Which of the words we learned yesterday do you think was fun or interesting to talk about? Why? Turn to your partner.*

PROMPT: "I think the word [*preposterous*] was [fun/interesting] to talk about because…."

PRACTICE USING THE WORDS

2 Play "Does That Make Sense?"

Explain that partners will play "Does That Make Sense?" You will read a scenario that includes one of the vocabulary words. Partners will decide whether or not the word makes sense in the scenario and why they think so.

Point to the word *clang*, and explain that the first scenario includes the word *clang*.

Then read the following scenario aloud twice:

- *Jocelyn is setting up a display of cereal boxes on a table. Just as she puts the last box of cereal on top of the display, a shopping cart hits the table. The boxes clang against each other as they fall to the floor.*

Ask:

Q *Does the word* clang *make sense in the scenario? Why do you think that? Turn to your partner.*

PROMPT: "The word *clang* [does/does not] make sense in the sentence because…."

In the same way, discuss:

[on pins and needles]

- *Pablo was on pins and needles while he waited for his turn to give his report.*

[preposterous]

- *Jennie told her mother that if she eats too many blueberries, her skin will turn blue. Her mother said, "Jennie, that is the most preposterous thing I have ever heard."*

◀ **Teacher Note**

If the students struggle to answer the questions, call for attention. Reread the scenario aloud, and explain that *clang* does not make sense because cereal boxes are not made of metal. They would not clang against each other. Then read the next scenario.

EXTENSION

An Interesting Fact About *Preposterous*

Explain that *preposterous* comes from the Latin *prae* meaning "before" and *posterous* meaning "coming behind." Literally, the word *preposterous* means "before-behind." Explain that when someone does something first that should be done later, it is preposterous, or contrary to the way we think it should be done. Tell the students that the phrase "topsy-turvy" and the idiom "put the cart before the horse" have similar meanings.

Day 3

Week 23 ▶ Day 3

Introduce *Master, Mystify,* and *Momentous*

Words Taught

master (p. 10)
If you master a skill, you become very good at it.

mystify
Mystify means "confuse, bewilder, or puzzle."

momentous
Momentous means "very important or meaningful."

Materials

- *Harry Houdini*
- Word chart from Day 1
- A marker

INTRODUCE AND PRACTICE USING *MASTER*

▶ 1 Introduce and Define *Master*

Open the book to page 10, and review that Harry Houdini was a great magician and escape artist. Read the following sentences from page 10 aloud, emphasizing the word *master*: "Some people thought he was born with magical powers. But this was not true. He became a master magician only after long years of hard work."

Tell the students that the first word they will learn today is *master* and that if you master a skill, you become very good at it. Explain that Houdini practiced hard for many years to master, or become very good at, performing magic tricks.

Have the students say the word *master*, and write it on the chart.

Grade Five | 515

Week 23 ▶ Day 3

2 Discuss Mastering a Skill

Explain that by practicing a skill such as drawing, singing, riding a bike, or flying a kite, a person can master the skill, or become very good at it. Give a few examples of skills you have mastered or are trying to master. (You might say, "After knitting for many years, I have finally mastered, or become very good at, making slippers. I am trying to master playing the guitar. Right now, I am just learning how to play and am trying to master all of the chords.")

Use "Think, Pair, Share" to discuss:

Q *What is a skill you have mastered or are trying to master?* [pause] *Turn to your partner.*

PROMPT: "A skill [I have mastered/I am trying to master] is…."

Have volunteers share their thinking.

Follow up by asking:

Q *What [did you do/are you doing] to master [doing a back flip off the diving board]?*

PROMPT: "To master [doing a back flip off the diving board], I…."

Review the pronunciation and meaning of the word.

> **Teacher Note**
>
> Support struggling students by giving examples of skills or subjects the students might have mastered or be trying to master (for example, dribbling a basketball, playing an instrument, or playing a video game).

INTRODUCE AND PRACTICE USING *MYSTIFY*

3 Introduce and Define *Mystify* and Review Synonyms

Open the book to page 11, and review that Ehrich (Houdini's real name was Ehrich Weiss) started practicing tricks and escapes when he was nine years old. Then read the first part of the first full paragraph on page 11 aloud, starting with, "He also practiced rope escapes," and stopping after, "How had he escaped?"

516 | Making Meaning® Vocabulary

Week 23 ▶ Day 3

Tell the students that the next word they will learn today is *mystify* and that *mystify* means "confuse, bewilder, or puzzle." Explain that *mystify*, *confuse*, *bewilder*, and *puzzle* are synonyms.

Explain that, when Ehrich escaped from the ropes, his friends were mystified, or bewildered or puzzled, about how he was able to do it.

Have the students say the word *mystify*, and write it on the chart.

◀ **Teacher Note**

If you started a synonym chart, add *mystify* and its synonyms to it.

4 ▶ Discuss Being Mystified

Remind the students that, when you are mystified, you are confused or puzzled by something, and give examples of times you have been mystified. (You might say, "I was mystified when I read an article about cloning. I was confused about how scientists can create two animals that are exactly alike. I was watching a mystery on TV, and I could not figure out who had committed the crime. I was completely mystified, or puzzled.")

Use "Think, Pair, Share" to discuss:

Q *When have you been mystified? Why were you mystified?* [pause] *Turn to your partner.*

PROMPT: "I was mystified when [I went outside and saw that my bicycle was gone from the yard] because…."

Review the pronunciation and meaning of the word.

◀ **Teacher Note**

Support struggling students by asking questions such as, "When have you been mystified, or confused, about how to do something?" "When have you been mystified, or bewildered, about something that someone did or said to you?" and "When have you been reading a book or watching a TV show or movie and been mystified, or puzzled, by what was happening?"

INTRODUCE AND PRACTICE USING *MOMENTOUS*

5 ▶ Introduce and Define *Momentous*

Open the book to page 15. Review that, when Erich was seventeen years old, he found a book about the life of Robert-Houdin, a famous magician. Then read the following sentence on page 15 aloud, "It was a moment that changed his life."

Grade Five | 517

Week 23 ▶ Day 3

Tell the students that the last word they will learn today is *momentous*, and explain that *momentous* means "very important or meaningful."

Explain that finding the book about Robert-Houdin was momentous, or very important or meaningful, for Ehrich, because after reading the book, he realized that he wanted to become a magician.

Have the students say the word *momentous*, and write it on the chart.

6 ▶ Discuss *Momentous*

Explain that, when we say an event is momentous, we mean that it is so important or meaningful that it changes our life in some way. Give examples of momentous events that have happened to you or someone you know. (You might say, "When I was your age, my family moved from the country to a big city. That was a momentous event, because it changed my life. I had to go to a new school and make new friends. For my daughter, taking gymnastic classes turned out to be momentous. Gymnastics has become the most important thing in her life. She wants to be an Olympic gymnast some day.")

Use "Think, Pair, Share" to discuss:

Q *What has been a momentous event in your life? Why was it momentous?* [pause] *Turn to your partner.*

PROMPT: "[Getting a baby brother] was a momentous event in my life because…."

Review the pronunciation and meaning of the word.

Teacher Note

Support struggling students by asking questions such as, "What is something that has happened to you that has changed your life in some way?" "What is something that happened to you that you will never forget because it made you very happy?" "When have you worked really hard to get or earn something?" and "What is something momentous that has happened to your family?"

If the students continue to struggle, name a few events that might be momentous for them (for example, moving, getting a pet, getting a sibling, being in a play or on a sports team, or doing something for the first time without help).

518 | Making Meaning® Vocabulary

Day 4

Review *Master, Mystify,* and *Momentous*

Words Reviewed

master
If you master a skill, you become very good at it.

mystify
Mystify means "confuse, bewilder, or puzzle."

momentous
Momentous means "very important or meaningful."

Materials
- Word chart from Day 3
- A marker

REVIEW THE WORDS

1 Briefly Review the Words

Review the pronunciation and meaning of each word.

Ask:

Q *If you could master any skill, what skill would you master? Why? Turn to your partner.*

PROMPT: "If I could master any skill, I would master [karate] because…."

In the same way, discuss:

Q *If you were mystified by a math problem, what might you do to try to solve it? Why? Turn to your partner.*

Grade Five | 519

Week 23 ▶ Day 4

PROMPT: "If I were mystified by a math problem, I might try to solve it by…."

Q *If you were making a momentous decision, whom would you ask for advice? Why? Turn to your partner.*

PROMPT: "If I were making a momentous decision, I would ask [my friend Eric] for advice because…."

PRACTICE USING THE WORDS

2 Do the Activity "What Do You Think About?"

Explain that partners will do the activity "What Do You Think About?" Point to the words on the chart, and explain that you want the students to notice what they think about, or what picture comes into their minds, when they hear each of the words.

Have the students close their eyes. Then use "Think, Pair, Share" to discuss:

Q *What do you think about when you hear the word* master*? Why?* [pause] *Open your eyes and turn to your partner.*

PROMPT: "When I hear the word *master*, I think of [chess] because…."

▶ Discuss the remaining words the same way.

Teacher Note

If the students struggle to make associations, call for attention and think aloud about what comes into your mind when you hear the word *master*. (You might say, "When I hear the word *master*, I think about tennis, because that is a sport I would like to master one day. I also think about my son Alex, because he has mastered skateboarding.")

If the students continue to struggle, support them by asking questions such as, "What is a skill you have mastered?" and "Who do you know who has mastered a skill?"

Teacher Note

Support struggling students by thinking aloud about what you picture in your mind when you hear the word or by asking questions such as, [*mystify*] "How do you feel when you are mystified?" "What might you say or do if you are mystified?" and "What kinds of things mystify you?" [*momentous*] "What is a momentous decision you have made?" and "What might be a momentous occasion in your future?"

520 | Making Meaning® Vocabulary

Day 5

Ongoing Review

Words Reviewed

academic
Academic means "having to do with school, studying, and learning."

consume/consumer
Consume means "buy and use products and services." A *consumer* is "a person who consumes."

dependent
Dependent means "relying on or needing someone or something for help or support."

influence
Influence means "affect the way someone develops, behaves, or thinks."

range
Range means "vary or change within certain limits."

Materials

- Pocket chart
- Word cards 81, 95, 96, 98, 100
- Charted sentences or transparency (BLM19) for "What's the Missing Word?" (see Step 2 on page 522)
- (Optional) Overhead projector and marker

REVIEW THE WORDS

1 Display the Word Cards and Briefly Review the Words

Review the pronunciation and meaning of the words.

Week 23 ▶ Day 5

PRACTICE USING THE WORDS

▶ **2 Play "What's the Missing Word?"**

Display the transparency or write the following sentences (without the answers) on the board or a sheet of chart paper, leaving blanks as shown:

> Some people think video games are a negative _____ on children. (influence)
>
> When Alicia broke her leg, she was _____ on her crutches to help her walk. (dependent)
>
> The wind speed of a hurricane can _____ from 74 miles per hour to over 155 miles per hour. (range)
>
> A _____ might use coupons if he wants to save money on groceries. (consumer)
>
> Of all the _____ subjects, social studies is my favorite. (academic)

Explain that partners will play the game "What's the Missing Word?" Direct the students' attention to the sentences, and point out that a word is missing from each sentence. Explain that you will read each sentence aloud and partners will discuss which vocabulary word could replace the missing word and why they think so.

Begin by pointing to this sentence and reading it aloud twice:

- *Some people think video games are a negative _____ on children.*

Ask:

Q *What is the missing word? Why do you think that? Turn to your partner.*

PROMPT: "I think [*influence*] is the missing word because...."

Have volunteers share their thinking with the class. Then reread the sentence, replacing the blank with the vocabulary word.

Discuss the remaining sentences the same way.

Teacher Note

You might invite partners to work together to create their own "What's the Missing Word?" sentences and have them share their sentences with the class.

Week 24 Overview

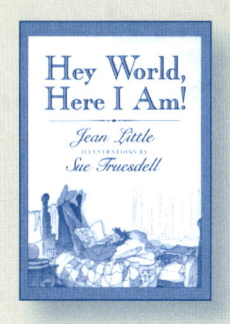

"**Mrs. Buell**" in *Hey World, Here I Am!*
by Jean Little,
illustrated by Sue Truesdell
(HarperTrophy, 1990)

Words Taught

dilapidated

cantankerous

disposition

lose your nerve

trickle

vexed

Word-learning Strategies

- Recognizing idioms (review)
- Recognizing words with multiple meanings (review)

Words Reviewed: defenseless, disperse, drastic, procedure, tranquil

DO AHEAD

- Prior to Day 5, collect these word cards for Ongoing Review: 103, 114, 119, 121 and 124.

Grade Five | 523

Week 24 ▶ Day 1

Day 1

Introduce *Dilapidated*, *Cantankerous*, and *Disposition*

Materials

- "Mrs. Buell" in *Hey World, Here I Am!*
- Chart paper
- A marker

Words Taught

dilapidated
Dilapidated means "old, broken, and in very bad condition."

cantankerous
Cantankerous means "grouchy or disagreeable."

disposition
Someone's disposition is his or her usual mood, or the way he or she usually acts or behaves.

INTRODUCE AND PRACTICE USING *DILAPIDATED*

▶ **1 Introduce and Define *Dilapidated***

Review "Mrs. Buell."

Remind the students that at the beginning of the story the narrator describes Buells, the corner store where she buys candy and comic books, and an encounter she has with the owner, Mrs. Buell.

Open the book to page 42, and read the first two sentences of the story aloud.

Tell the students that the first word they will learn today is *dilapidated* and that *dilapidated* means "old, broken, and in very bad condition." Explain that the store is old, run-down, and not very clean; it is dilapidated.

524 | Making Meaning® Vocabulary

Have the students say the word *dilapidated*, and then write it on a sheet of chart paper.

2. Do the Activity "Imagine That!"

Explain that something that is dilapidated has deteriorated. It was once new and in good condition, but over time it has become old or has been broken and is in very bad condition.

> **Teacher Note**
> You might review that *deteriorate* means "become worse."

Give examples of dilapidated things you have seen. (You might say, "There is a dilapidated building downtown that has been abandoned. The dilapidated building has broken windows and missing doors, and the sign has fallen off. I have a dilapidated copy of my favorite book at home. It has a worn cover, torn pages, and faded pictures.")

Have the students close their eyes and imagine:

- *You are driving through the country. You see a dilapidated barn in a field.*

Use "Think, Pair, Share" to discuss:

Q *What does the dilapidated barn look like?* [pause] *Open your eyes and turn to your partner.*

PROMPT: "The dilapidated barn…."

In the same way, discuss:

- *You are looking through a trunk in your attic. You find a dilapidated photo album.*
- *You are walking to school. You see a dilapidated car parked on the side of the street.*

Review the pronunciation and meaning of the word.

Week 24 ▶ Day 1

INTRODUCE AND PRACTICE USING *CANTANKEROUS*

▶ 3 Introduce and Define *Cantankerous*

Open to page 42 again, and review that Mrs. Buell is the owner of the corner store. Read the first three sentences of the second paragraph aloud.

Tell the students that the next word they will learn today is *cantankerous* and that *cantankerous* means "grouchy or disagreeable." Explain that, because Mrs. Buell never smiles or asks how her customers are doing, people think she is cantankerous, or grouchy.

Have the students say the word *cantankerous*, and write it on the chart.

▶ 4 Play "Is Tulip's Family Cantankerous?"

Remind the students that cantankerous people are grouchy, grumpy, or cranky. Explain that animals can also be cantankerous. For example, a wild bear might be cantankerous when it is looking for food or protecting its cub. A cat might be cantankerous when it is sick and does not want to be bothered.

Tell the students that you will describe a person or pet in Tulip's family and partners will discuss whether the person or pet is cantankerous or not and why they think so.

Begin with:

- *Tulip's Great Aunt Fern grunts at people instead of saying hello, and she yells at anyone who tries to help her.*

Ask:

Q *Do you think Great Aunt Fern is cantankerous? Why? Turn to your partner.*

PROMPT: "Great Aunt Fern [is/is not] cantankerous because…."

526 | Making Meaning® Vocabulary

In the same way, discuss:

- *Tulip's Uncle Elmer is very sociable. He always jokes and laughs with Tulip and her friends.*
- *Tulip's dog Daisy is very old and does not like to be petted. Whenever a person comes near her, she growls and backs away.*

Review the pronunciation and meaning of the word.

◄ **Teacher Note**
You might review that *sociable* means "friendly or liking to be with others."

INTRODUCE AND PRACTICE USING *DISPOSITION*

5 **Introduce and Define** *Disposition*

Open to page 43. Tell the students that the last word they will learn today is *disposition*, and explain that someone's disposition is his or her usual mood, or the way he or she usually acts or behaves.

Explain that Mrs. Buell has a cantankerous disposition—she is usually grouchy and mean—but on one occasion her disposition changes. Explain that, as you read about that occasion, you want the students to listen for the way that Mrs. Buell's disposition changes. Then read page 43 aloud, stopping after, "And I wasn't looking straight at her."

Discuss as a class:

Q *How does Mrs. Buell's disposition change? Why do you say that?*

PROMPT: "Mrs. Buell's disposition changes [when/because]…."

Explain that Mrs. Buell's disposition, or the way she usually acts and behaves, changes when the narrator falls down. The usually grouchy Mrs. Buell becomes caring and kind. She picks up the narrator, sits her down, and cleans and bandages her scraped knee.

Have the students say the word *disposition*, and write it on the chart.

Grade Five | 527

Week 24 ▶ Day 1

6 Discuss *Disposition*

Remind the students that someone's disposition is his or her usual mood, or the way he or she usually acts or behaves. Explain that, if someone is usually happy and good natured, we say that person has a happy or cheerful disposition. If someone is usually mean and does not like to be around people, we say the person has a cantankerous or unfriendly disposition. If someone is shy, we say the person has a quiet or bashful disposition.

Explain that you will read a description of a person or animal. Partners will discuss what word they would use to describe the disposition of the person or animal and why.

Read the following description aloud twice:

- *Selma is always happy. She makes everyone around her laugh and smile, and she tries to see the good in everyone.*

Ask:

Q *What word would you use to describe Selma's disposition? Why? Turn to your partner.*

PROMPT: "I would use the word [*happy*] to describe Selma's disposition, because…."

In the same way, discuss:

- *Cal always feels uneasy about trying new things. He is afraid to go to new places and will not go near animals because he does not want to be bitten.*

- *Gertrude is a cat who loves people. She rubs against people's legs, sits in their laps, and licks their hands.*

Discuss as a class:

Q *What words would you use to describe your own disposition? Why?*

PROMPT: "I would use the words [*friendly* and *helpful*] to describe my disposition because…."

Review the pronunciation and meaning of the word.

Teacher Note

If the students struggle to answer the question, think aloud about words you would use to describe Selma's disposition. (You might say, "I would use the word *happy*, *cheerful*, or *friendly* to describe Selma's disposition, because she is always happy and because she makes the people around her happy, too.") Then read the next description.

Teacher Note

Support struggling students by asking questions such as, "What word would you use to describe someone who is uneasy about trying new things? Why?" and "Do you think Cal has a [nervous/anxious/worried] disposition? Why?"

Teacher Note

Possible responses include *gentle*, *loving*, and *affectionate*.

Making Meaning® Vocabulary

Day 2

Week 24 ▶ Day 2

Review *Dilapidated, Cantankerous,* and *Disposition*

Words Reviewed

dilapidated
Dilapidated means "old, broken, and in very bad condition."

cantankerous
Cantankerous means "grouchy or disagreeable."

disposition
Someone's disposition is his or her usual mood, or the way he or she usually acts or behaves.

Materials
- Word chart from Day 1

REVIEW THE WORDS

1 Briefly Review the Words

Review the pronunciation and meaning of each word.

Use "Think, Pair, Share" to discuss:

Q *Which of the words we learned yesterday might you use if you were writing a story about a grouchy old man? How might you use the word?* [pause] *Turn to your partner.*

PROMPT: "I might use the word [*cantankerous*]. I might write…."

◀ **Teacher Note**

If the word *cantankerous* is the students' only response, ask, "How might you use the word [*disposition/dilapidated*] in a story about a grouchy old man?"

Grade Five | 529

Week 24 ▶ Day 2

PRACTICE USING THE WORDS

2 Discuss What You Might Say or Do

Explain that you will describe a situation and partners will discuss what they might say or do in it.

Begin with:

- *Your little brother wants to give you a gift. He hands you a dilapidated toy fire truck.*

Ask:

Q *What might you say or do if your little brother gave you a dilapidated toy fire truck as a gift? Why? Turn to your partner.*

PROMPT: "If my little brother gave me a dilapidated toy fire truck, I might [give it back to him] because…."

In the same way, discuss:

- *You are walking home from school, and a cantankerous dog is blocking the sidewalk ahead of you.*

Q *What might you say or do if a cantankerous dog were blocking the sidewalk? Why? Turn to your partner.*

PROMPT: "If a cantankerous dog were blocking the sidewalk, I might [cross the street] because…."

- *You are in a play. You are playing a character that has a nervous disposition.*

Q *What might you say or do to show that your character had a nervous disposition? Why? Turn to your partner.*

PROMPT: "To show that my character had a nervous disposition, I might [pretend to bite my nails] because…."

Day 3

Week 24 ▶ Day 3

Introduce "Lose Your Nerve," *Trickle*, and *Vexed*

Words Taught

lose your nerve (p. 44)
"Lose your nerve" means "lose the courage or confidence to do something."

trickle (p. 44)
A *trickle* is "a small amount." *Trickle* also means "move or flow in small groups or amounts."

vexed
Vexed means "irritated or annoyed."

Materials

- "Mrs. Buell" in *Hey World, Here I Am!*
- Word chart from Day 1
- A marker

INTRODUCE AND PRACTICE USING "LOSE YOUR NERVE"

1 Introduce and Define "Lose Your Nerve" and Review Idioms

Open to page 43 of "Mrs. Buell," and review that Mrs. Buell briefly becomes gentle and nice, but her cantankerous disposition quickly returns. Read the paragraph that starts at the bottom of page 43 and continues on the top of page 44 aloud, emphasizing the words "lost my nerve."

Tell the students that they will start their vocabulary work today by discussing the idiom "lose your nerve." Explain that "lose your nerve" means "lose the courage or confidence to do something." Explain that the narrator wants to thank Mrs. Buell for helping her and buy some candy, but she loses her nerve, or loses her courage or confidence, and leaves the store instead.

Grade Five | 531

Week 24 ▶ Day 3

Have the students say "lose your nerve," and write it on the chart.

Remind the students that an *idiom* is "an expression or phrase that means something different from what it appears to mean." Explain that when we say people "lose their nerve," we do not mean that they actually lose a nerve in their bodies. Instead, we mean that they lose the courage or confidence to do something.

Teacher Note ▶

If you started an idiom chart, add "lose your nerve" to it.

2 ▶ Discuss "Lose Your Nerve"

Review that, when people intend to do things, but lose the courage or confidence to do them, we say they lose their nerve. Explain that most people lose their nerve at one time or another, and give a few examples of times you have lost your nerve. (You might say, "I was going to learn how to drive a motorcycle, but I lost my nerve. I was afraid the motorcycle would tip over. Last weekend I went to the lake to go swimming, but when I felt how cold the water was, I lost my nerve and didn't go in.")

Use "Think, Pair, Share" to discuss:

Q *When have you lost your nerve? Why did you lose your nerve?* [pause] *Turn to your partner.*

Teacher Note ▶

Support struggling students by asking questions such as, "When have you wanted to try something new, but lost your nerve?" and "When have you wanted to talk to someone about something, but lost your nerve?"

PROMPT: "I wanted to [learn how to rollerblade], but I lost my nerve, because…."

Review the pronunciation and meaning of the word.

INTRODUCE AND PRACTICE USING *TRICKLE*

3 ▶ Introduce and Define *Trickle*

Open the book to page 44. Review that the children in the neighborhood do not pay much attention to Mrs. Buell or think about her much. Then read the third full paragraph on page 44 aloud, beginning with, "She never took days off." Emphasize the word *trickle*.

Week 24 ▶ Day 3

Tell the students that the next word they will learn is *trickle* and that a *trickle* is "a small amount." Explain that Mrs. Buell does not make much money in her store because she mainly sells stuff to kids. She earns only a trickle, or small amount, of change each day.

4 ▶ Discuss *Trickle*

Explain that we can use the word *trickle* to talk about a small amount of many different things. For example, we might squirt a trickle, or small amount, of mustard on a sandwich. We might notice a trickle of ketchup on someone's chin. We might see a trickle of paint on the floor.

Discuss as a class:

Q *When might you use a trickle of glue?*

PROMPT: "You might use a trickle of glue when [you are gluing something little that doesn't need much glue]."

In the same way, discuss:

Q *Would you wear a raincoat if the weather forecast said we could expect a trickle of rain? Why or why not?*

PROMPT: "I [would/would not] wear a raincoat if the forecast said we could expect a trickle of rain because…."

Have the students say the word *trickle*, and write it on the chart.

5 ▶ Discuss Another Meaning of *Trickle*

Remind the students that words often have more than one meaning, and explain that *trickle* can also mean "move or flow in small groups or amounts." Explain that, when something trickles, it moves little by little. For example, if you are collecting food for a charity and people are not very willing to donate, donations might trickle in, or arrive in small amounts.

Week 24 ▸ Day 3

Discuss as a class:

Q *What do we mean when we say people are trickling out of a building?*

PROMPT: "When people are trickling out of a building, we mean [only one or two people are coming out of the building at a time]."

Explain that the word *trickle* is often used to talk about liquids that flow or move slowly. For example, blood might trickle from a scrape, water might trickle out of a leaking faucet, or the last drops of milk might trickle out of a milk carton.

Ask:

Q *What other liquids might trickle? When might they trickle? Turn to your partner.*

PROMPT: "[Ketchup] might trickle [out of a bottle] when…."

Review the pronunciation and meaning of the word.

INTRODUCE AND PRACTICE USING *VEXED*

6 Introduce and Define *Vexed*

Open to page 45. Review that one day the narrator walks into Buells and sees a man and a woman she does not know. Read pages 45–46 aloud, beginning with, "I think I must have made a sound then" on page 45, and ending with, "'If you don't want anything, beat it,' she told me" on page 46. Use a sharp, irritated tone when reading what the daughter says.

Tell the students that the last word they will learn today is *vexed* and that *vexed* means "irritated or annoyed." Explain that Mrs. Buell's daughter is vexed, or irritated or annoyed, because she has to clean out her mother's store and because Harry did not lock the door.

Have the students say the word *vexed*, and write it on the chart.

7 ▶ Discuss Being Vexed

Explain that all of us are vexed, or irritated or annoyed, from time to time, and give examples of times you have been vexed. (You might say, "I was vexed when my dog chewed a hole in my favorite blanket. I was really annoyed with him. I was vexed when I arrived at the store and found out that it had closed early.")

Ask:

Q *When have you been vexed? Why were you vexed? Turn to your partner.*

PROMPT: "I was vexed when [my model airplane broke] because…."

Review the pronunciation and meaning of the word.

EXTENSION

Illustrate Idioms

Write the following idioms on the board, or post the idioms chart where students can see it:

   Blow off steam

   Get on board

   Hair-raising

   On pins and needles

   Lose your nerve

Direct the students' attention to the idioms, and remind them that they have learned these idioms. Review that an *idiom* is "an expression or phrase that means something different from what it appears to mean," and review the meaning of each idiom.

Give each student a sheet of paper. Have each student choose one of the idioms and illustrate either what it appears to mean or what it actually means.

Teacher Note

You might have students continue the activity by investigating the meaning of and illustrating other idioms such as, "lend a hand," "bend over backwards," "bite off more than you can chew," "chip on his shoulder," and "crack someone up."

Week 24 ▶ Day 4

Day 4

Review "Lose Your Nerve," *Trickle*, and *Vexed*

Materials
- Word chart from Day 3
- A marker

Words Reviewed

lose your nerve
"Lose your nerve" means "lose the courage or confidence to do something."

trickle
A *trickle* is "a small amount." *Trickle* also means "move or flow in small groups or amounts."

vexed
Vexed means "irritated or annoyed."

REVIEW THE WORDS

1 Briefly Review the Words

Review the pronunciation and meaning of each word.

Ask:

Q *Which of the words we learned yesterday might you use when you are talking with your friends or family? How might you use the word? Turn to your partner.*

PROMPT: "I might use the word [*vexed*] when I'm talking with [my annoying cousin]. I might say…."

Week 24 ▸ Day 4

PRACTICE USING THE WORDS

▷ 2 Do the Activity "Which Word Goes With?"

Tell the students that partners will do the activity "Which Word Goes With?" Review that you will write a word on the board and partners will discuss which of the vocabulary words they learned yesterday goes with the word you write. Then you will ask some pairs to share their thinking with the class.

Write the words *hot sauce* on the board, and read them aloud. Use "Think, Pair, Share" to discuss:

Q *Which of yesterday's words do you think goes with* hot sauce? *Why do you think that?* [pause] *Turn to your partner.*

PROMPT: "I think ['lose your nerve'] goes with *hot sauce* because…."

Write the word *audience* on the board, and read the word aloud.

Use "Think, Pair, Share" to discuss:

Q *Which of yesterday's words do you think goes with* audience? *Why do you think that?* [pause] *Turn to your partner.*

PROMPT: "I think [*trickle*] goes with *audience* because…."

When most pairs have finished talking, ask one or two pairs to share their thinking with the class.

Remember that there are no right or wrong responses. What is important is that the students explain the thinking behind their associations and demonstrate an understanding of the word's meaning.

Teacher Note

If the students struggle to answer the questions, think aloud about associations you might make and why. (You might say, "I think 'lose your nerve' goes with *hot sauce*, because you might think you want to taste it, but then you lose your nerve at the last second. I think *trickle* goes with *hot sauce*, too, because you can trickle hot sauce on your food. I think *vexed* can go with *hot sauce* also, because if you put too much hot sauce on your food, you might be vexed.") Then discuss the word *audience* as a class, rather than in pairs.

Teacher Note

If the students struggle to make associations, think aloud about associations you might make, or ask questions such as, "What places might you see an audience trickle into or out of? Why might an audience trickle out of a show?" "How might 'lose your nerve' go with *audience*? When might someone lose her nerve in front of an audience?" and "How might the word *vexed* go with *audience*? Why might an audience become vexed during a movie? If you were in an audience, what might someone do to vex you?"

Teacher Note

For a crossword puzzle you can use to review words taught during weeks 23 and 24, visit Developmental Studies Center's website at www.devstu.org.

Grade Five | 537

Week 24 ▶ Day 5

Day 5

Ongoing Review

Materials
- Pocket chart
- Word cards 103, 114, 119, 121, 124

Words Reviewed

defenseless
Defenseless means "without defense, helpless, or unprotected."

disperse
Disperse means "scatter in different directions."

drastic
Drastic means "harsh, extreme, or very severe."

procedure
A *procedure* is "a way to do something, or method of doing it, especially by a series of steps."

tranquil
Tranquil means "calm or peaceful."

REVIEW THE WORDS

1 Display the Word Cards and Briefly Review the Words

Review the pronunciation and meaning of the words.

PRACTICE USING THE WORDS

2 Play "Finish the Story"

Tell the students that partners will play "Finish the Story." Explain that you will tell a story, leaving off the last word. Point to the word chart, and explain that partners will finish the story by choosing the word on the chart that makes the best ending for it.

Begin by reading the following story aloud twice:

- *Emma's father is teaching her how to fish. Emma carefully watches how her father ties a hook to her fishing line so that she can learn the _____. (procedure)*

Ask:

Q *Which word makes the best ending for the story? Why? Turn to your partner.*

PROMPT: "I think [*procedure*] makes the best ending because…."

Retell the story, adding the word *procedure* at the end.

Continue the activity using the following stories:

- *Emma casts her fishing line into the lake and waits for a bite. She leans against a rock and enjoys the breeze and the warmth of the sun on her face. She thinks to herself, "This place is so _____." (tranquil)*

- *Emma is startled when she feels a tug on her line. She screams and yells for her father. Her father says, "Emma, it's just the wind. Your reaction is a bit _____." (drastic)*

- *Emma settles down and tries again. While she is waiting for a fish to take the bait, she sticks her toes in the water. Tiny tadpoles swim toward her feet, and when she wiggles her toes, the tadpoles suddenly _____. (disperse)*

- *While Emma is watching the tadpoles, her father catches a fish. When he pulls the fish out of the water, Emma feels a bit sad because now the fish is_____. (defenseless)*

Week 24 ▶ Day 5

CLASS VOCABULARY PROGRESS ASSESSMENT

As you observe the students, ask yourself:

- Are the students able to choose the best word to finish each story?
- Are they able to use the words to explain their thinking?
- Are they using the words spontaneously and accurately in conversations outside of vocabulary time?

For more information about reviewing and practicing the words, see "Retaining the Words" on pages xviii–xix.

INDIVIDUAL VOCABULARY PROGRESS ASSESSMENT

Before continuing with week 25, take this opportunity to assess individual students' understanding of words taught in weeks 21–24 by administering "Word Check 6" (BLM28). Please refer to pages 630–631 for instructions on administering the assessment.

STUDENT SELF-ASSESSMENT

In addition to or in place of the Individual Vocabulary Progress Assessment, have the students evaluate their understanding of words taught in weeks 21–24 through this self-assessment (BLM30). For instructions on administering the assessment, see pages 634–635.

Week 25

Overview

"Zoo"
by Edward D. Hoch

Words Taught

significant

insignificant

intrigue

cluster

grotesque

throng

Word-learning Strategy

- Recognizing antonyms (review)

Words Reviewed: ascend, deteriorate, heartless, inundate, resolve

DO AHEAD

- Prior to Day 5, collect these word cards for Ongoing Review: 109, 116, 125, 126, and 129.

Grade Five

Week 25 ▶ Day 1

Day 1

Introduce *Significant, Insignificant,* and *Intrigue*

Materials

- "Zoo" (see pages 559–561)
- Chart paper
- A marker
- (Optional) *Making Meaning Student Response Book*

Words Taught

significant
Significant means "very important or noticeable."
Something significant matters a lot to you.

insignificant
Insignificant means "not very important or not noticeable."
Something insignificant does not matter a lot to you.

intrigue
Intrigue means "fascinate or stir up curiosity or interest."

INTRODUCE AND PRACTICE USING *SIGNIFICANT*

1 Introduce and Define *Significant*

Teacher Note

You might have the students bring their *Making Meaning Student Response Books* to the rug and follow along as you read from the story.

Briefly review "Zoo."

Review that children look forward each year to the arrival of Professor Hugo's Interplanetary Zoo. Then read the first paragraph on page 559 aloud.

Tell the students that the first word they will learn today is *significant* and that *significant* means "very important or noticeable." Explain that something significant matters a lot to you. Explain that August 23 is a significant, or very important, date to the children because it is the day Professor Hugo's zoo comes to town.

542 | Making Meaning® Vocabulary

Discuss as a class:

Q *What is a day or date that is significant, or very important, to you? Why?*

PROMPT: "[Next Friday] is a significant day because [I am going camping after school]."

Have the students say the word *significant*, and then write it on a sheet of chart paper.

2 Discuss Significant People and Changes

Remind the students that *significant* means "very important."

Ask:

Q *Who are some significant people in your life? Why are they significant? Turn to your partner.*

PROMPT: "[My mom and dad] are significant people in my life because…."

Review that *significant* can also mean "noticeable." Explain that, when we say there has been a significant change in something, we mean there has been a noticeable or very obvious change. For example, dying her hair blue would make a significant change in a friend's appearance. You would notice that. Building a brand new gymnasium at our school would be a significant change to the school.

Use "Think, Pair, Share" to discuss:

Q *What might be a significant, or noticeable, change we could make to our classroom?* [pause] *Turn to your partner.*

PROMPT: "A significant change to our classroom might be [painting all the walls bright blue]."

Review the pronunciation and meaning of the word.

Week 25 ▶ Day 1

INTRODUCE AND PRACTICE USING *INSIGNIFICANT*

3 **Introduce and Define *Insignificant* and Review Antonyms**

Tell the students that the next word they will learn today is *insignificant*. Have the students say *insignificant*, and then write it on the chart.

> **Teacher Note**
>
> If you started an antonym chart, add *significant* and *insignificant* to it.

Explain that *significant* and *insignificant* are antonyms, or words with opposite meanings. Then discuss as a class:

Q *If* significant *means "very important or noticeable" and* significant *and* insignificant *are antonyms, what do you think* insignificant *means?*

PROMPT: "I think *insignificant* means ['not very important or not noticeable']."

If necessary, explain that *insignificant* means "not very important or not noticeable." Explain that something insignificant does not matter a lot to you.

> **Teacher Note**
>
> You might explain that *in-* in *insignificant* is a prefix that means "not" and that *insignificant* means "not significant, or not very important or not noticeable." The prefix *in-* is formally taught in grade 4 of *Making Meaning Vocabulary*.

4 **Play "Significant or Insignificant?"**

Remind the students that something significant matters a lot to you because it is very important. Something insignificant does not matter a lot to you because it is not very important.

Explain that partners will play "Significant or Insignificant?" Explain that you will describe a situation the students might face. Partners will discuss whether the situation would be significant, or very important, to them, or insignificant, or not very important, and why. Explain that partners may disagree, and that is fine.

Begin with:

- *You get mud all over your favorite sneakers.*

Ask:

Q *Would getting mud all over your favorite sneakers be significant or insignificant to you? Why? Turn to your partner.*

PROMPT: "Getting mud all over my favorite sneakers would be [significant/insignificant] to me because…."

In the same way, discuss:

- *You find out that your best friend was not truthful with you about something.*

Q *Would finding out that your best friend was not truthful with you be significant or insignificant? Why? Turn to your partner.*

PROMPT: "Finding out that my best friend was not truthful with me would be [significant/insignificant] because…."

- *Your parents decide you cannot watch TV on school nights.*

Q *Would not being allowed to watch TV on school nights be significant or insignificant to you? Why? Turn to your partner.*

PROMPT: "Not being allowed to watch TV on school nights would be [significant/insignificant] to me because…."

Review the pronunciation and meaning of the words.

INTRODUCE AND PRACTICE USING *INTRIGUE*

5 Introduce and Define *Intrigue*

Review that every year crowds of people come to see the peculiar creatures in Professor Hugo's Interplanetary Zoo. Read the second paragraph on page 559 aloud.

◀ **Teacher Note**

Using a previously taught word, like *peculiar*, to discuss a text is an excellent way to review the word. You might review that *peculiar* means "strange or odd."

Week 25 ▶ Day 1

Tell the students that the last word they will learn today is *intrigue* and that *intrigue* means "fascinate or stir up curiosity or interest." Explain that Professor Hugo's zoo intrigues, or fascinates, the people of Earth. Point out that people are so intrigued by, or curious about, the creatures on the ship that they wait in long lines and pay money to see them.

Teacher Note ▶

You might explain that *intrigue* and *fascinate* are synonyms and add the words to the synonym chart.

Have the students say the word *intrigue*, and write it on the chart.

6 ▶ Discuss *Intrigue*

Remind the students that something that intrigues them fascinates them or stirs up their curiosity or interest, and give examples of things that intrigue you or someone you know. (You might say, "Dolphins intrigue me because I think the way they communicate is very interesting. Venus flytraps also intrigue me because I think carnivorous plants are fascinating. My son is intrigued by outer space, especially the possibility that there might be life on other planets. He reads a lot about space, and he spends hours looking through his telescope at the stars and planets.")

Use "Think, Pair, Share" to discuss:

Q *What is something that intrigues you? Why does it intrigue you?* [pause] *Turn to your partner.*

Teacher Note ▶

Support struggling students by asking questions such as, "What is something you have seen or heard about on TV that really interests you?" "What is something you would like to learn more about?" and "What is something you are curious about?"

PROMPT: "[Gila monsters] intrigue me because…."

Review the pronunciation and meaning of the word.

546 | Making Meaning® Vocabulary

Day 2

Week 25 ▸ Day 2

Review *Significant, Insignificant,* and *Intrigue*

Words Reviewed

significant
Significant means "very important or noticeable."
Something significant matters a lot to you.

insignificant
Insignificant means "not very important or not noticeable."
Something insignificant does not matter a lot to you.

intrigue
Intrigue means "fascinate or stir up curiosity or interest."

Materials
- Word chart from Day 1

REVIEW THE WORDS

1 Briefly Review the Words

Review the pronunciation and meaning of each word.

Discuss as a class:

Q *Would a week of gray, rainy weather have a significant effect on your mood? Why?*

PROMPT: "A week of gray, rainy weather [would/would not] have a significant effect on my mood because…."

In the same way, discuss:

Q *If you had an insignificant stain on your shirt, would you change it? Why?*

Grade Five | 547

Week 25 ▶ Day 2

PROMPT: "If I had an insignificant stain on my shirt, I [would/would not] change it because…."

Q *What do you do when something intrigues you? Why?*

PROMPT: "If something intrigues me, I [try to find out more about it] because…."

PRACTICE USING THE WORDS

2 ▶ Do the Activity "Tell Me a Story"

Explain that partners will do the activity "Tell Me a Story." Review that you will tell the beginning of a story that includes one of the vocabulary words. The students will use what they know about the word and their imaginations to make up an ending for the story.

Begin by reading the following story aloud twice, slowly and clearly:

- *A scientist named Lora Lookabout disappeared while exploring a rain forest. When she was found a year later, there was a significant change in her appearance. The significant change was….*

Use "Think, Pair, Share" to discuss:

Q *How might you finish the story? What significant change might there be in the explorer's appearance?* [pause] *Turn to your partner.*

PROMPT: "The significant change was…."

In the same way, discuss:

- *Ten-year-old Joaquin is easily upset. He becomes upset over insignificant things like….*

Q *How might you finish the story? What insignificant things might upset Joaquin?* [pause] *Turn to your partner.*

PROMPT: "Joaquin becomes upset over insignificant things like…."

- *"I like reading about animals that are big or dangerous," said Nora. "I'm especially intrigued by…."*

Q *How might you finish the story? What big or dangerous animals might especially intrigue Nora? [pause] Turn to your partner.*

PROMPT: "I'm especially intrigued by…."

Week 25 ▶ Day 3

Day 3

Introduce *Cluster*, *Grotesque*, and *Throng*

Materials

- "Zoo" (see pages 559–561)
- Word chart from Day 1
- A marker
- (Optional) *Making Meaning Student Response Book*

Words Taught

cluster (p. 559)
Cluster means "stand or grow close together."

grotesque
Grotesque means "ugly or strange in a way that is unpleasant or frightening."

throng
A *throng* is "a large crowd of people."

INTRODUCE AND PRACTICE USING *CLUSTER*

▶ **1 Introduce and Define *Cluster***

Remind the students that crowds of children and adults come to see the peculiar creatures in Professor Hugo's zoo. Then read this sentence from the third paragraph of page 559 aloud, emphasizing the word *clustered*, "The citizens of Earth clustered around as Professor Hugo's crew quickly collected the waiting dollars, and soon the good Professor himself made an appearance, wearing his many-colored rainbow cape and top hat."

Teacher Note
You might have the students bring their *Making Meaning Student Response Books* to the rug and follow along as you read from the story.

Tell the students that the first word they will learn today is *cluster* and that *cluster* means "stand or grow close together." Explain that people cluster, or stand close together, around the crew so that they can be among the first to pay their dollars and see the creatures up close.

Have the students say the word *cluster*, and write it on the chart.

550 | Making Meaning® Vocabulary

Week 25 ▶ Day 3

2 Discuss *Cluster*

Review that when people cluster, they stand close together. Remind the students that in the story, people cluster around the crew because they are eager to pay their money and see the creatures. Point out that in school students sometimes cluster around a teacher because they are curious to hear what the teacher is saying or see what she is doing.

Use "Think, Pair, Share" to discuss:

Q *What is another time or place you might see people cluster, or stand close together?* [pause] *Turn to your partner.*

PROMPT: "People might cluster [at a bus stop while they are waiting to get on the bus]."

Remind the students that *cluster* also means "grow close together," and explain that grapes cluster, or grow close together, on a vine.

Discuss as a class:

Q *If you saw flowers clustered on a bush, what would that look like?*

PROMPT: "Flowers clustered on a bush would look like…."

Review the pronunciation and meaning of the word.

ELL Note

You might invite a group of volunteers to cluster around you and then have the students discuss what they notice.

Teacher Note

Support struggling students by asking questions such as, "When might you see people cluster [in the hallways at school/in the cafeteria/on the playground/at a movie theater/on a sidewalk or street corner/at a zoo or park]?"

INTRODUCE AND PRACTICE USING *GROTESQUE*

3 Introduce and Define *Grotesque*

Review that the professor brought the horse-spider people of Kaan in his interplanetary zoo. Then read the last paragraph beginning on page 559 aloud, beginning with, "And the crowds slowly filed by…."

Tell the students that the next word they will learn today is *grotesque* and that *grotesque* means "ugly or strange in a way that is unpleasant or frightening."

Grade Five | 551

Week 25 ▶ Day 3

Explain that, to the people of Earth, these creatures that look like horses but run up walls like spiders are grotesque, or ugly or strange in a way that is unpleasant and frightening. They are both horrified and intrigued by these grotesque creatures.

Have the students say the word *grotesque*, and write it on the chart.

4 ▶ Do the Activity "Imagine That!"

Remind the students that something grotesque is ugly or strange in a way that is unpleasant or frightening, and explain that science fiction stories, like "Zoo," sometimes have grotesque creatures, like the horse-spider people of Kaan.

Ask the students to imagine they are writing a science fiction story about a grotesque creature from outer space. Have them close their eyes and picture in their minds what their grotesque creature might look like. Help them form mental pictures by asking these questions, pausing between the questions to give them time to think:

Q *What size is your grotesque creature?*

Q *What do the creature's eyes look like? Mouth? Nose? Teeth?*

Q *What does its body look like?*

Q *How does your grotesque creature move?*

Then say "turn to your partner" and have partners take turns describing their grotesque creatures.

PROMPT: "My grotesque creature…."

Review the pronunciation and meaning of the word.

INTRODUCE AND PRACTICE USING *THRONG*

5 Introduce and Define *Throng*

Remind the students that the crowd pays money to see the horse-spider people of Kaan. Then read the following sentence from page 560 aloud, "All day long it went like that, until ten thousand people had filed by the barred cages set into the side of the spaceship."

Tell the students that the last word they will learn today is *throng* and that a *throng* is "a large crowd of people." Review that, by the end of the day, a throng, or large crowd, of ten thousand people had seen the horse-spider people.

Have the students say the word *throng*, and write it on the chart.

◀ **Teacher Note**

You might explain that *throng* and *crowd* are synonyms and add the words to the synonym chart.

6 Discuss Throngs of People

Review that a *throng* is a "large crowd of people," and give a few examples of times you have seen or been in a throng of people. (You might say, "When I was at the beach, a throng of people was waiting in line to rent umbrellas. Whenever I visit the aquarium, there is always a throng of people in front of the otter exhibit. On TV, you see throngs of people at baseball games and other sporting events.")

Ask:

Q *When have you seen or been in a throng of people? Turn to your partner.*

PROMPTS: "I saw a throng of people…" or "I was in a throng of people when…."

Review the pronunciation and meaning of the word.

◀ **Teacher Note**

You might explain that the word *throng* can also be a verb and that, when we say people throng to a place, we mean that large numbers of people go to the place (for example, during the holidays people throng to shopping malls).

Week 25 ▶ Day 4

Day 4

Review *Cluster*, *Grotesque*, and *Throng*

Materials
- Word chart from Day
- A marker

Words Reviewed

cluster
Cluster means "stand or grow close together."

grotesque
Grotesque means "ugly or strange in a way that is unpleasant or frightening."

throng
A *throng* is "a large crowd of people."

REVIEW THE WORDS

1 Briefly Review the Words

Review the pronunciation and meaning of each word.

Ask:

Q Which of the words we learned yesterday do you think was especially interesting or fun to talk about? Why? Turn to your partner.

PROMPT: "I think the word [*grotesque*] was especially [interesting/fun] to talk about because…."

PRACTICE USING THE WORDS

2 Think More About the Words

Explain that you will ask the students questions that include yesterday's words and words they learned earlier.

Ask:

Q *Would you be mystified if you woke up one morning and there was a crowd of people clustered around your bed? Why? Turn to your partner.*

PROMPT: "I [would/would not] be mystified if I woke up and there was a crowd of people clustered around my bed because…."

◀ **Teacher Note**
You might review that *mystify* means "confuse, bewilder, or puzzle."

In the same way, discuss:

Q *What might a throng of people gathered outside a building be clamoring for? Turn to your partner.*

PROMPT: "A throng of people gathered outside a building might be clamoring for…."

◀ **Teacher Note**
You might review that *clamor* means "demand or ask for something loudly."

Q *Would you be petrified if you saw a grotesque shadow on your bedroom wall? Turn to your partner.*

PROMPT: "I [would/would not] be petrified if I saw a grotesque shadow on my bedroom wall because…."

◀ **Teacher Note**
You might review that *petrified* means "unable to move or act because you are extremely frightened."

Week 25 ▶ Day 5

Day 5

Ongoing Review

Materials
- Pocket chart
- Word cards 109, 116, 125, 126, 129

Words Reviewed

ascend
Ascend means "go up, move up, or climb."

deteriorate
Deteriorate means "become worse."

heartless
Heartless means "without heart (kindness or compassion), unkind, or cruel."

inundate
Inundate means "fill or cover completely with water." *Inundate* also means "overwhelm with a large amount of something."

resolve
Resolve means "find an answer or solution to a problem."

REVIEW THE WORDS

▶ **1** **Display the Word Cards and Briefly Review the Words**
Review the pronunciation and meaning of the words.

Week 25 ▶ Day 5

PRACTICE USING THE WORDS

▶2 Play "Make a Choice"

Explain that partners will use the words to play "Make a Choice." Point to the word *ascend*, and tell the students that they will play the first round of the game with the word *ascend*.

Read the following question aloud twice:

Q *Which of these would you use to ascend to the fifth floor of a building: the stairs or the elevator? Why? Turn to your partner.*

PROMPT: "To ascend to the fifth floor of a building, I would use [the stairs] because…."

In the same way, discuss:

[deteriorate]

Q *Which of these might cause the flow of traffic to deteriorate: road construction or a pedestrian crossing the street? Why? Turn to your partner.*

PROMPT: "I think [road construction] would cause the flow of traffic to deteriorate because…."

[heartless]

Q *Which of these people is heartless: a woman who ignores an abandoned kitten or a woman who takes an abandoned kitten to an animal shelter? Why? Turn to your partner.*

PROMPT: "I think [a woman who ignores an abandoned kitten] is heartless because…."

◀ **Teacher Note**

For a fully written-out example of the activity, see page 88.

ELL Note

Rather than having the students choose between two scenarios, you might have them discuss each one individually by first asking, "Would you use the stairs to ascend to the fifth floor of a building? Why?" and then asking, "Would you use an elevator to ascend to the fifth floor of a building? Why?"

Grade Five | 557

Week 25 ▸ Day 5

[inundate]

Q *Which of these would you rather be inundated with: homework or chores? Why? Turn to your partner.*

PROMPT: "I would rather be inundated with [homework] because…."

[resolve]

Q *Which of these people would you ask for advice if you wanted to resolve a problem: your best friend or your parents? Why? Turn to your partner.*

PROMPT: "If I wanted to resolve a problem, I would ask [my parents] for advice because…."

Short Story

Zoo

by Edward D. Hoch

The children were always good during the month of August, especially when it began to get near the twenty-third. It was on this day that Professor Hugo's Interplanetary Zoo settled down for its annual six-hour visit to the Chicago area.

Before daybreak the crowds would form, long lines of children and adults both, each one clutching his or her dollar, and waiting with wonderment to see what race of strange creatures the Professor had brought this year.

In the past they had sometimes been treated to three-legged creatures from Venus, or tall, thin men from Mars, or even snakelike horrors from somewhere more distant. This year, as the great round ship settled slowly to earth in the huge tri-city parking area just outside of Chicago, they watched with awe as the sides slowly slid up to reveal the familiar barred cages. In them were some wild breed of nightmare—small, horselike animals that moved with quick, jerking motions and constantly chattered in a high-pitched tongue. The citizens of Earth clustered around as Professor Hugo's crew quickly collected the waiting dollars, and soon the good Professor himself made an appearance, wearing his many-colored rainbow cape and top hat. "Peoples of Earth," he called into his microphone.

The crowd's noise died down as he continued. "Peoples of Earth, this year you see a real treat for your single dollar—the little-known horse-spider people of Kaan—brought to you across a million miles of space at great expense. Gather around, study them, listen to them, tell your friends about them. But hurry! My ship can remain here only six hours!"

And the crowds slowly filed by, at once horrified and fascinated by these strange creatures that looked like horses but ran up the walls

continues

Zoo

continued

of their cages like spiders. "This is certainly worth a dollar," one man remarked, hurrying away. "I'm going home to get the wife."

All day long it went like that, until ten thousand people had filed by the barred cages set into the side of the spaceship. Then, as the six-hour limit ran out, Professor Hugo once more took microphone in hand. "We must go now, but we will return next year on this date. And if you enjoyed our zoo this year, phone your friends in other cities about it. We will land in New York tomorrow, and next week on to London, Paris, Rome, Hong Kong, and Tokyo. Then on to other worlds!"

He waved farewell to them, and as the ship rose from the ground the Earth peoples agreed that this had been the very best Zoo yet….

Some two months and three planets later, the silver ship of Professor Hugo settled at last onto the familiar jagged rocks of Kaan, and the queer horse-spider creatures filed quickly out of their cages. Professor Hugo was there to say a few parting words, and then they scurried away in a hundred different directions, seeking their homes among the rocks.

In one, the she-creature was happy to see the return of her mate and offspring. She babbled a greeting in the strange tongue and hurried to embrace them. "It was a long time you were gone! Was it good?"

And the he-creature nodded. "The little one enjoyed it especially. We visited eight worlds and saw many things."

continues

Zoo

continued

The little one ran up the wall of the cave. "On the place called Earth it was the best. The creatures there wear garments over their skins, and they walk on two legs."

"But isn't it dangerous?" asked the she-creature.

"No," her mate answered. "There are bars to protect us from them. We remain right in the ship. Next time you must come with us. It is well worth the nineteen commocs it costs."

And the little one nodded. "It was the very best Zoo ever…."

Week 26 Overview

"12 seconds from death"
in *Heroes*
by Paul Dowswell
(Usborne, 2007)

Words Taught

plummet

knowledgeable

lurch

impact

billow

engrossed

Word-learning Strategies

- Using context to determine word meanings (review)

- Recognizing words with multiple meanings (review)

Words Reviewed: cantankerous, engrossed, on pins and needles, vexed, wide-eyed

DO AHEAD

- Prior to Day 1, write the context sentences from "12 seconds from death" on the board or a sheet of chart paper or make a transparency of the sentences (BLM20). (See Step 1 on page 564.)

- Prior to Day 1, review More Strategy Practice on pages 569–570. Write the "Use the Clues" sentences on the board or a sheet of chart paper or make a transparency of the sentences (BLM21).

- Prior to Day 5, collect these word cards for Ongoing Review: 131, 134, 140, 144, and 156.

Grade Five | 563

Week 26 ▶ Day 1

Day 1

Introduce *Plummet, Knowledgeable,* and *Lurch*

Materials

- "12 seconds from death"
- Chart paper
- A marker
- Context sentences or transparency (BLM20; see Step 1 below)
- (Optional) *Making Meaning Student Response Book*
- (Optional) "Use the Clues" sentences or transparency (BLM21; see More Strategy Practice on pages 569–570)
- (Optional) Overhead projector and marker

Words Taught

plummet (p. 22)
Plummet means "fall suddenly and very quickly from a high place." *Plummet* also means "decrease suddenly by a large amount."

knowledgeable
If you are knowledgeable about something, you know a lot about it.

lurch (p. 23)
Lurch means "lean or roll suddenly forward or to one side."

INTRODUCE AND PRACTICE USING *PLUMMET*

▶ **1 Introduce *Plummet* and Use Context Clues to Figure Out Its Meaning**

Teacher Note ▶

You might have the students bring their *Making Meaning Student Response Books* to the rug and follow along as you read from the story.

Briefly review "12 seconds from death."

Display the transparency or write the context sentences below on the board or a sheet of chart paper, and underline the word *plummet*:

> Richard Maynard was making his first jump. He had paid a substantial fee to <u>plummet</u> from 3,600m (12,000ft), strapped to Mike Smith, a skilled parachute instructor.

Review that, at the beginning of the story, Richard Maynard is in a plane getting ready to skydive for the first time. Then read the second paragraph on page 22 aloud, emphasizing the word *plummet*.

564 | Making Meaning® Vocabulary

Tell the students that the first word they will learn today is *plummet*. Remind them that sometimes you can figure out the meaning of a word by rereading the sentence that includes the word, or the sentence before or after it, looking for clues.

Direct the students' attention to the context sentences, and explain that, as you reread the sentence that includes the word *plummet* and the sentence before it, you want them to think about what the word might mean and what words in the sentences are clues to the meaning of *plummet*.

Read the sentences aloud twice, slowly and clearly. Then point to the word *plummet*, and discuss as a class:

Q *Based on what you just heard, what do you think the word* plummet *might mean? What words in the sentences are clues to the meaning of* plummet?

PROMPT: "I think *plummet* might mean ['fall']. The words ['jump'] and ['from 3,600m'] are clues that tell you that *plummet* means 'fall.'"

If necessary, explain that *plummet* means "fall suddenly and very quickly from a high place." Explain that, when people skydive, they jump out of a plane and then plummet, or fall suddenly and very quickly, until they open their parachutes to slow their descent. Point out that the words "jump," "from 3,600m," and "strapped to Mike Smith, a skilled parachute instructor" are clues to the meaning of *plummet*.

Have the students say the word *plummet*, and then write it on a sheet of chart paper.

2 Discuss *Plummet*

Review that *plummet* means "fall suddenly and very quickly from a high place." Explain that during an avalanche, snow and ice plummet, or fall suddenly and very quickly, down the side of a mountain. During wars, planes that are shot down plummet into the ground or ocean.

Teacher Note

If the students do not immediately determine the meaning of *plummet* from the context, give them the definition, rather than have them guess.

Teacher Note

You might underline the context clues. For more practice with context clues, see More Strategy Practice on pages 569–570.

Teacher Note

You might explain that *plummet* and *fall* are synonyms. If you started a synonym chart, add *plummet* and *fall* to it. (You might also tell the students that *plunge* is a synonym of *plummet* and *fall*. The word *plunge* is taught in grade 4 of *Making Meaning Vocabulary*.)

Discuss as a class:

Q *When might a bird plummet from the sky?*

PROMPT: "A bird might plummet from the sky when…."

3 ▶ Introduce Another Meaning of *Plummet*

Review that words often have more than one meaning, and explain that *plummet* can also mean "decrease suddenly by a large amount." Explain that, if the cost of an airplane ticket decreased in a week from $400 to $100, we would say the cost of the ticket plummeted. If the number of people attending baseball games dropped in a week from fifty thousand people to five thousand people, we would say attendance at the games plummeted.

4 ▶ Play "Is It Plummeting?"

Remind the students that *plummet* can mean "fall suddenly and very quickly from a high place" or "decrease suddenly by a large amount." Explain that you will describe a situation and partners will decide whether or not someone or something in the situation is plummeting and why they think so.

Begin with:

- *A mountain climber loses her footing and tumbles hundreds of feet down the mountain.*

Ask:

Q *Is the mountain climber plummeting? Why? Turn to your partner.*

PROMPT: "The mountain climber [is/is not] plummeting because…."

In the same way, discuss:

- *A feather drifts slowly out of a bird's nest onto the ground.*
- *The temperature goes from 60 degrees to 10 degrees in a few hours.*
- *The price of a slice of pizza drops from $1.50 to $1.45 over the weekend.*

INTRODUCE AND PRACTICE USING *KNOWLEDGEABLE*

5 Introduce and Define *Knowledgeable*

Remind the students that, when Richard Maynard made his first parachute jump, he did not jump alone. Then reread this sentence from the second paragraph of page 22 aloud, "He had paid a substantial fee to plummet from 3,600m (12,000ft), strapped to Mike Smith, a skilled parachute instructor."

Tell the students that the next word they will learn is *knowledgeable*, and explain that, if you are knowledgeable about something, you know a lot about it. Explain that Mike Smith is knowledgeable about skydiving—he knows a lot about it. That is why Richard Maynard paid Mike Smith to jump with him.

Have the students say the word *knowledgeable*, and write it on the chart.

◀ **Teacher Note**

You might point out that the words *know* and *knowledge* are part of the word *knowledgeable*.

6 Discuss Things We Are Knowledgeable About

Remind the students that, if you are knowledgeable about something, you know a lot about it. For example, doctors are knowledgeable, or know a lot, about the human body and how it works. Auto mechanics are knowledgeable about the way cars work and how to fix them.

Ask:

Q *What is a topic or subject you are knowledgeable about? Turn to your partner.*

PROMPT: "I am knowledgeable about…."

Have volunteers share their thinking.

Follow up by asking:

Q *How did you become knowledgeable about [mummies]?*

PROMPT: "I became knowledgeable about [mummies] by…."

Discuss as a class:

Q *What is a subject or topic you would like to become more knowledgeable about? Why?*

PROMPT: "I would like to become more knowledgeable about [the ocean] because…."

Review the pronunciation and meaning of the word.

INTRODUCE AND PRACTICE USING *LURCH*

7 Introduce and Define *Lurch*

Review that, when O'Brien saw that Smith and Maynard's parachute did not open, he dove quickly through the air to catch the plummeting pair and release their parachute. Read the following sentences from page 23 aloud, emphasizing the word *lurch*: "But diving at the same speed was extremely difficult. O'Brien would be within arm's length of the falling men and then lurch out of reach."

Tell the students that the last word they will learn today is *lurch* and that *lurch* means "lean or roll suddenly forward or to one side." Explain that, when O'Brien was close enough to Smith and Maynard to open their parachute, his body would lurch, or roll suddenly forward or to one side, making the men suddenly out of reach.

Have the students say the word *lurch*, and write it on the chart.

8 Do the Activity "Imagine That!"

Have the students close their eyes and imagine:

- *You are on an amusement park ride. The ride turns and twists and causes you to lurch from side to side.*

Use "Think, Pair, Share" to discuss:

Q *What might it look or feel like to lurch from side to side on an amusement park ride? [pause] Open your eyes and turn to your partner.*

PROMPT: *"Lurching from side to side might [look/feel] like…."*

Invite a volunteer to act out the way lurching from side to side on a ride might look.

In the same way, discuss:

- *You are riding in a car. The car stops suddenly, causing you to lurch forward.*

MORE STRATEGY PRACTICE

Play "Use the Clues"

Display the transparency, or write the following sentences on the board or a sheet of chart paper, leaving blanks as shown:

> As the wrecking ball struck the windows, the glass _____ into tiny pieces and then fell to the ground like rain.
>
> After many hours, the demolition was finally _____, and the construction crew began to sort through the rubble and haul it away.

Explain that partners will play the game "Use the Clues," in which they use clues to figure out a word that is missing from a sentence. Direct the students' attention to the example sentences, and review that, as you read the sentences aloud, you want them to think about what the missing word might be and what words in the sentences are clues to the missing word. Remind them that more than one word might make sense as the missing word and that the word does not have to be a vocabulary word.

continues

Week 26 ▶ Day 1

Teacher Note

Listen as partners share. If the students suggest words that are not supported by the context, call for attention. Provide a word and point out the context clues. Then have the students discuss the second example in pairs. ▶

Teacher Note

Although *broke* and *shattered* are logical responses, the students may reasonably argue that *burst*, *exploded*, or another word is also supported by the clues in the sentence. ▶

Teacher Note ▶

Possible responses include *done*, *finished*, *completed*, and *through*.

MORE STRATEGY PRACTICE *continued*

Read the first sentence aloud twice, slowly and clearly, saying "blank" for the missing word.

Use "Think, Pair, Share" to discuss:

Q *What's the missing word? What words are clues to the missing word?* [pause] *Turn to your partner.*

Have a few pairs share their ideas with the class.

If necessary, explain that the missing word might be *broke* or *shattered* and that the words "struck the window" and "tiny pieces" are clues that the window was destroyed.

Discuss the second sentence the same way.

570 | Making Meaning® Vocabulary

Day 2

Week 26 ▶ Day 2

Review *Plummet, Knowledgeable,* and *Lurch*

Words Reviewed

plummet
Plummet means "fall suddenly and very quickly from a high place." *Plummet* also means "decrease suddenly by a large amount."

knowledgeable
If you are knowledgeable about something, you know a lot about it.

lurch
Lurch means "lean or roll suddenly forward or to one side."

Materials
- Word chart from Day 1

REVIEW THE WORDS

1 Briefly Review the Words

Review the pronunciation and meaning of each word.

Discuss as a class:

Q *Which of the words might you use in a story about two friends who build their own spaceship? How might you use the words?*

PROMPT: "I might use the word [*knowledgeable*]. I might write that [the boys were really knowledgeable about outer space and rocket technology]."

Grade Five | 571

Week 26 ▶ Day 2

PRACTICE USING THE WORDS

2▶ Do the Activity "Create a Sentence"

Explain that partners will do the activity "Create a Sentence." Review that partners will work together to create sentences that use the vocabulary words.

Point to the word *plummet* on the chart, and review that *plummet* means "fall suddenly and very quickly from a high place" and "decrease suddenly by a large amount."

Use "Think, Pair, Share" to discuss:

Q *How might you use the word* plummet *in a sentence?* [pause] *Turn to your partner.*

Have a few pairs share their sentences.

Follow up by asking:

Q *Does it make sense to say, ["The kite plummeted from the sky when the wind suddenly stopped blowing"]? Why?*

In the same way, have partners work together to use *knowledgeable* and *lurch* in sentences.

Teacher Note

Support struggling students by asking questions such as, "When might you see something plummet from the sky?" and "What might cause a person's math grade to plummet?" If they continue to struggle, provide a sentence starter such as, "The kite plummeted from the sky when…" or "Attendance at school plummeted when…."

Teacher Note

[*knowledgeable*] Support struggling students by asking questions such as, "What is something you are knowledgeable about?" and "How might someone become knowledgeable about a topic?" If they continue to struggle, provide a sentence starter such as, "I am knowledgeable about…" or "Jay became knowledgeable about plants by…."

[*lurch*] Support struggling students by asking questions such as, "What might cause a car to lurch?" and "When have you lurched to avoid something?" If they continue to struggle, provide a sentence starter such as, "A car might lurch when…" or "I lurched forward when…."

Day 3

Week 26 ▸ Day 3

Introduce *Impact, Billow,* and *Engrossed*

Words Taught

impact (p. 24)
Impact means "a violent collision or the forceful striking of one thing against another." *Impact* also means "the effect that something has on a person or thing."

billow (p. 25)
Billow means "swell out or puff up."

engrossed
Engrossed means "so interested in something that you do not notice anything else."

Materials
- "12 seconds from death"
- Word chart from Day 1
- A marker
- (Optional) *Making Meaning Student Response Book*

INTRODUCE AND PRACTICE USING *IMPACT*

1 Introduce and Define *Impact*

Show pages 24–25. Point to page 24, and remind the students that this page shows the sequence of the events in the story. Remind the students that Ronnie O'Brien saw Richard Maynard and Mike Smith spinning out of control and tried to help them. Then read the following caption from page 24 aloud, emphasizing the word *impact*: "2,500–1,500m (7,000–5,000ft) O'Brien catches up with tandem divers but slips underneath them (25 seconds to impact)."

Tell the students that the first word they will learn today is *impact* and that *impact* means "a violent collision or the forceful striking of one thing against another." Explain that "25 seconds to impact" means that O'Brien had only 25 seconds to reach Maynard and

◂ **Teacher Note**
You might have the students bring their *Making Meaning Student Response Books* to the rug and follow along as you read from the story.

Grade Five | 573

Smith before impact, or before the moment when Maynard and Smith would violently collide with the ground.

Have the students say the word *impact*, and write it on the chart.

2 ▶ Discuss *Impact*

Explain that an impact, or violent collision, often causes a loud noise or damage. For example, in a car accident the impact of one car hitting another causes a loud smashing noise and results in dented fenders and other damage. The impact of a baseball bat striking a ball causes a loud cracking sound.

Ask:

Q *If you ran into a tree with your bike, what sounds might you hear at the moment of impact? Turn to your partner.*

PROMPT: "At the moment of impact, I might hear…."

Discuss as a class:

Q *What damage might the impact cause?*

PROMPT: "The impact might cause…."

In the same way, discuss:

Q *How might the impact feel?*

PROMPT: "The impact might feel…."

3 ▶ Discuss Another Meaning of *Impact*

Remind the students that words often have more than one meaning and that sometimes the meanings are very different. Explain that *impact* can also mean "the effect that something has on a person or thing."

Explain that something that has an impact on you changes the way you feel, think, or behave. For example, seeing a sad movie might have an impact on, or effect, the way you feel, changing your happy mood to a sad mood. Seeing a TV show about global warming might have an impact on the way you think, causing you to want to do something to fight global warming. Discovering that exposure to the sun can lead to skin cancer might have an impact on your behavior, causing you to use sunscreen regularly.

Ask:

Q *What might be the impact, or effect, of eating too much candy? Turn to your partner.*

PROMPT: "The impact of eating too much candy might be…."

In the same way, discuss:

Q *If you have a problem, what might be the impact of talking about the problem with a friend? Turn to your partner.*

PROMPT: "The impact of talking about the problem might be…."

Review the pronunciation and meaning of the word.

◀ **Teacher Note**

Support struggling students by asking questions such as, "What impact might eating too much candy have on your teeth? The way your body feels? Your energy level? Your weight?"

INTRODUCE AND PRACTICE USING *BILLOW*

4 Introduce and Define *Billow*

Review that O'Brien finally caught up with Maynard and Smith and released Smith's parachute. Read the following sentence from page 25 aloud, emphasizing the word *billowed*, "With barely 12 seconds before they hit the ground, O'Brien found the handle, and the large main chute billowed out above them."

Tell the students that the next word they will learn today is *billow* and that *billow* means "swell out or puff up." Show pages 24–25 and point to the illustration on the bottom of page 24. Explain that when the parachute was released, it billowed, or swelled out or puffed up with air, above Maynard and Smith.

Have the students say the word *billow*, and write it on the chart.

Week 26 ▶ Day 3

5 ▶ Act Out Billowing Our Cheeks

Tell the students that sometimes people billow their cheeks, or puff them up with air, when they are holding their breath or blowing out candles on a birthday cake. Explain that you want partners to take turns acting out billowing their cheeks as if to blow out candles on a cake. Explain that afterwards you will ask a volunteer to show the class what it looks like to billow your cheeks.

Give partners a few moments to act out billowing their cheeks. Then have a volunteer act out billowing his cheeks for the class.

Discuss as a class:

Q *What did you see [Jordan] doing when [he] billowed [his] cheeks?*

PROMPT: "When [Jordan] billowed [his] cheeks, [he]…."

ELL Note

Acting out words or seeing words acted out is especially beneficial to English Language Learners, who may struggle to understand verbal definitions.

6 ▶ Do the Activity "Imagine That!"

Remind the students that a parachute billows, or swells out or puffs up, in the wind, and tell them that other things billow in the wind. Explain that you will ask the students to imagine a thing that is billowing. Then partners will discuss what they imagined.

Have the students close their eyes and imagine:

- *A flag billowing in the wind*

Use "Think, Pair, Share" to discuss:

Q *What might a flag billowing in the wind look like? Sound like? [pause] Open your eyes and turn to your partner.*

PROMPT: "A flag billowing in the wind might [look/sound] like…."

In the same way, discuss:

- *Clothes billowing on a clothesline*

Q *What might clothes billowing on a clothesline look like? Sound like? [pause] Open your eyes and turn to your partner.*

576 | Making Meaning® Vocabulary

PROMPT: "Clothes billowing on a clothesline might [look/sound] like…."

Discuss as a class:

Q *What else might billow in the wind?*

PROMPT: "[Sails on a boat] might billow in the wind."

Review the pronunciation and meaning of the word.

◀ **Teacher Note**

If the students struggle to answer the question, call for attention and think aloud about other things that might billow in the wind (for example, sheets, windsocks, and kites).

INTRODUCE AND PRACTICE USING *ENGROSSED*

7 Introduce and Define *Engrossed*

Review that O'Brien was able to release Maynard and Smith's parachute, and all three of the skydivers landed safely. Read the last paragraph on page 25 aloud.

Tell the students that the last word they will learn today is *engrossed* and that *engrossed* means "so interested in something that you do not notice anything else." Explain that Maynard was so engrossed, or interested, in the excitement of his jump that he did not realize that anything had gone wrong.

Have the students say the word *engrossed*, and write it on the chart.

8 Discuss Being Engrossed

Review that, when you are engrossed in something, you are very, very interested in it—so interested that you do not notice anything else. Explain that, when a person is engrossed in something, it can be difficult to get her attention, or it might seem like the person is ignoring you. Give examples of times you or someone you know has been engrossed. (You might say, "Last night I was so engrossed in reading your creative writing assignments that I forgot to eat dinner. This morning my husband was engrossed in an article in the newspaper. When I asked him if he wanted more coffee, he did not answer me.")

Grade Five | 577

Explain that we sometimes get engrossed in activities that we especially enjoy. Ask:

Q *What is an activity you get engrossed in? What happens when you get engrossed in the activity? Turn to your partner.*

PROMPT: "I get engrossed in [playing video games]. When I am engrossed in [my game], I…."

Review the pronunciation and meaning of the word.

Week 26 ▶ Day 4

Day 4

Review *Impact, Billow,* and *Engrossed*

Words Reviewed

impact
Impact means "a violent collision or the forceful striking of one thing against another." *Impact* also means "the effect that something has on a person or thing."

billow
Billow means "swell out or puff up."

engrossed
Engrossed means "so interested in something that you do not notice anything else."

Materials
- Word chart from Day 3
- A marker

REVIEW THE WORDS

1 ▶ Briefly Review the Words

Review the pronunciation and meaning of each word.

Ask:

Q *Which of the words we learned yesterday might you use in your writing? How might you use the word? Turn to your partner.*

PROMPT: "I might use the word [*billow*]. I might write…."

Grade Five | 579

Week 26 ▸ Day 4

PRACTICE USING THE WORDS

2 Play "Does That Make Sense?"

Explain that partners will play the game "Does That Make Sense?" Explain that you will read a scenario that includes one of the vocabulary words. Partners will decide whether or not the word makes sense in the scenario and why they think so.

Point to the word *impact* and explain that the first scenario includes the word *impact*.

Then read the following scenario aloud twice:

- *The scientist did an experiment to find out if adding salt to the soil would have an impact on a plant's growth.*

Ask:

Q *Does the word* impact *make sense in the scenario? Why do you think that? Turn to your partner.*

PROMPT: "The word *impact* [does/does not] make sense in the scenario because…."

In the same way, discuss:

[billow]

- *When Jen opened the window, the curtains billowed in the breeze.*

[engrossed]

- *Caleb was so engrossed in his book that he talked to anyone who walked by.*

Teacher Note

If the students struggle to answer the questions, call for attention. Reread the scenario aloud, and explain that *impact* does make sense. Explain that *impact* means "effect" and that the scientist wanted to see if adding salt to the soil would have a noticeable effect on the growth of plants. Then read the scenario that uses the word *billow* and discuss it in pairs.

Teacher Note

For a crossword puzzle you can use to review words taught during weeks 25 and 26, visit Developmental Studies Center's website at www.devstu.org.

580 | Making Meaning® Vocabulary

Day 5

Ongoing Review

Words Reviewed

cantankerous
Cantankerous means "grouchy or disagreeable."

engrossed
Engrossed means "so interested in something that you do not notice anything else."

on pins and needles
"On pins and needles" means "very nervous or uneasy."

vexed
Vexed means "irritated or annoyed."

wide-eyed
Wide-eyed means "with the eyes wide open, especially because you are amazed or surprised."

Materials
- Pocket chart
- Word cards 131, 134, 140, 144, 156

REVIEW THE WORDS

1 Display the Word Cards and Briefly Review the Words
Review the pronunciation and meaning of the words.

Week 26 ▶ Day 5

PRACTICE USING THE WORDS

2 Do the Activity "Describe the Character"

Explain that partners will do the activity "Describe the Character." Explain that you will read a scenario aloud and partners will discuss which vocabulary word or idiom best describes the main character of the scenario and why they think so.

Teacher Note ▶
For a fully written-out example of the activity, see page 223.

Explain that the main character of the first scenario is Elliott. Then read the following scenario aloud twice:

- At the amusement park, Elliott is waiting in line to ride the hair-raising "Tornado Twirler." As he watches the ride spin and twist around, he starts feeling nervous about going on the ride. The longer he waits in the line, the more nervous he becomes. (on pins and needles)

Teacher Note ▶
You might review that *hair-raising* means "exciting, thrilling, or terrifying."

Point to the vocabulary words and ask:

Q Which word or idiom best describes Elliott? Why? Turn to your partner.

PROMPT: "['On pins and needles'] best describes Elliott because…."

Teacher Note ▶
If the students struggle to answer the questions, call for attention, reread the scenario, and think aloud about which word or idiom best describes Elliott. (You might say, "I think 'on pins and needles' best describes Elliott, because when someone is on pins and needles, the person is nervous or anxious. Elliott is on pins and needles while he waits for his turn on the scary ride.") Then read the next scenario.

In the same way, discuss:

- After spending the day cleaning her house, Tabitha went out to dinner. When she got home, she discovered that her dog Prince had tracked mud all over the floors and furniture. "You are a bad dog, Prince," Tabitha scolded. "I am really angry with you." (vexed)

- Old Mr. Riverton is a grump. If you say hello to him, either he ignores you or grunts or snarls at you. (cantankerous or vexed)

- Lora is watching a scary movie. The movie intrigues her so much that she does not notice the spider crawling across her foot. (engrossed)

Teacher Note ▶
You might review that *intrigue* means "fascinate or stir up curiosity or interest."

- Carlos is at a magic show. With every trick the magician completes, Carlos becomes more amazed, and his eyes grow bigger and bigger. (wide-eyed)

582 | Making Meaning® Vocabulary

CLASS VOCABULARY PROGRESS ASSESSMENT

As you observe the students, ask yourself:

- Can the students identify the vocabulary words?
- Do their explanations show that they understand the words' meanings?
- Are they using the synonyms they are learning in their writing?

For more information about reviewing and practicing the words, see Retaining the Words on pages xviii–xix.

Week 27

Overview

Articles

"Is Dodge Ball Too Dangerous?"
by Dina Maasarani
from *TIME For Kids* (timeforkids.com, May 15, 2001)

"Turn It Off!"
by Kathryn R. Hoffman
from *TIME For Kids* (timeforkids.com, April 12, 2002)

Words Taught

disallow

fiddle

avid

participant

excessive

motivate

Word-learning Strategies

- Using the prefix *dis-* to determine word meanings (review)

- Recognizing antonyms (review)

- Using context to determine word meanings (review)

Words Reviewed: cluster, lose your nerve, significant, sufficient, vivid

DO AHEAD

- Prior to Day 1, collect a paperclip and a pencil. You and a student volunteer will use the objects to act out the word *fiddle*.

- Prior to Day 3, write the context sentences from "Turn It Off!" on the board or a sheet of chart paper or make a transparency of the sentences (BLM22). (See Step 1 on page 593.)

- Prior to Day 5, collect these word cards for Ongoing Review: 123, 130, 142, 145, and 148.

Grade Five | 585

Week 27 ▶ Day 1

Day 1

Introduce *Disallow*, *Fiddle*, and *Avid*

Materials

- "Is Dodge Ball Too Dangerous?" (see pages 603–604)
- "Turn It Off!" (see pages 605–606)
- Chart paper
- A marker
- A paperclip and a pencil (see Step 5 on page 588)
- (Optional) *Making Meaning Student Response Book*

Words Taught

disallow
Disallow means "not allow or ban."

fiddle (p. 605)
When you fiddle with something, you keep moving or touching it, especially because you are bored or nervous.

avid (p. 605)
If you are avid about something, you are very enthusiastic about it and you do it as much as possible.

INTRODUCE AND PRACTICE USING *DISALLOW*

1 ▶ Introduce *Disallow*

Teacher Note

You might have the students bring their *Making Meaning Student Response Books* to the rug and follow along as you read from the articles.

Briefly review "Is Dodge Ball Too Dangerous?"

Remind the students that many people think that dodge ball is too dangerous for kids to play at school. Read the following sentence from the first paragraph of the article aloud, "More and more schools are banning dodge ball, a game in which kids throw balls at other kids who have to avoid—or dodge—them."

Explain that dodge ball is disallowed in many schools, and tell the students that *disallow* is the first word they will learn today.

Ask the students to say the word *disallow*, and then write it on a sheet of chart paper.

586 | Making Meaning® Vocabulary

Week 27 ▶ Day 1

2 Use the Prefix *dis-* to Determine the Meaning of *Disallow* and Review Antonyms

Point to the prefix *dis-* in *disallow* on the chart, and review that *dis-* is a prefix that means "not" or "the opposite of." Explain that when you add *dis-* to the word *allow*, you make the word *disallow*.

Discuss as a class:

Q *Based on what you know about the prefix* dis- *and the word* allow, *what do you think* disallow *means? What happens when a game like dodge ball is disallowed?*

PROMPTS: "I think *disallow* means…" or "When a game like dodge ball is disallowed…."

Explain that *disallow* means "not allow or ban" and that *disallow* and *allow* are antonyms. Review that some schools have disallowed, or banned, dodge ball.

◀ **Teacher Note**

You might remind the students that they learned the word *ban* earlier and that something that is banned is not allowed. You might explain that *disallow* and *ban* are synonyms and add them to the synonym chart. If you started an antonym chart, add *allow* and *disallow* to it.

3 Discuss *Disallow*

Review that many schools disallow dodge ball because they consider it to be a dangerous game. Discuss as a class:

Q *What games are disallowed at our school? Why?*

PROMPT: "[Handball] is disallowed because [too many people were getting hurt]."

Explain that things other than games can be disallowed at school, and give a few examples of things that are disallowed at your school. (You might say, "Bringing toys and video games to school is disallowed at our school. Fighting is also disallowed.")

Use "Think, Pair, Share" to discuss:

Q *What other things are disallowed at school? Why?* [pause] *Turn to your partner.*

PROMPT: "[Taking food out of the lunch room] is disallowed because…."

Teacher Note

Support struggling students by asking questions such as, "What things are disallowed in the [hallways/lunchroom/library]?" "What things are disallowed on the playground?" and "What things are disallowed in our classroom?"

Grade Five | 587

Week 27 ▸ Day 1

Discuss as a class:

Q *What do your parents disallow at home? Why?*

PROMPT: "My parents disallow [watching TV before my homework is done] because…."

Teacher Note ▶ Review the pronunciation and meaning of the word.

If you started a chart of dis- words, add disallow to it.

INTRODUCE AND PRACTICE USING *FIDDLE*

4 Introduce and Define *Fiddle*

Briefly review "Turn It Off!"

Review that TV-Turnoff Week is a time when millions of TV screens go blank. Read the following sentence from the first paragraph of the article aloud, emphasizing the word *fiddling*, "But instead of fiddling with the remote or calling the cable company, avid TV watchers everywhere will take drastic action."

Teacher Note ▶

You might review that drastic means "harsh, extreme, or very severe."

Tell the students that the next word they will learn today is *fiddle*, and explain that, when you fiddle with something, you keep moving or touching it, especially because you are bored or nervous.

Explain that, when TV screens suddenly go blank, people sometimes fiddle with, or touch, the buttons on the remote control to try to turn the TV back on. Point out that during TV-Turnoff Week people do not need to fiddle with the remote, because nothing is actually wrong with their TVs. They choose to turn the TVs off.

Have the students say the word *fiddle*, and write it on the chart.

5 Discuss Fiddling with Things

Remind the students that we often fiddle with things, or keep moving them or touching them, when we are bored or nervous. Act out fiddling with a paperclip as if you are bored or nervous.

588 | Making Meaning® Vocabulary

Week 27 ▶ Day 1

Point out that, when people are bored or nervous, they might fiddle with other objects, like pens, pencils, coins, or rubber bands. Explain that you will ask a volunteer to act out fiddling with a pencil and that you want the students to watch carefully. Then have a volunteer act out fiddling with a pencil.

Discuss as a class:

Q *What did you see [Margaret] do when [she] fiddled with [her] pencil?*

PROMPT: "When [Margaret] fiddled with [her] pencil, [she]…."

Ask:

Q *What do you fiddle with when you are nervous or bored? Turn to your partner.*

PROMPT: "When I am nervous or bored, I fiddle with [my hair]."

Explain that people sometimes fiddle with broken things, or keep moving or touching them, to try to fix them or get them to work.

Discuss as a class:

Q *When have you or someone you know fiddled with something to try to fix it or to get it to work?*

PROMPT: "[My dad] fiddled with [the kitchen faucet when it was leaking]."

Review the pronunciation and meaning of the word.

ELL Note

Acting out words or seeing words acted out is especially beneficial to English Language Learners, who may struggle to understand verbal definitions.

INTRODUCE AND PRACTICE USING *AVID*

6 Introduce and Define *Avid*

Review that during TV-Turnoff Week, millions of people turn off their TVs. Then reread the second sentence of the article, emphasizing the word *avid*.

Grade Five | 589

Week 27 ▶ Day 1

Tell the students that the last word they will learn today is *avid*, and explain that, if you are avid about something, you are very enthusiastic about it and you do it as much as possible.

Explain that avid TV watchers are people who are very enthusiastic about TV and spend a lot of time watching it. Explain that TV-Turnoff Week challenges avid TV watchers to spend their time doing other activities, like riding their bikes or playing games with friends.

Discuss as a class:

Q *Do you consider yourself to be an avid TV watcher? Why?*

PROMPT: "I [do/do not] consider myself to be an avid TV watcher because…."

Have the students say the word *avid*, and write it on the chart.

7 Discuss Things We Are Avid About

Review that a person who is avid about something is very enthusiastic about it and does it as much as possible. Give examples of things you or someone you know is avid about. (You might say, "I'm avid about baseball. I love the game and go to as many games as I can during the summer. I'm also avid about reading. I'm especially avid about nonfiction. I really enjoy reading about real people and events. My son is avid about karate. He practices constantly and wants to become an expert one day.")

Use "Think, Pair, Share" to discuss:

Q *What is something you are avid about? What do you do that shows you are avid about it?* [pause] *Turn to your partner.*

PROMPT: "I am avid about [skateboarding]. I show I am avid by…."

Review the pronunciation and meaning of the word.

590 | Making Meaning® Vocabulary

Day 2

Review *Disallow*, *Fiddle*, and *Avid*

Words Reviewed

disallow
Disallow means "not allow or ban."

fiddle
When you fiddle with something, you keep moving or touching it, especially because you are bored or nervous.

avid
If you are avid about something, you are very enthusiastic about it and you do it as much as possible.

Materials
- Word chart from Day 1

REVIEW THE WORDS

1 Briefly Review the Words

Review the pronunciation and meaning of each word.

Ask:

Q *Which of the words we learned yesterday might you use in a conversation with your family or friends? How might you use the word? Turn to your partner.*

PROMPT: "I might use the word [*fiddle*] when I talk with [my little brother]. I might say…."

Grade Five | 591

Week 27 ▶ Day 2

PRACTICE USING THE WORDS

2 ▶ **Do the Activity "Which Word Goes With?"**

Tell the students that partners will do the activity "Which Word Goes With?" Review that you will write a word on the board and partners will discuss which of the words they learned yesterday goes with the word you write. Then you will ask some pairs to share their thinking with the class.

Write the words *baseball card* on the board, and read them aloud. Use "Think, Pair, Share" to discuss:

▶ **Q** *Which of yesterday's words do you think goes with* baseball card? *Why do you think that?* [pause] *Turn to your partner.*

PROMPT: "I think [*disallow*] goes with *baseball card* because…."

Write the word *radio* on the board, and read the word aloud.

Use "Think, Pair, Share" to discuss:

▶ **Q** *Which of yesterday's words do you think goes with* radio? *Why do you think that?* [pause] *Turn to your partner.*

PROMPT: "I think [*avid*] goes with *radio* because…."

When most pairs have finished talking, ask one or two pairs to share their thinking with the class.

Teacher Note

If the students struggle to answer the questions, think aloud about associations you might make and why. (You might say, "I think *disallow* goes with *baseball card* because baseball cards are disallowed at our school. I think *fiddle* goes with *baseball card,* too, because you might fiddle with a baseball card if you are nervous or bored. I think *avid* can go with *baseball card* also, because someone who is an avid baseball fan might collect baseball cards.") Then discuss the word *radio* as a class, rather than in pairs.

Teacher Note

If the students have trouble making associations, think aloud about associations you might make, or ask questions such as, "How might *disallow* go with *radio*? When or where might listening to a radio be disallowed?" "How might *fiddle* go with *radio*? Why might someone fiddle with a radio?" and "How might *avid* go with *radio*? Why might a person be avid about listening to the radio? What would a person who is avid about listening to a radio do?"

592 | Making Meaning® Vocabulary

Day 3

Week 27 ▶ Day 3

Introduce *Participant, Excessive,* and *Motivate*

Words Taught

participant (p. 605)
A *participant* is "someone who participates in, or takes part in, an activity or event."

excessive (p. 605)
Excessive means "too much or too great."

motivate
Motivate means "inspire and encourage someone to do something."

Materials

- "Turn It Off!" (see pages 605–606)
- Word chart from Day 1
- A marker
- Context sentences or transparency (BLM22; see Step 1 below)
- (Optional) *Making Meaning Student Response Book*
- (Optional) Overhead projector and marker

INTRODUCE AND PRACTICE USING *PARTICIPANT*

1 **Introduce *Participant* and Use Context Clues to Figure Out Its Meaning**

Briefly review "Turn It Off!"

Display the transparency or write the context sentences below on the board or a sheet of chart paper and underline the word *participants*:

> In the beginning, only a few thousand people took part. This year, there will be participants in every state and more than 12 countries.

Remind the students that TV-Turnoff Week is an annual event that was started in 1995. Then read the following sentences from the second paragraph of the article aloud, emphasizing the word *participants*: "In the beginning, only a few thousand people took

Teacher Note

You might have the students bring their *Making Meaning Student Response Books* to the rug and follow along as you read from the article.

Grade Five | 593

Week 27 ▶ Day 3

part. This year, there will be participants in every state and more than 12 countries."

Tell the students that the first word they will learn today is *participant*. Remind them that sometimes you can figure out the meaning of a word by rereading the sentence that includes the word, or the sentence before or after it, looking for clues.

Direct the students' attention to the context sentences, and explain that, as you reread the sentence that includes the word *participant*, you want them to think about what the word might mean and what words in the sentences are clues to the meaning of *participant*.

Read the sentences aloud twice, slowly and clearly. Then point to the word *participants* and discuss as a class:

Q *Based on what you just heard, what do you think the word* participant *might mean? What words in the sentences are clues to the meaning of* participant*?*

▶ **Teacher Note**

If the students do not immediately determine the meaning of *participant* from the context, give them the definition, rather than have them guess.

PROMPT: "I think *participant* means ['a person who does something with other people']. I think the words 'a few thousand people took part' are clues to the meaning of *participant*."

If necessary, explain that a *participant* is "someone who participates in, or takes part in, an activity or event." Point out that the words "people" and "took part" are clues to the meaning of *participant*. Explain that the number of participants, or people who take part in TV-Turnoff Week, gets larger every year.

▶ **Teacher Note**

You might underline the context clues.

Have the students say the word *participant*, and write it on the chart.

▶ **2** **Discuss Being a Participant**

Explain that all of us are participants in, or people who take part in, activities. Explain that at this moment the students are participants in a vocabulary lesson. At recess or during PE, they are participants in various games and activities.

594 | Making Meaning® Vocabulary

Ask:

Q *What is a fun activity you were a participant in recently? Turn to your partner.*

PROMPT: "A fun activity I was a participant in recently was…."

Discuss as a class:

Q *Why might a person not want to be a participant in an activity?*

PROMPT: "A person might not want to be a participant in an activity because…."

Review the pronunciation and meaning of the word.

INTRODUCE AND PRACTICE USING *EXCESSIVE*

3 Introduce and Define *Excessive*

Review that there are many groups, like the American Medical Association, that are concerned about the effects that watching too much television can have on people. Read the following sentence from "TV's Many Turnoffs" aloud, emphasizing the word *excessive*, "They point to studies that link excessive TV viewing to such problems as bad eating habits, lack of exercise, obesity, and violent behavior."

Tell the students that the next word they will learn today is *excessive* and that *excessive* means "too much or too great." Explain that studies have shown that watching an excessive amount of TV, or too much TV, might lead to health problems and violent behavior.

Have the students say the word *excessive*, and write it on the chart.

Week 27 ▶ Day 3

▶ 4 Discuss *Excessive*

Review that *excessive* means "too much or too great." Then ask:

Q *If a person uses an excessive amount of ketchup on his hamburger, what might that look like? Turn to your partner.*

PROMPT: "If a person uses an excessive amount of ketchup on his hamburger…."

Explain that, when a person does something a lot or too much, we say that the person does it excessively. Then ask:

Teacher Note ▶
The suffix *-ly* is formally taught in grade 4 of *Making Meaning Vocabulary*.

Q *If a person brushes her teeth excessively, what might that look like? Turn to your partner.*

PROMPT: "If a person brushes her teeth excessively, she might…."

In the same way, discuss:

Q *If a person talks excessively, what might that look like? Turn to your partner.*

PROMPT: "If a person talks excessively, he might…."

Review the pronunciation and meaning of the word.

INTRODUCE AND PRACTICE USING *MOTIVATE*

▶ 5 Introduce and Define *Motivate*

Remind the students that the TV-Turnoff Network is the organization that sponsors TV-Turnoff Week. Then read the first paragraph of "Enjoying Life, Unplugged" aloud.

Teacher Note ▶
The word *inspire* is taught in grade 4 of *Making Meaning Vocabulary*. *Inspire* means "make someone feel that he or she wants to do something and can do it."

Tell the students that the last word they will learn today is *motivate* and that *motivate* means "inspire and encourage someone to do something."

Explain that the goal of TV-Turnoff Week is to motivate, or inspire and encourage, people to participate in other activities so that they do not watch as much TV.

Have the students say the word *motivate*, and write it on the chart.

6 Discuss People Who Motivate Us

Review that *motivate* means "inspire and encourage someone to do something," and explain that teachers motivate, or encourage and inspire, their students to learn by creating interesting lessons and working with them to help them do their best work.

Explain that sometimes friends, family members, or other people motivate us, as well. Give examples of people who have motivated you and things they did to motivate you. (You might say, "My friend Christine motivated me to start running. She motivated me by running with me and encouraging me to participate in races. All of you motivate, or inspire, me to work hard to be the best teacher I can be. You motivate me by being eager to learn and by being curious about what we are studying.")

Use "Think, Pair, Share" to discuss:

Q *Who has motivated you to do something? What did he or she do to motivate you?* [pause] *Turn to your partner.*

PROMPT: "[My friend Todd] motivated me to [try karate]. [He] motivated me by…."

Discuss as a class:

Q *When have you motivated someone? What did you do to motivate the person?*

PROMPT: "I motivated [my friend Ernie to try out for Little League by telling him how much fun it was]."

Review the pronunciation and meaning of the word.

◀ **Teacher Note**

Support struggling students by asking questions such as, "Who has encouraged you to try something you did not think you could do? What did the person do to motivate you?" "What is something you have done with a friend that you would not have done on your own?" and "When has someone inspired you to try something new?"

Week 27 ▶ Day 4

Day 4

Review *Participant, Excessive,* and *Motivate*

Materials
- Word chart from Day 3
- A marker

Words Reviewed

participant
A *participant* is "someone who participates in, or takes part in, an activity or event."

excessive
Excessive means "too much or too great."

motivate
Motivate means "inspire and encourage someone to do something."

REVIEW THE WORDS

1 Briefly Review the Words

Review the pronunciation and meaning of each word.

Discuss a class:

Q *Which of the words we learned yesterday do you think was especially interesting or fun to talk about? Why?*

PROMPT: "I think the word [*motivate*] was especially [interesting/fun] to talk about because…."

598 | Making Meaning® Vocabulary

PRACTICE USING THE WORDS

2 Discuss "Would You?" Questions

Point to the word *participant* and ask:

Q *Would you get on board with being a participant in a rope-climbing contest? Why? Turn to your partner.*

PROMPT: "I [would/would not] get on board with being a participant in a rope-climbing contest because…."

◀ **Teacher Note**

You might review that "get on board" means "accept or go along with something."

In the same way, discuss:

[excessive]

Q *Would you regret eating an excessive amount of food? Why? Turn to your partner.*

PROMPT: "I [would/would not] regret eating an excessive amount of food because…."

◀ **Teacher Note**

You might review that *regret* means "feel sorry about something you have done and wish you had not done it."

[motivate]

Q *Would you be motivated to go to a party if you were feeling sick? Why? Turn to your partner.*

PROMPT: "I [would/would not] be motivated to go to a party if I were feeling sick because…."

Teacher Note

For a crossword puzzle you can use to review words taught during week 27, visit Developmental Studies Center's website at www.devstu.org.

Week 27 ▸ Day 5

Day 5

Ongoing Review

Materials
- Pocket chart
- Word cards 123, 130, 142, 145, 148

Words Reviewed

cluster
Cluster means "stand or grow close together."

lose your nerve
"Lose your nerve" means "lose the courage or confidence to do something."

significant
Significant means "very important or noticeable." Something significant matters a lot to you.

sufficient
Sufficient means "enough or adequate."

vivid
Vivid means "sharp and clear." *Vivid* also means "bright and strong."

REVIEW THE WORDS

▶ **1** **Display the Word Cards and Briefly Review the Words**
Review the pronunciation and meaning of the words.

PRACTICE USING THE WORDS

2 **Do the Activity "Imagine That!"**

Have the students imagine the following scene:

- *You are walking through the park. You see people clustering around a fountain.*

Ask:

Q *What do people clustering around a fountain look like? Turn to your partner.*

PROMPT: "People clustering around a fountain look like…."

Follow up by discussing as a class:

Q *Why might people cluster around a fountain?*

PROMPT: "People might cluster around a fountain because…."

In the same way, discuss:

- *You put your hand out to pet a baby alligator, but you lose your nerve.*

Q *Why might you lose your nerve? Turn to your partner.*

PROMPT: "I might lose my nerve because…."

- *You have just finished writing a report about your trip to the Grand Canyon. Your friend suggests that you include some pictures with your report.*

Q *Would including pictures with your report be a significant change? Why? Turn to your partner.*

PROMPT: "Including pictures [would/would not] be a significant change because…."

Week 27 ▶ Day 5

- *You have half an hour to get ready for school. You still need to get dressed, eat breakfast, brush your teeth, and finish your homework.*

Q *Is 30 minutes a sufficient amount of time to get ready for school? Why? Turn to your partner.*

PROMPT: "Thirty minutes [is/is not] a sufficient amount of time because…."

- *You walk outside after a rainstorm, and you see a vivid rainbow in the sky.*

Q *What does the vivid rainbow look like? Turn to your partner.*

PROMPT: "The vivid rainbow…."

INDIVIDUAL VOCABULARY PROGRESS ASSESSMENT

Take this opportunity to assess individual students' understanding of the words taught in weeks 25–27 by administering "Word Check 7" (BLM29). Please refer to pages 632–633 for instructions on administering the assessment.

STUDENT SELF-ASSESSMENT

In addition to or in place of the Individual Vocabulary Progress Assessment, have the students evaluate their understanding of the words taught in weeks 25–27 through this self-assessment (BLM30). For instructions on administering the assessment, see pages 634–635.

Article

by Dina Maasarani

from *TIME For Kids* (timeforkids.com, May 15, 2001)

Is Dodge Ball Too Dangerous?
Many schools are banning a gym game they say is too violent

Is dodge ball on the verge of being tossed out? Dodge ball, one of the most popular games in gym class, is now also being called one of the most dangerous. More and more schools are banning dodge ball, a game in which kids throw balls at other kids who have to avoid—or dodge—them. Now, the game itself is having to dodge some pretty serious criticism.

Why Ban Dodge Ball?
What's all the fuss about a game that's been played across the country for decades? School districts in states such as Texas, Virginia, Maine and Massachusetts have banned it because many educators and parents say dodge ball is a violent and aggressive game. They say a game where there is a "human target" makes it more likely for kids to get hurt.

Neil Williams, an Eastern Connecticut State University physical education professor, has created a Physical Education Hall of Shame. He considers dodge ball (also known as bombardment, burning ball, killer ball, prison ball, and ball chaser) the most shameful school sport on his list. "It allows the stronger kids to pick on and target the weaker kids," Williams says. Critics also complain the game is not a good form of exercise because it requires kids who are eliminated (or hit by the ball) to sit on the sidelines while others get to keep playing. "If a boy doesn't throw hard and make a hit, the other boys call him a girl," says Lilla Atherton, a fifth grader in Fairfax County, Virginia, where the game has been banned.

continues

Is Dodge Ball Too Dangerous?
continued

Dodge Ball Defenders
Fans of the classic game say it's simple and fun and helps kids improve their reflexes and hand-eye coordination. Dodge ball supporters also say injuries are rare because most gym teachers do not allow students to aim for the head and because most balls are made from foam or other soft materials. Martha Kupferschmidt, an official at the Murray school district in Utah, wonders why dodge ball is being singled out when other sports like football, kickball and wrestling are also aggressive. "If we are going to ban dodge ball for aggressiveness, we would have to look at a whole gamut of sports," she says.

While some adults are debating whether kids should be playing dodge ball, others are starting to play the game themselves. The first-ever world dodge ball indoor championship for adults was held in Schaumburg, Illinois in January. "Dodge Ball Day 2001" is scheduled for July 28, also in Illinois.

Changing the Rules of the Game
Some school districts that do not want to ban dodge ball have instead decided to change the rules to make it less violent. In several districts, kids who are hit with the ball get to re-enter the game so there are no hurt feelings. In other schools, kids aim at a deflated ball instead of other kids.

Article

by Kathryn R. Hoffman

from *TIME For Kids* (timeforkids.com, April 12, 2002)

Turn It Off!
Next week, millions of people will go TV-free. How about you?

On April 22, millions of TVs around the world will go blank. But instead of fiddling with the remote or calling the cable company, avid TV watchers everywhere will take drastic action. Entire families will go outside to ride bikes; groups of friends will play games. Will you join in—or will you just sit there and watch?

April 22–28 is TV-Turnoff Week. TV-Turnoff Network, a nonprofit organization, has promoted the annual event since 1995. In the beginning, only a few thousand people took part. This year, there will be participants in every state and more than 12 countries.

TV's Many Turnoffs

Each year, kids in the U.S. spend more time glued to the tube than doing anything else—except for sleeping! People have worried about the effects of TV ever since the 1940s, when television became popular. Over the years, health care groups like the American Academy of Pediatrics and the American Medical Association have voiced their concern. They point to studies that link excessive TV viewing to such problems as bad eating habits, lack of exercise, obesity and violent behavior.

Two weeks ago, a new study published in the journal *Science* gave fresh evidence of a connection between TV viewing and violence. Psychologist Jeffrey G. Johnson and his research team followed children in 707 families for 17 years. The researchers found that kids who watched more than one hour of TV a day were more likely than other kids to take part in aggressive and violent behavior as they grew older. Says Johnson, the link between TV, with all its violent shows, and aggressive behavior "has gotten to the point where it's overwhelming."

continues

Turn It Off!
continued

Others worry about the impact of commercials on kids. One study found that during four hours of Saturday-morning cartoons, TV networks ran 202 ads for junk foods. The steady stream of reminders to buy sugary soda, cereal and candy are one reason that more than one in eight American kids is overweight. Long hours sitting in front of the tube are another reason. "Almost anything uses more energy than watching TV," says Dr. William H. Dietz of the U.S. Centers for Disease Control and Prevention in Atlanta, Georgia.

Enjoying Life, Unplugged
TV-Turnoff Network wants to encourage life outside the box. "We're not anti-TV," says the group's director, Frank Vespe. The goal is to help kids tune into real life so that "they won't have time for TV."

But this is an adult speaking. Is it really possible to live without popular TV shows? Sarah Foote, of Burke, Virginia, says she made it through TV-Turnoff Week last year—and enjoyed herself! After a few days, says Sarah, 10, "I thought, 'Why did I ever need TV?'" Her brother Nathaniel, 8, agrees: "There are about 8,000 other things you can do."

Still, some kids can't picture life without TV. Christian Cardenas, 10, of New York City, doesn't plan on tuning out. "It entertains you on rainy days," he says.

Could you go without TV for a whole week? Says TV-Turnoff veteran Carly Cara, 11, of Niles, Illinois: "You're doing so many fun things that before you know it, it's over!"

Appendices

Making Meaning Vocabulary Lessons and Making Meaning

This table shows each week of *Making Meaning Vocabulary*, the text used during the week, and the corresponding *Making Meaning, Second Edition* week. We suggest that you teach each vocabulary week a week after its corresponding *Making Meaning* week.

Making Meaning Vocabulary	Read-aloud Text	Making Meaning
Week 1	*The Lotus Seed; Something to Remember Me By*	Unit 1: Week 1
Week 2	*Everybody Cooks Rice*	Unit 1: Week 2
Week 3	*Life in the Rain Forests*	Unit 2: Week 1
Week 4	"Follow That Ball!"; "All Work and No Play"	Unit 2: Week 2
Week 5	*Chinese Americans*	Unit 2: Week 3
Week 6	*Big Cats*	Unit 3: Week 1
Week 7	*Big Cats*	Unit 3: Week 2
Week 8	*The Summer My Father Was Ten; Uncle Jed's Barbershop*	Unit 4: Week 1
Week 9	*Star of Fear, Star of Hope*	Unit 4: Week 2
Week 10	*The Van Gogh Cafe:* "The Cafe," "The Possum"	Unit 5: Week 1
Week 11	"Speech Class"	Unit 5: Week 2
Week 12	"Eraser and School Clock"	Unit 5: Week 3
Week 13	*Richard Wright and the Library Card*	Unit 6: Week 1
Week 14	*Wildfires*	Unit 6: Week 2
Week 15	*Earthquakes*	Unit 6: Week 3
Week 16	"Copycats: Why Clone?"; "The Debate on Banning Junk Food Ads"	Unit 7: Week 1
Week 17	"All-girls' and All-boys' Schools: Better for Kids"; "Do Kids Really Need Cell Phones?"	Unit 7: Week 2
Week 18	"How to Make an Origami Cup"; "Ashton Hammerheads Schedule for July, 2008"; "Frontier Fun Park" Ticket Prices	Unit 7: Week 3
Week 19	*Survival and Loss: Native American Boarding Schools*	Unit 7: Week 4
Week 20	*Survival and Loss: Native American Boarding Schools*	Unit 7: Week 5
Week 21	*Letting Swift River Go*	Unit 8: Week 1
Week 22	*A River Ran Wild*	Unit 8: Week 2
Week 23	*Harry Houdini: Master of Magic*	Unit 8: Week 3
Week 24	*Hey World, Here I Am!* "Mrs. Buell"	Unit 8: Week 4
Week 25	"Zoo"	Unit 9: Week 1
Week 26	*Heroes:* "12 seconds from death"	Unit 9: Week 2
Week 27	"Is Dodgeball Too Dangerous?"; "Turn It Off!"	Unit 9: Week 3

Grade 5 Words and Definitions

This table shows the words taught in grade 5 in alphabetical order, the definition, the lesson in which the word is introduced, and the number of the word card.

Word	Definition	Lesson	Card
a shambles	When a place is a shambles, it is very messy or in complete disorder or ruin.	15	86
academic	*Academic* means "having to do with school, studying, and learning."	17	98
adapt	*Adapt* means "change your behavior or ideas because you are in a new situation."	5	28
advantage	An *advantage* is "something that is helpful or useful." An advantage can help you do something better or succeed at something.	6	35
apprehensive	*Apprehensive* means "uneasy or worried and slightly afraid."	13	75
ascend	*Ascend* means "go up, move up, or climb."	21	125
avid	If you are avid about something, you are very enthusiastic about it and you do it as much as possible.	27	159
ban	A *ban* is "a rule or law that says people must not do something." Something that is banned is not allowed.	5	26
batter	*Batter* means "pound repeatedly with heavy blows."	15	90
befuddled	*Befuddled* means "completely confused."	20	115
billow	*Billow* means "swell out or puff up."	26	155
blow off steam	"Blow off steam" means "do or say something that helps you get rid of energy or strong feelings."	4	23
blunt	*Blunt* means "not sharp or pointed." *Blunt* also means "straightforward and honest in what you say."	7	41
bundle	*Bundle* means "wrap or tie things together."	8	46
calamity	A *calamity* is "a terrible disaster."	14	80
cantankerous	*Cantankerous* means "grouchy or disagreeable."	24	140
churn	*Churn* means "stir or move about with force."	15	88
claim	*Claim* means "state as a fact something that may or may not be true."	5	27
clamor	*Clamor* means "demand or ask for something loudly."	1	1
clang	*Clang* means "make a loud, ringing sound."	23	133
clash	*Clash* means "fight or argue."	19	113
cluster	*Cluster* means "stand or grow close together."	25	148
compel	*Compel* means "force."	19	110
comply	*Comply* means "do what you are asked to do or what a law or rule requires you to do."	19	111
comrade	A *comrade* is "a good friend or companion."	11	61
conspicuous	*Conspicuous* means "obvious or noticeable." Something that is conspicuous stands out and can be seen easily.	10	58
consume/ consumer	*Consume* means "buy and use products and services." A *consumer* is "a person who consumes."	16	96
cuisine	A *cuisine* is "a style of cooking."	2	10
defenseless	*Defenseless* means "without defense, helpless, or unprotected."	19	114
delectable	*Delectable* means "delicious, or very good to taste or smell."	2	8
deliberately	*Deliberately* means "intentionally or on purpose."	20	118

Grade 5 Words and Definitions

Word	Definition	Lesson	Card
dependent	*Dependent* means "relying on or needing someone or something for help or support."	17	100
deprive	*Deprive* means "prevent from having something or take something away."	14	84
desert/deserter	*Desert* means "abandon, or leave someone or something that should not be left behind." A *deserter* is "a person who deserts."	11	66
desirable	*Desirable* means "worth having or wishing for."	16	93
deteriorate	*Deteriorate* means "become worse."	22	129
devastate	*Devastate* means "destroy or badly damage."	3	14
device	A *device* is "a tool, machine, or piece of equipment that does a particular job."	17	101
devour	*Devour* means "eat something quickly and hungrily."	7	37
dignified	*Dignified* means "confident, calm, and in control."	7	38
dilapidated	*Dilapidated* means "old, broken, and in very bad condition."	24	139
disadvantage	A *disadvantage* is "something that causes a problem or makes it harder to succeed."	6	36
disallow	*Disallow* means "not allow or ban."	27	157
discontinue	*Discontinue* means "not continue something, or stop doing, using, or making something."	4	22
discourteous	*Discourteous* means "not courteous, or disrespectful or rude."	13	76
discriminate	*Discriminate* means "treat one person or group differently from another, often in an unfair way."	5	25
disperse	*Disperse* means "scatter in different directions."	21	124
disposition	Someone's *disposition* is his or her usual mood, or the way he or she usually acts or behaves.	24	141
dissatisfied	*Dissatisfied* means "not satisfied or happy with the way things are." When you are dissatisfied, you want something more or something different.	4	21
drastic	*Drastic* means "harsh, extreme, or very severe."	20	119
dumbfounded	*Dumbfounded* means "so surprised that you cannot speak."	12	72
dwelling	A *dwelling* is "a place where someone lives, such as a house or an apartment."	22	128
engrossed	*Engrossed* means "so interested in something that you do not notice anything else."	26	156
episode	An *episode* is "an event or series of events in a person's life."	13	78
ethical	*Ethical* means "right according to a society's beliefs." When people think something is ethical, they believe it is the right thing to do.	16	91
excessive	*Excessive* means "too much or too great."	27	161
extend	*Extend* means "lengthen or stretch out." *Extend* also means "offer or give."	6	34
fanciful	*Fanciful* means "imaginary, or not real."	12	71
fiddle	When you fiddle with something, you keep moving or touching it, especially because you are bored or nervous.	27	158
flourish	*Flourish* means "grow well or be successful."	14	83
forceful	*Forceful* means "powerful and strong."	9	54
frugal	*Frugal* means "careful in spending money or not wasteful."	13	73
get on board	"Get on board" means "accept or go along with something."	17	99
grotesque	*Grotesque* means "ugly or strange in a way that is unpleasant or frightening."	25	149
guarantee	*Guarantee* means "promise or make certain that something will happen or be done."	3	13
gush	*Gush* means "flow or pour out quickly."	15	89
hair-raising	*Hair-raising* means "exciting, thrilling, or terrifying."	18	107

Grade 5 Words and Definitions

Word	Definition	Lesson	Card
harbor	*Harbor* means "protect or shelter."	10	55
heartless	*Heartless* means "without heart (kindness or compassion), unkind, or cruel."	20	116
hospitable	*Hospitable* means "friendly, welcoming, and generous to visitors."	2	9
hunger	*Hunger* is "a strong desire or want."	13	74
impact	*Impact* means "a violent collision or the forceful striking of one thing against another." *Impact* also means "the effect that something has on a person or thing."	26	154
indicate	*Indicate* means "point out or show." *Indicate* also means "be a sign of."	18	105
influence	*Influence* means "affect the way someone develops, behaves, or thinks."	16	95
injustice	An *injustice* is "a situation in which people are treated very unfairly."	20	120
insignificant	*Insignificant* means "not very important or not noticeable." Something insignificant does not matter a lot to you.	25	146
insufficient	*Insufficient* means "not enough or not adequate."	21	122
interact	*Interact* means "talk or work with people."	17	97
international	*International* means "having to do with more than one country."	2	12
intrigue	*Intrigue* means "fascinate or stir up curiosity or interest."	25	147
inundate	*Inundate* means "fill or cover completely with water." *Inundate* also means "overwhelm with a large amount of something."	21	126
irate	*Irate* means "furious, or extremely angry."	9	52
jumble	A *jumble* is "a messy mixture of things."	12	67
knowledgeable	If you are knowledgeable about something, you know a lot about it.	26	152
lifeless	*Lifeless* means "without life or living things such as people, animals, or plants."	3	15
lose your nerve	"Lose your nerve" means "lose the courage or confidence to do something."	24	142
lurch	*Lurch* means "lean or roll suddenly forward or to one side."	26	153
master	If you master a skill, you become very good at it.	23	136
memento	A *memento* is "something given or kept as a reminder of a person, place, or experience."	1	4
merge	*Merge* means "combine or join together to form one thing."	14	79
momentous	*Momentous* means "very important or meaningful."	23	138
moocher	A *moocher* is "a person who tries to get something without paying or working for it."	2	7
motionless	*Motionless* means "without motion, still, or not moving."	12	68
motivate	*Motivate* means "inspire and encourage someone to do something."	27	162
mystify	*Mystify* means "confuse, bewilder, or puzzle."	23	137
on pins and needles	"On pins and needles" means "very nervous or uneasy."	23	134
opportunity	An *opportunity* is "a chance to do something."	5	29
ordeal	An *ordeal* is "a very difficult or bad experience."	12	69
pandemonium	*Pandemonium* is "chaos or confusion."	1	2
paradise	A *paradise* is "a place, situation, or activity that is extremely pleasant, beautiful, or enjoyable."	3	16
participant	A *participant* is "someone who participates in, or takes part in, an activity or event."	27	160
peculiar	*Peculiar* means "strange or odd."	10	57
petrified	*Petrified* means "unable to move or act because you are extremely frightened."	9	50
picturesque	*Picturesque* means "beautiful or pleasant to look at."	10	56
plight	A *plight* is "a very serious or dangerous situation."	3	18

Grade 5 Words and Definitions

Word	Definition	Lesson	Card
plummet	*Plummet* means "fall suddenly and very quickly from a high place." *Plummet* also means "decrease suddenly by a large amount."	26	151
prearrange	*Prearrange* means "arrange or plan something before it happens."	9	51
prejudice	*Prejudice* is "an unfair opinion of someone based on the person's race, religion, or other characteristic."	13	77
preposterous	*Preposterous* means "completely ridiculous." If something is preposterous, it is too silly or fantastic to be believed.	23	135
preserve	*Preserve* means "protect from harm or damage."	3	17
preteen	A *preteen* is "a boy or girl before he or she becomes a teenager." A preteen is between the ages of 8 and 12.	17	102
priority	A *priority* is "something that is more important or more urgent than other things."	18	108
procedure	A *procedure* is "a way to do something, or method of doing it, especially by a series of steps."	18	103
quality	A *quality* is "a special characteristic, or feature, of a person's personality or character." Friendliness and honesty are examples of qualities a person might have.	20	117
range	*Range* means "vary or change within certain limits."	14	81
reassure	When you reassure someone, you make the person feel less worried. You calm the person and give the person courage or confidence.	1	5
regret	*Regret* means "feel sorry about something you have done and wish you had not done it."	9	53
regulate	*Regulate* means "control or manage, usually through rules or laws."	16	94
resilient	*Resilient* means "able to recover from or adjust to misfortune or change."	8	48
resolve	*Resolve* means "find an answer or solution to a problem."	19	109
restore	*Restore* means "bring something back to its original condition."	22	132
restriction	A *restriction* is "a rule or law that limits what a person can do or what is allowed to happen."	4	24
reverie	A *reverie* is "a pleasant daydream."	12	70
revive	*Revive* means "bring back to a healthy, active condition or give new strength or freshness to."	14	82
scarce	*Scarce* means "difficult to get or find." If something is scarce, there is very little of it.	7	40
selfless	*Selfless* means "unselfish, or without thought for yourself." When you are selfless, you are more concerned about others than about yourself.	8	47
sequence	A *sequence* is "a series of events or objects in a particular order."	18	104
significant	*Significant* means "very important or noticeable." Something significant matters a lot to you.	25	145
sociable	*Sociable* means "friendly or liking to be with others."	6	33
solitary	*Solitary* means "living or being alone."	6	32
spectacle	A *spectacle* is "an unusual or remarkable sight."	10	60
squander	*Squander* means "carelessly waste something such as money, time, or opportunities."	19	112
stamina	*Stamina* is "the energy and strength to keep doing something for a long time."	4	20
strive	*Strive* means "try very hard."	11	64
stun	*Stun* means "make unconscious or unable to think clearly." *Stun* also means "shock or greatly surprise."	6	31
sufficient	*Sufficient* means "enough or adequate."	21	123
suit	Something that suits you is right for you or meets your needs.	10	59

Grade 5 Words and Definitions

Word	Definition	Lesson	Card
supporter	A *supporter* is "someone who supports, or helps or favors, a particular person, group, or plan."	22	127
supreme	*Supreme* means "the best or the highest in quality, power, or rank."	18	106
surge	A *surge* is "a sudden increase or a sudden strong rush."	4	19
sympathize	*Sympathize* means "understand how someone feels."	11	65
tattered	*Tattered* means "torn and ragged."	1	6
tend	*Tend* means "take care of." *Tend* also means "be likely." If something tends to happen, it is likely to happen or usually or often happens.	8	43
thoughtful	*Thoughtful* means "full of thought for the feelings or needs of others."	11	63
thoughtless	*Thoughtless* means "without thought for the feelings or needs of others."	11	62
throng	A *throng* is "a large crowd of people."	25	150
thrust	*Thrust* means "push or shove suddenly or with force."	15	87
thunderous	*Thunderous* means "making a loud, rumbling noise like thunder."	7	39
topple	*Topple* means "fall over or make something fall over."	15	85
towering	*Towering* means "very tall."	1	3
trample	*Trample* means "damage or crush by walking or stepping on something heavily."	8	45
tranquil	*Tranquil* means "calm or peaceful."	21	121
trickle	A *trickle* is "a small amount." *Trickle* also means "move or flow in small groups or amounts."	24	143
trudge	*Trudge* means "walk with slow, heavy steps because you are tired or it is difficult to walk."	8	44
uneasy	*Uneasy* means "nervous, worried, or anxious."	9	49
unethical	*Unethical* means "wrong according to a society's beliefs." When people think something is unethical, they believe it is the wrong thing to do.	16	92
values	*Values* are "a person's beliefs about what is right and wrong or about what is important in life."	5	30
vary	*Vary* means "are different."	2	11
vexed	*Vexed* means "irritated or annoyed."	24	144
vivid	*Vivid* means "sharp and clear." *Vivid* also means "bright and strong."	22	130
wide-eyed	*Wide-eyed* means "with the eyes wide open, especially because you are amazed or surprised."	22	131
widespread	*Widespread* means "spread, scattered, or happening over a large area."	7	42

Independent Word-learning Strategies

The tables that follow show the weeks in which each independent word-learning strategy is introduced and reviewed, and when it is practiced in More Strategy Practice (MSP) activities. The words used to introduce and review the strategy are also listed. In some weeks, words used to review a prefix or suffix are not words formally taught in the program. Asterisks identify these words.

Using context to determine word meanings

Week	Words
1	towering MSP: Play "Use the Clues"
6	solitary sociable
7	devour
8	tend MSP: Play "Use the Clues"
15	MSP: Play "Use the Clues"
16	regulate MSP: Play "Use the Clues"
26	plummet MSP: Play "Use the Clues"
27	participant

Using the prefix *dis-* to determine word meanings

Week	Words
4	dissatisfied discontinue MSP: *distrust, *disobey, *disbelieve
6	disadvantage
13	discourteous
27	disallow

Using the prefix *pre-* to determine word meanings

Week	Words
9	prearrange MSP: *preview, *preheat, *preorder
13	prejudice
17	preteen MSP: *prepaid

Grade Five | 615

Independent Word-learning Strategies

Using the suffix -er to determine word meanings

Week	Words
2	moocher MSP: *explorer, *entertainer
11	deserter
16	consumer MSP: *rapper, *learner, *skier, *tickler, *wanderer
22	supporter MSP: *trader, *settler, *dweller

Using the suffix -less to determine word meanings

Week	Words
3	lifeless MSP: *homeless
8	selfless
11	thoughtless
12	motionless MSP: *shoeless, *penniless, *shapeless, *useless, *weightless
19	defenseless
20	heartless

Recognizing words with multiple meanings

Week	Words
6	stun extend
7	blunt
8	tend
10	MSP: harbor
11	MSP: thoughtful
14	MSP: range
18	indicate
21	inundate
22	vivid
24	trickle
26	plummet, impact

Independent Word-learning Strategies

Recognizing idioms

Week	Words
4	blow off steam MSP: Discuss Idioms
17	get on board
18	hair-raising
23	on pins and needles
24	lose your nerve

Recognizing antonyms

Week	Words
4	dissatisfied, satisfied discontinue, continue MSP: Start an Antonym Chart
6	solitary, sociable disadvantage, advantage
11	thoughtful, thoughtless
12	fanciful, real
13	discourteous, courteous
16	unethical, ethical
20	heartless, kind
21	sufficient, insufficient MSP: Play "Antonym Match"
25	insignificant, significant
27	disallow, allow

Grade Five | 617

Independent Word-learning Strategies

Recognizing synonyms

Week	Words
2	delectable (delicious) MSP: Start a Synonym Chart
3	devastate (destroy)
5	opportunity (chance)
6	stun (shock, surprise) MSP: Play "Synonym Match"
7	devour (eat)
9	uneasy (nervous, worried, anxious) irate (furious, angry) forceful (powerful, strong)
10	peculiar (strange, odd)
14	calamity (disaster)
15	topple (fall) thrust (push, shove) MSP: Play "Synonym Match"
18	hair-raising (exciting, thrilling, terrifying)
19	compel (force) clash (fight, argue) MSP: Play "Synonym Match"
20	befuddled (confused) heartless (unkind, cruel)
21	tranquil (calm, peaceful)
23	mystify (confuse, bewilder, puzzle)

Extension Activities

The table below shows the weeks in which Extension activities appear. The activities are an opportunity to introduce the students to independent word-learning strategies not formally taught in the program, as well as onomatopoeia, homophones, and other interesting aspects of words. The table shows the week of the activity, the activity, and the word or words used in the activity.

Week	Activity
7	Introduce and Discuss the Suffix -ous (thunderous)
9	Discuss Other Words with the Suffix -ful (forceful)
10	Fun with Puns
11	Discuss the Suffix -ful (thoughtful, forceful, regretful) Discuss Desert and Other Heteronyms Discuss Desert and Dessert and Other Homophones
13	Exploring Roots (prejudice, spectacle)
14	An Interesting Fact About Revive
16	Discuss Other Words with the Prefix un- (unethical, unbundled, undesirable, undignified)
17	Introduce and Discuss the Prefix inter- (interact)
18	Explore the Suffix -tion (indication, regulation, interaction)
20	Give Your Best Friend a New Name (quality)
21	Discuss Other Words with the Prefix in- (inaccurate, inactive, inconsiderate, inconspicuous, inhospitable)
22	Discuss Vivid Language (vivid) Discuss Vivid Verbs (devour, gush, trudge)
23	Discuss Onomatopoeia (clang) An Interesting Fact About Preposterous
24	Illustrate Idioms (blow off steam, get on board, hair-raising, on pins and needles, lose your nerve)

Word Check 1: Which Word Am I?

Word Check 1: Which Word Am I?

This Individual Vocabulary Progress Assessment helps you assess individual students' understanding of words taught in weeks 1–4. For more information about assessing the students, see "Assessment" on page xx.

Materials

- Word Check 1 answer sheet, one for each student (BLM23)
- (Optional) Transparency of the Word Check 1 answer sheet

Conducting the Assessment

1. Distribute a Word Check 1 answer sheet to each student.

2. Tell the students that they will think more about the words they have been learning by doing the activity "Which Word Am I?" Explain that you will give a clue about one of the words and they will circle the word that fits the clue.

3. Explain that the first clue is about one of these words, which are written next to the number 1 on the answer sheet: *paradise*, *pandemonium*, or *moocher*.

4. Read clue number 1 aloud twice. (See "Which Word Am I?" on the following page.)

5. Have the students circle the word that fits the clue.

6. Read the remaining clues the same way.

▶ **Teacher Note**

If the students are not familiar with this multiple-choice format, you might make a transparency of the answer sheet and point to each vocabulary word as you pronounce it. You might discuss the first few clues as a class and model circling the answers. The transparency is also useful for discussing the activity after the students complete it.

Discussing the Students' Responses

To fully assess the students' understanding of the words, it is important to discuss the activity with them after they have completed it. Discuss each question with the class or individual students. Have them explain the thinking behind their responses by asking questions such as:

Q Why did you say the word [pandemonium] *is what you might see when a fire breaks out in an apartment building? What do you know about the word* [pandemonium]?

Q *What do you know about the word* [paradise/moocher]?

620 | Making Meaning® Vocabulary

Which Word Am I?

1. I'm what you might see when a fire breaks out in an apartment building.

    Q *Which word am I:* **paradise**, **pandemonium**, *or* **moocher**? (pandemonium)

2. I'm what you do when you go for a long, hard bike ride to get rid of built-up anger.

    Q *Which word or idiom am I:* **preserve**, **clamor**, *or* **"blow off steam"**? (blow off steam)

3. I might include foods like fresh fish, fruits, and rice.

    Q *Which word am I:* **cuisine**, **memento**, *or* **surge**? (cuisine)

4. I'm what a company does when it promises to fix or replace a television if it should break.

    Q *Which word am I:* **varies**, **discontinues**, *or* **guarantees**? (guarantees)

5. I'm how a poster might look if it has been hanging on a wall outside for months.

    Q *Which word am I:* **tattered**, **towering**, *or* **delectable**? (tattered)

6. I'm what you need in order to work all day under a hot sun.

    Q *Which word am I:* **plight**, **stamina**, *or* **restriction**? (stamina)

7. I'm what a wrecking ball does when it hits a building.

    Q *Which word am I:* **reassures**, **devastates**, *or* **preserves**? (devastates)

8. I'm how you describe a business that has offices in many different countries.

    Q *Which word am I:* **international**, **lifeless**, *or* **dissatisfied**? (international)

Word Check 2: What's the Missing Word?

Word Check 2: What's the Missing Word?

This Individual Vocabulary Progress Assessment helps you assess individual students' understanding of words taught in weeks 5–8. For more information about assessing the students, see "Assessment" on page xx.

Materials

- Word Check 2 answer sheet, one for each student (BLM24)
- (Optional) Transparency of the Word Check 2 answer sheet

Conducting the Assessment

1. Distribute a Word Check 2 answer sheet to each student.

2. Tell the students that they will think more about the words they have been learning by doing the activity "What's the Missing Word?" Explain that you will read a sentence that has a word missing and they will circle the vocabulary word that can replace the missing word.

> **Teacher Note**
>
> If the students are not familiar with this multiple-choice format, you might make a transparency of the answer sheet and point to each vocabulary word as you pronounce it. You might discuss the first few sentences as a class and model circling the answers. The transparency is also useful for discussing the activity after the students complete it.

3. Explain that one of these words can replace the missing word in the first sentence: *bans*, *values*, or *disadvantages*. Then read sentence number 1 aloud, saying the word "blank" for the missing word. (See "What's the Missing Word?" on the following page.)

4. Have the students circle the word that can replace the missing word.

5. Read the remaining sentences the same way.

Discussing the Students' Responses

To fully assess the students' understanding of the words, it is important to discuss the activity with them after they have completed it. Discuss each question with the class or with individual students. Have them explain the thinking behind their responses by asking questions such as:

Q *Why did you say the word* [values] *can replace the missing word? What do you know about the word* [value]?

Q *What do you know about the word* [bans/disadvantages]?

Making Meaning® Vocabulary

Word Check 2: What's the Missing Word?

What's the Missing Word?

1. Jo thinks honesty and kindness are important _____, so she tries hard to be honest and kind.

    Q *What's the missing word:* **bans**, **values**, *or* **disadvantages**? (values)

2. Mr. Quinby is _____; he stops frequently when he is out walking to visit with his neighbors.

    Q *What's the missing word:* **solitary**, **sociable**, *or* **thunderous**? (sociable)

3. The hungry children quickly _____ all the food at the picnic.

    Q *What's the missing word:* **stunned**, **devoured**, *or* **extended**? (devoured)

4. After the storm, children had to _____ through deep snow to get to school.

    Q *What's the missing word:* **bundle**, **trample**, *or* **trudge**? (trudge)

5. Ty is a _____ person. He puts the needs of others ahead of his own needs.

    Q *What's the missing word:* **blunt**, **resilient**, *or* **selfless**? (selfless)

6. After she broke her leg, Yi-Min had to _____ to using crutches. She had never used crutches before.

    Q *What's the missing word:* **adapt**, **claim**, *or* **tend**? (adapt)

7. The rainstorm caused _____ flooding. Thousands of acres of farmland were under water.

    Q *What's the missing word:* **scarce**, **dignified**, *or* **widespread**? (widespread)

8. Abe did not know anything about computers. That was a big _____ when he tried to get a job at a computer repair shop.

    Q *What's the missing word:* **disadvantage**, **advantage**, *or* **opportunity**? (disadvantage)

Word Check 3: Which Word Is It?

Word Check 3: Which Word Is It?

This Individual Vocabulary Progress Assessment helps you assess individual students' understanding of words taught in weeks 9–12. For more information about assessing the students, see "Assessment" on page xx.

Materials

- Word Check 3 answer sheet, one for each student (BLM25)
- (Optional) Transparency of the Word Check 3 answer sheet

Conducting the Assessment

1. Distribute a Word Check 3 answer sheet to each student.

2. Tell the students that they will think more about the words they have been learning by doing the activity "Which Word Is It?" Explain that you will read a clue about one of the words and they will circle the word that fits the clue.

3. Explain that the first clue is about one of these words, which are written next to the number 1 on the answer sheet: *uneasy*, *conspicuous*, or *thoughtless*.

4. Read clue number 1 aloud twice. (See "Which Word Is It?" on the following page.)

5. Have the students circle the word that fits the clue.

6. Read the remaining clues the same way.

Discussing the Students' Responses

To fully assess the students' understanding of the words, it is important to discuss the activity with them after they have completed it. Discuss each question with the class or with individual students. Have them explain the thinking behind their responses by asking questions such as:

Q *Why did you say the word* [conspicuous] *fits the clue? What do you know about the word* [conspicuous]*?*

Q *What do you know about the word* [uneasy/thoughtless]*?*

> **Teacher Note**
>
> If the students are not familiar with this multiple-choice format, you might make a transparency of the answer sheet and point to each vocabulary word as you pronounce it. You might discuss the first few clues as a class and model circling the answers. The transparency is also useful for discussing the activity after the students complete it.

624 | Making Meaning® Vocabulary

Which Word Is It?

1. This is how you describe a street sign that stands out and can be easily seen.

    Q *Which word is it:* **uneasy, conspicuous,** *or* **thoughtless**? (conspicuous)

2. This is a pleasant daydream you have while you lie in a hammock on a hot summer day.

    Q *Which word is it:* **reverie, jumble,** *or* **ordeal**? (reverie)

3. This is what you do when you work really hard in school.

    Q *Which word is it:* **harbor, strive,** *or* **sympathize**? (strive)

4. This is a person with whom you like to spend time.

    Q *Which word is it:* **deserter, spectacle,** *or* **comrade**? (comrade)

5. This is how you describe a story about a friendly talking dragon.

    Q *Which word is it:* **irate, fanciful,** *or* **motionless**? (fanciful)

6. This is what you do when you make plans to spend the night at your friend's house.

    Q *Which word is it:* **prearrange, desert,** *or* **suit**? (prearrange)

7. This is what you are doing when you wish you had been nicer to someone you mistreated.

    Q *Which word is it:* **regretting, harboring,** *or* **deserting**? (regretting)

8. This is how you describe a person who brings flowers to a sick friend.

    Q *Which word is it:* **forceful, thoughtful,** *or* **peculiar**? (thoughtful)

Word Check 4: Yes or No?

This Individual Vocabulary Progress Assessment helps you assess individual students' understanding of words taught in weeks 13–16. For more information about assessing the students, see "Assessment" on page xx.

Materials
- Word Check 4 answer sheet, one for each student (BLM26)
- (optional) Transparency of the Word Check 4 answer sheet

Conducting the Assessment

1. Distribute a Word Check 4 answer sheet to each student.

2. Tell the students that they will think more about the words they have been learning by answering questions that use the words. Explain that you will ask a question and they will answer it by circling "yes" or "no" on the answer sheet.

3. Explain that the first question is about these two words: *flourish* and *deprived*. Then read question number 1 aloud twice. (See "Yes or No?" on the following page.)

4. Have the students circle "yes" or "no" to answer the question.

5. Read the remaining questions the same way.

Discussing the Students' Responses

To fully assess the students' understanding of the words, it is important to discuss the activity with them after they have completed it. Discuss each question with the class or with individual students. Have them explain the thinking behind their responses by asking questions such as:

Q *Why did you say a baby [can/cannot] flourish if he is deprived of care?*

Q *What do you know about the word [flourish]?*

Q *What do you know about the word [deprive]?*

> **Teacher Note** ▶
> You might write the questions on a sheet of chart paper.

Word Check 4: Yes or No?

Yes or No?

1. Can a baby *flourish* if he is *deprived* of care?

    Q *Yes* or *No?* (No)

2. Would it be a *calamity* if an earthquake left an entire city in *a shambles*?

    Q *Yes* or *No?* (Yes)

3. Would you *hunger* to tell others about an embarrassing *episode* in your life?

    Q *Yes* or *No?* (No)

4. Is it smart to be a *frugal consumer*?

    Q *Yes* or *No?* (Yes)

5. Would it be *desirable* to have a *discourteous* friend?

    Q *Yes* or *No?* (No)

6. Is it *ethical* to be *prejudiced* against someone because of that person's race?

    Q *Yes* or *No?* (No)

7. Would you be *apprehensive* if you cut your finger and blood *gushed* from the wound?

    Q *Yes* or *No?* (Yes)

8. Is it *unethical* to *batter* someone?

    Q *Yes* or *No?* (Yes)

Word Check 5: I'm Thinking of a Word

This Individual Vocabulary Progress Assessment helps you assess individual students' understanding of words taught in weeks 17–20. For more information about assessing the students, see "Assessment" on page xx.

Materials

- Word Check 5 answer sheet, one for each student (BLM27)
- (Optional) Transparency of the Word Check 5 answer sheet

Conducting the Assessment

1. Distribute a Word Check 5 answer sheet to each student.

2. Tell the students that they will think more about the words they have been learning by doing the activity "I'm Thinking of a Word." Explain that you will give a clue about one of the words and they will circle the word that fits the clue.

3. Explain that the first clue is about one of these words, which are written next to the number 1 on the answer sheet: *interact*, *compel*, or *resolve*.

4. Read clue number 1 aloud twice. (See "I'm Thinking of a Word" on the following page.)

5. Have the students circle the word that fits the clue.

6. Read the remaining clues the same way.

Discussing the Students' Responses

To fully assess the students' understanding of the words, it is important to discuss the activity with them after they have completed it. Discuss each question with the class or with individual students. Have them think more deeply about the word or explain the thinking behind their responses by asking questions such as:

Q *How might you use the word* [resolve] *in a sentence? When have you had a problem that was difficult to resolve?*

Q *What do you know about the word* [interact/compel]*?*

> **Teacher Note**
>
> If the students are not familiar with this multiple-choice format, you might make a transparency of the answer sheet and point to each vocabulary word as you pronounce it. You might discuss the first few clues as a class and model circling the answers. The transparency is also useful for discussing the activity after the students complete it.

Word Check 5: I'm Thinking of a Word

I'm Thinking of a Word

1. I'm thinking of a word that means "find an answer or solution to a problem."

    Q *Which word am I thinking of:* **interact**, **compel**, *or* **resolve**? (resolve)

2. I'm thinking of a word that means "a series of events or objects in a particular order."

    Q *Which word am I thinking of:* **sequence**, **priority**, *or* **quality**? (sequence)

3. I'm thinking of a word that means "completely confused."

    Q *Which word am I thinking of:* **defenseless**, **heartless**, *or* **befuddled**? (befuddled)

4. I'm thinking of a word that means "fight or argue."

    Q *Which word am I thinking of:* **squander**, **clash**, *or* **comply**? (clash)

5. I'm thinking of a word that means "harsh, extreme, or very severe."

    Q *Which word am I thinking of:* **drastic**, **hair-raising**, *or* **supreme**? (drastic)

6. I'm thinking of a word that means "a way to do something."

    Q *Which word am I thinking of:* **injustice**, **device**, *or* **procedure**? (procedure)

7. I'm thinking of a word or phrase that means "point out or show."

    Q *Which word or idiom am I thinking of:* **indicate**, **interact**, *or* **"get on board"**? (indicate)

8. I'm thinking of a word that means "the best or highest in quality."

    Q *Which word am I thinking of:* **academic**, **dependent**, *or* **supreme**? (supreme)

Grade Five | 629

Word Check 6: Which Word Am I?

Word Check 6: Which Word Am I?

This Individual Vocabulary Progress Assessment helps you assess individual students' understanding of words taught in weeks 21–24. For more information about assessing the students, see "Assessment" on page xx.

Materials

- Word Check 6 answer sheet, one for each student (BLM28)
- (Optional) Transparency of the Word Check 6 answer sheet

Conducting the Assessment

1. Distribute a Word Check 6 answer sheet to each student.

2. Tell the students that they will think more about the words they have been learning by doing the activity "Which Word Am I?" Explain that you will give a clue about one of the words and they will circle the word that fits the clue.

3. Explain that the first clue is about one of these words, which are written next to the number 1 on the answer sheet: *wide-eyed*, *vexed*, or *dilapidated*.

4. Read clue number 1 aloud twice. (See "Which Word Am I?" on the following page.)

5. Have the students circle the word that fits the clue.

6. Read the remaining clues the same way.

Discussing the Students' Responses

To fully assess the students' understanding of the words, it is important to discuss the activity with them after they have completed it. Discuss each question with the class or with individual students. Have them explain the thinking behind their responses by asking questions such as:

Q *Why did you say the word* [wide-eyed] *describes how a person looks when she sees something amazing? What do you know about the word* [wide-eyed]?

Q *What do you know about the word* [vexed/dilapidated]?

> **Teacher Note**
>
> If the students are not familiar with this multiple-choice format, you might make a transparency of the answer sheet and point to each vocabulary word as you pronounce it. You might discuss the first few clues as a class and model circling the answers. The transparency is also useful for discussing the activity after the students complete it.

Word Check 6: Which Word Am I?

Which Word Am I?

1. I'm how people look when they see something amazing.

    Q *Which word am I:* **wide-eyed**, **vexed**, *or* **dilapidated**? (wide-eyed)

2. I'm what you do when you start to do something and then stop because you are afraid.

    Q *Which word or idiom am I:* **disperse**, **restore**, *or* "**lose your nerve**"? (lose your nerve)

3. I'm a fan who goes to every game to cheer for my hometown team.

    Q *Which word am I:* **supporter**, **dwelling**, *or* **trickle**? (supporter)

4. I'm how you describe an event that changes your life.

    Q *Which word am I:* **tranquil**, **momentous**, *or* **cantankerous**? (momentous)

5. I'm what a bird does as it flies higher and higher into the sky.

    Q *Which word am I:* **inundates**, **ascends**, *or* **clangs**? (ascends)

6. I'm how you describe the supply of cups when you have enough for a party.

    Q *Which word am I:* **vivid**, **insufficient**, *or* **sufficient**? (sufficient)

7. I'm what you do when you learn a foreign language well enough to speak, read, and write it.

    Q *Which word am I:* **master**, **deteriorate**, *or* **mystify**? (master)

8. I'm how you describe a rusty old truck with a cracked windshield, no doors, and worn tires.

    Q *Which word or idiom am I:* **dilapidated**, **preposterous**, *or* "**on pins and needles**"? (dilapidated)

Word Check 7: Yes or No?

This Individual Vocabulary Progress Assessment helps you assess individual students' understanding of words taught in weeks 25–27. For more information about assessing the students, see "Assessment" on page xx.

Materials

- Word Check 7 answer sheet, one for each student (BLM29)
- (Optional) Transparency of the Word Check 7 answer sheet

Conducting the Assessment

1. Distribute a Word Check 7 answer sheet to each student.

2. Tell the students that they will think more about the words they have been learning by answering questions that use the words. Explain that you will ask a question and they will answer it by circling "yes" or "no" on the answer sheet.

3. Explain that the first question is about these two words: *billow* and *plummeted*. Then read question number 1 aloud twice. (See "Yes or No?" on the following page.)

4. Have the students circle "yes" or "no" to answer the question.

5. Read the remaining questions the same way.

Discussing the Students' Responses

To fully assess the students' understanding of the words, it is important to discuss the activity with them after they have completed it. Discuss each question with the class or with individual students. Have them explain the thinking behind their responses by asking questions such as:

Q *Why did you say a rock [would/would not] billow if it plummeted off a cliff?*

Q *What do you know about the word [billow]?*

Q *What do you know about the word [plummet]?*

▶ **Teacher Note**
You might write the questions on a sheet of chart paper.

Word Check 7: Yes or No?

Yes or No?

1. Would a rock *billow* if it *plummeted* off a cliff?

   Q *Yes* or *No?* (No)

2. If you were an *avid* baseball player, would you be *knowledgeable* about the rules of the game?

   Q *Yes* or *No?* (Yes)

3. Would it be *significant* if a city received an *excessive* amount of snowfall?

   Q *Yes* or *No?* (Yes)

4. If you were *intrigued* by birds, would you be *motivated* to learn about them?

   Q *Yes* or *No?* (Yes)

5. Might you see a *throng* at a rock concert *clustered* around the stage?

   Q *Yes* or *No?* (Yes)

6. If you were a *participant* in an activity you didn't enjoy, would you be *engrossed* in the activity?

   Q *Yes* or *No?* (No)

7. If touching an object is *disallowed*, should you *fiddle* with it?

   Q *Yes* or *No?* (No)

8. If you were in a car, would the *impact* of a collision cause you to *lurch*?

   Q *Yes* or *No?* (Yes)

Student Self-assessment Instructions

The Student Self-assessment gives the students an opportunity to reflect on how well they know the words they are learning and gives you the chance to identify words in need of further review and practice. We recommend that the Student Self-assessment be administered every three or four weeks in place of or in addition to the Individual Vocabulary Progress Assessment. For more information about assessing the students, see "Assessment" on page xx.

Materials

- "Which Words Do I Know?" response sheet, one for each student (see BLM30)
- Transparency of the response sheet
- Overhead projector and a marker

Conducting the Assessment

1. Identify the words to be assessed. We recommend that you select from eight to twelve words from the previous three or four weeks of vocabulary instruction.

2. Write the words on a master copy of the response sheet and make photocopies of the sheet for each student. Make a transparency of the response sheet with the words.

3. Place the transparency on the overhead projector and distribute the response sheets.

4. Tell the students that today they will have an opportunity to think about how well they know the words they have been learning. Point to the list of words on the transparency and explain that these are some vocabulary words they have talked about recently. Explain that you will read each word and give the students a few moments to think about the word. Then they will put a checkmark in the column that tells how well they know the word.

    Explain that if they are sure they know what the word means, they will put a checkmark in the "I know this word!" column. If they think they know what the word means but are not sure, they will put a checkmark in the "I think I know this word, but I'm not sure" column. If they do not know what the word means or cannot remember, they will put a checkmark in the "I don't know this word" column.

> **Teacher Note**
>
> You might prefer to write the words on the board or a sheet of chart paper and have the students copy the words onto their response sheets.

Student Self-assessment Instructions

Tell the students that the purpose of the activity is to help them figure out which words they know well and which words they need to review and practice. Explain that it is OK if the students are not sure about a word or do not know what it means.

5. Point to the first word on the transparency, read it aloud, and give the students a few moments to think about the word. Then have them put a checkmark in the column that tells how well they know the word.

6. Follow the same procedure with the remaining words.

Using the Assessment Results

Here are some suggestions for ways you might use the results of the assessment:

- Ask the students to circle on their response sheet any word they are not sure they know or do not know. Then have them discuss with a partner what they might do to review and practice those words. If the students have difficulty thinking of ideas, suggest a few of your own. For example, they might use word cards to review the words by themselves or with a partner, or they might take the word cards home and practice the words with a family member. (For blackline masters of the word cards, see BLM33–BLM56.) They might also write stories using the words, draw pictures about the words, or act out the words with a partner.

- Briefly review the meaning of each word by having the students tell what they know about the word. If the students are not sure or do not know what a word means, write that word on the board. During the next few days, review the word's meaning periodically and look for opportunities to use the word. Encourage the students to use the word in conversations with classmates and others and in their writing.

- Collect the response sheets. Identify words that many students are not sure of or do not know and review them as a class or in groups. For suggestions for reviewing words, see "Retaining the Words" on pages xviii–xix.

Vocabulary Words K–6

Grade K Word List

active
allow
amusing
assist
assortment
clear
clever
collide
comfort
comfortable
communicate
companion
complete
concerned
confident
construct
container
courageous
cozy
creature
creep
crowded
cupboard
decide
depart
determined
disappear
disappointed
doubtful
drowsy
eager
edge
energetic
enjoy
enormous
entire
evening
exhausted
explore
fact
filthy
fits
frustrated
furious
future
generous
glance
gooey
grin
haul
healthy
imitate
important
injure
kind
land
load
mend
moan
nuisance
object
observe
passenger
patient
pedestrian
peer
persistent
pleasant
pleased
pounce
practice
prevent
prey
proud
pursue
recover
remarkable
repair
scoop
scramble
scrumptious
signal
similar
slam
snatch
snooze
soar
soggy
straight
structure
stuck
swiftly
switch
tame
tangled
transportation
travel
uncomfortable
uncrowded
unkind
unpleasant
unusual
upset
useful
various
visible
wade
warn
welcome
whirl
wide
wild

Grade 1 Word List

admire
adventure
affectionate
appear
appetite
arrange
arrive
astonish
audible
beam
bob
bold
chomp
collapse
commotion
contents
cooperate
crabby
curious
dart
delicious
delighted
destination
discover
disgusting
doze
dump
ear-splitting
essential
evidence
exclaim
excursion
extraordinary
faint
fatigued
ferocious
firm
fond
frigid
gather
gigantic
glide
glow
hero
hope
humorous
impolite
impossible
inaudible
independent
inspect
lickety-split
lunge
masterpiece
meadow
memory
miserable
munch
mushy
mutter
neighborhood
ordinary
peaceful
perilous
persevere
pile
plenty
popular
possession
possible
pout
powerful
private
protect
provide
public
quarrel
rapidly
refreshed
release
remain
rescue
resent
respect
rumble
rush
scold
scoot
sob
solid
spring
squint
stomp
store
surroundings
survive
tag along
thrilling
tidy
timid
tip
track
tremble
tug
untidy
vegetation
wobble
wonder

Grade 2 Word List

accompany
advice
annoy
approve
attach
attract
beneficial
blob
broad
bulge
chaos
characteristic
compassionate
complex
congratulate
conserve
consume
content
convince
create
damage
delightful

636 | Making Meaning® Vocabulary

Vocabulary Words K–6

disapprove
disguise
disobedient
downcast
dreadful
dull
duplicate
eavesdropper
ecstatic
embarrass
encourage
expand
expert
fabulous
fade
familiar
fearful
fearless
fetch
flap
flexible
flop
fresh
genius
glee
grasp
gratitude
grip
grumble
guide
hospitality
host
huddle
include
insist
introduce
miniature
murmur
narrow
necessary
notorious
numerous
obedient
occasionally
optional
overjoyed
panic
ponder
precaution
predicament

predict
prefer
prepare
rarely
recreation
reluctant
remedy
risky
routine
ruckus
scrunch
shelter
shimmer
shriek
snap
solution
steer clear
stream
strenuous
stunned
sturdy
successful
support
swirl
terrific
tumble
unique
unwelcome
vanish
variety
victory
whimper

Grade 3 Word List

achieve
adjust
adventuresome
advise
aggressive
appetizing
aroma
astounding
available
avoid
bare
barricade
bask
belongings
bewildered

bounce back
bound
caretaker
celebration
challenge
cherish
clatter
clench
cling
clutch
coax
collaborate
command
commence
considerate
contentment
cross
customary
dazzle
deadly
delirious
demolish
determination
differ
diligent
dim
disaster
display
distress
diverse
dodge
donate
doubtful
ease
energize
evacuate
exhilarated
faint
fantasize
fantastic
fierce/fiercest
flabbergasted
flashy
flick
flimsy
floppy
flutter
fortunate
frank
frantic

fret
frolic
fury
gasp
ghastly
graceful
gruff
headstrong
heap
heartbreaking
identify
image
immature
immense
intense
involved
joyful
likely
lively
long
magnificent
mature
memorable
mighty
moist
motion
nifty
obstinate
original
overwhelmed
particularly
permissible
persist
plain
predator
prey
proper
prowl
quiver
rap
realize
recall
reconsider
refreshing
retrieve
reunite
reuse
roam
rubble
satisfied

savory
seldom
self-confident
shuffle
skillful
slink
slither
slog
slump
snap
snug
sorrowful
speck
spectacular
speechless
speedy
squirm
strain
swarm
sway
terrifying
threatened
tingle
ultimate
unaggressive
unfinished
unfortunate
ungrateful
unlikely
urgent
whiz
wind
wondrous
wriggle
zoom

Grade 4 Word List

adequate
adore
alternative
ambition
amiable
analyze
anticipate
apprehensive
approach
bellow
bizarre
bliss

Grade Five | 637

Vocabulary Words K–6

blotch	hitch	pay no mind	uniform	disallow
blurt out	humane	pelt	valiant	discontinue
boost	humble	perilous	vast	discourteous
ceremony	humdrum	permanent	vigilant	discriminate
circulate	ideal	pessimistic		disperse
circumstances	imposing	plunge	**Grade 5**	disposition
conceal	impressive	portray	**Word List**	dissatisfied
conditions	imprudent	precarious	a shambles	drastic
consistent	in the blink of	precise	academic	dumbfounded
consistently	an eye	prior to	adapt	dwelling
crave	inadequate	process	advantage	engrossed
creak	inclusive	proficient	apprehensive	episode
critical	inconsistent	prudent	ascend	ethical
dazed	indignantly	raises eyebrows	avid	excessive
defy	industrious	recede	ban	extend
dejected	inedible	reduce	batter	fanciful
dense	ineffective	refuge	befuddled	fiddle
desire	ineligible	reminisce	billow	flourish
desperate	inequitable	reputation	blow off steam	forceful
dissimilar	informal	resemble	blunt	frugal
distinguish	inhumane	revere	bundle	get on board
dubious	initial	rickety	calamity	grotesque
edible	inspire	rove	cantankerous	guarantee
eerie	integrate	rowdier	churn	gush
effective	intimidate	rowdy	claim	hair-raising
elated	intricate	rugged	clamor	harbor
eligible	jittery	rummage	clang	heartless
endure	jubilant	safeguard	clash	hospitable
engage	keen	sag	cluster	hunger
ensure	labor	sandwiched	compel	impact
enthusiastic	launch	scrutinize	comply	indicate
envision	lend a hand	secure	comrade	influence
equitable	lethal	seek	conspicuous	injustice
establish	limit	segregate	consume/consumer	insignificant
exclusive	loathe	sensitive	cuisine	insufficient
feat	luscious	serene	defenseless	interact
flee	lush	sidesplitting	delectable	international
focus	manually	speculate	deliberately	intrigue
formal	merit	stalk	dependent	inundate
fume	misfortune	survey	deprive	irate
function	misjudge	sustain	desert/deserter	jumble
get-up-and-go	mislead	taunt	desirable	knowledgeable
gleeful	mistreat	temporary	deteriorate	lifeless
glower	musty	thoroughly	devastate	lose your nerve
glum	nosing around	thrive	device	lurch
harass	note	transform	devour	master
hardship	obstacle	trend	dignified	memento
hazard	optimistic	trim	dilapidated	merge
hinder	partial	turbulent	disadvantage	momentous

638 | Making Meaning® Vocabulary

Vocabulary Words K–6

moocher
motionless
motivate
mystify
on pins and needles
opportunity
ordeal
pandemonium
paradise
participant
peculiar
petrified
picturesque
plight
plummet
prearrange
prejudice
preposterous
preserve
preteen
priority
procedure
quality
range
reassure
regret
regulate
resilient
resolve
restore
restriction
reverie
revive
scarce
selfless
sequence
significant
sociable
solitary
spectacle
squander
stamina
strive
stun
sufficient
suit
supporter
supreme
surge
sympathize

tattered
tend
thoughtful
thoughtless
throng
thrust
thunderous
topple
towering
trample
tranquil
trickle
trudge
uneasy
unethical
values
vary
vexed
vivid
wide-eyed
widespread

Grade 6 Word List

abruptly
abundant
access
accessible
acknowledge
acquire
acute
adept
adhere
adversity
appeal
arduous
aspire
assert
awkward
bark
beckon
bind
blare
blissful
bluff
bond
boom
bustle
carefree
catastrophe

clamp
commercial
compatible
conceivable
congenial
consider
cordial
counsel
cower
cruise
dead on your feet
debris
decrepit
desolate
detest
detestable
distinctive
document
dogged
down in the dumps
dramatic
encounter
enigma
erroneously
eventful
excel
external
extract
extreme
fit
forethought
forlorn
fretful
gargantuan
glint
go overboard
grim
grit
grueling
guidance
hardy
hideous
hobble
hoist
hostile
hurtle
hypocrite
idle
impermanent
incident

inconceivable
indispensable
insensitive
intensify
internal
intrude
isolated
leisure
livelihood
lumber
mistrustful
modify
monitor
mount
nimble
nonhuman
nontoxic
nonverbal
nonviolent
obligation
obsessed
official
on top of the world
ooze
overcome
overload
overpopulated
overtake
overworked
particular
pastime
perplexed
plot
pluck
precede
preferable
presentable
prohibited
prosperous
pry
rate
reasonable
recollect
rejuvenate
resident
resource
resourceful
salvage
scamper
scrawny

scurry
self-sufficient
shatter
sheepish
shield
shift
shrivel
skim
sleek
sling
solemn
sparse
step up to the plate
stew
stoop
storm
subterranean
summon
suppress
surreptitiously
tenacious
toil
toxic
trace
tribulation
trigger
trustworthy
understanding
unfit
unjust
unpredictable
unreasonable
vital
vulnerable
worthwhile
yearn

Grade Five | 639

Bibliography

Anderson, Richard C., Elfrieda H. Hiebert, Judith A. Scott, and Ian A. G. Wilkinson. *Becoming a Nation of Readers: The Report of the Commission on Reading.* Washington, DC: The National Institute of Education, 1985.

Bauman, James F. and Edward J. Kame'enui, eds. *Vocabulary Instruction: Research to Practice.* New York: The Guilford Press, 2004.

Bauman, James F., Edward J. Kame'enui, and Gwynne E. Ash. "Research on Vocabulary Instruction: Voltaire Redux." *Handbook of Research on Teaching the English Language Arts*, Second Edition, J. Flood, D. Lapp, J. R. Squire, and J. M. Jensen, eds. Mahwah, NJ: Lawrence Erlbaum Associates, 2003.

Beck, Isabel L., Margaret McKeown, and Linda Lucan. *Bringing Words to Life: Robust Vocabulary Instruction.* New York: The Guilford Press, 2002.

Freeman, Yvonne S. and David E. Freeman. *ESL/EFL Teaching: Principles for Success.* Portsmouth, NH: Heinemann, 1998.

Graves, Michael F. *The Vocabulary Book: Learning and Instruction.* New York: Teachers College Press, 2006.

Greenwood, Scott C. *Words Count: Effective Vocabulary Instruction in Action.* Portsmouth, NH: Heinemann, 2004.

Hiebert, Elfrieda H. "In Pursuit of an Effective, Efficient Vocabulary Curriculum for the Elementary Grades." *The Teaching and Learning of Vocabulary: Bringing Scientific Research to Practice*, E. H. Hiebert and M. Kamil, eds. Mahwah, NJ: Lawrence Erlbaum Associates, 2005.

Johnson, Dale D. *Vocabulary in the Elementary and Middle School.* Needham Heights, MA: Allyn and Bacon, 2001.

Krashen, S.D. *Second Language Acquisition and Second Language Learning.* New York, NY: Pergamon Press, 1981.

Krashen, S.D. *Principles and Practice in Second Language Acquisition.* New York: Prentice-Hall, 1982.

Krashen, S.D., and T. D. Terrell. *The Natural Approach: Language Acquisition in the Classroom.* Englewood Cliffs, N.J: Prentice Hall, 1983.

Morrow, Lesley Mandel, Linda B. Gambrell, and Michael Pressley. *Best Practices in Literacy Instruction*, Second Edition. New York: The Guilford Press, 2003.

Stahl, Steven A. *Vocabulary Development.* Newton Upper Falls, MA: Brookline Books, 1999.

White, T. G., J. Sowell, and A. Yanagihara. "Teaching Elementary Students to Use Word-Part Clues." *The Reading Teacher*, 1989.

Vocabulary for Making Meaning®
SECOND EDITION

Reorder Information

Grade K
Complete Classroom Package   MMV-CPK

Contents: Teacher's Manual, Picture Cards, Word Cards, and Pocket Chart

Available separately:
Picture Cards	MMV-PCSK
Pocket Chart	MMV-CHART
Teacher's Manual	MMV-TMK
Word Cards	MMV-WCSK

Grade 1
Complete Classroom Package   MMV-CP1

Contents: Teacher's Manual, Picture Cards, Word Cards, and Pocket Chart

Available separately:
Picture Cards	MMV-PCS1
Pocket Chart	MMV-CHART
Teacher's Manual	MMV-TM1
Word Cards	MMV-WCS1

Grade 2
Complete Classroom Package   MMV-CP2

Contents: Teacher's Manual, Word Cards, and Pocket Chart

Available separately:
Pocket Chart	MMV-CHART
Teacher's Manual	MMV-TM2
Word Cards	MMV-WCS2

Grade 3
Complete Classroom Package   MMV-CP3

Contents: Teacher's Manual, Word Cards, and Pocket Chart

Available separately:
Pocket Chart	MMV-CHART
Teacher's Manual	MMV-TM3
Word Cards	MMV-WCS3

Grade 4
Complete Classroom Package   MMV-CP4

Contents: Teacher's Manual, Blackline Masters, Word Cards, and Pocket Chart

Available separately:
Blackline Masters	MMV-BM4
Pocket Chart	MMV-CHART46
Teacher's Manual, vol. 1	MMV-TM4-V1
Teacher's Manual, vol. 2	MMV-TM4-V2
Word Cards	MMV-WCS4

Grade 5
Complete Classroom Package   MMV-CP5

Contents: Teacher's Manual, Blackline Masters, Word Cards, and Pocket Chart

Available separately:
Blackline Masters	MMV-BM5
Pocket Chart	MMV-CHART46
Teacher's Manual, vol. 1	MMV-TM5-V1
Teacher's Manual, vol. 2	MMV-TM5-V2
Word Cards	MMV-WCS5

Grade 6
Complete Classroom Package   MMV-CP6

Contents: Teacher's Manual, Blackline Masters, Word Cards, and Pocket Chart

Available separately:
Blackline Masters	MMV-BM6
Pocket Chart	MMV-CHART46
Teacher's Manual, vol. 1	MMV-TM6-V1
Teacher's Manual, vol. 2	MMV-TM6-V2
Word Cards	MMV-WCS6

Ordering Information:
To order call 800.666.7270 * fax 510.842.0348
log on to www.devstu.org * e-mail pubs@devstu.org

Or Mail Your Order to:
Developmental Studies Center * Publications Department
2000 Embarcadero, Suite 305 * Oakland, CA 94606-5300

DEVELOPMENTAL STUDIES CENTER™